FACT BOOK ON
HIGHER EDUCATION

FACT BOOK ON
HIGHER EDUCATION
1997 EDITION

Compiled by
CHARLES J. ANDERSEN

AMERICAN COUNCIL ON EDUCATION ★
ORYX PRESS ★
Series on Higher Education
1998

The rare Arabian oryx is believed to have inspired the myth of the unicorn. This desert antelope became virtually extinct in the early 1960s. At that time several groups of international conservationists arranged to have 9 animals sent to the Phoenix Zoo to be the nucleus of a captive breeding herd. Today the oryx population is over 1,000, and over 500 have been returned to the Middle East.

ISBN 0-89774-820-4
ISSN 0363-6720

Contents

Introduction   xi
Highlights on the Status of Minorities in Higher
    Education   xiii
Highlights on the Status of Women in Higher
    Education   xv

I. Demographic and Economic Data

    Demographic and Economic Data
    Highlights   3–4
1   U.S. Resident Population, by Sex, Race,
    and Age, Selected Years, 1900–2050   5
2   U.S. Resident Population, by Region and
    State, Selected Years, 1970–2010   6–7
3   Population, Age 18 Years Old, by Sex and
    Race, Selected Years, 1950–2050   8
4   Population, Ages 18–24, by Sex and Race,
    Selected Years, 1950–2050   9
5   Population, Ages 18–24, by Region and
    State, Selected Years, 1970–2000   10–11
6   Households, by Region and State,
    Selected Years, 1970–1994   12–13
7   Households and Families, Selected Years,
    1960–2010   14
8   Births and Birth Rates; Deaths and Death
    Rates, Selected Years, 1910–2000   15
9   Educational Attainment of the Population,
    25 Years Old and Over, by Region and
    State, 1990   16–17
10   High School Graduates, by Control of
    Institution, Selected Years, 1909–1999   18
11   College Enrollment of Recent High School
    Graduates, by Sex and Race/Ethnicity,
    Selected Years, 1960–1995   19
12   High School Completions, by Persons Aged
    18–24 and by Race/Ethnicity, 1975–1994   20
13   High School Graduates and College Enroll-
    ment as a Percentage of the 18–24-year-old
    Population, by Race/Ethnicity, Selected
    Years, 1980–1994   21
14   General Educational Development (GED)
    Testing Data, Selected Years, 1949–1995   22
15   Educational Attainment of Population Aged
    18 Years Old and Over, by Sex, Race/Ethnicity,
    and Age, 1995   23
16   Median Income, by Sex, Race/Ethnicity, and
    Educational Attainment, 1993 and 1995   24
17   Families, by Income Range and Race/Ethnicity,
    Selected Years, 1970–1994   25

18   Median Income of Families by Race/Ethnicity,
    Selected Years, 1950–1995, (in Current
    Dollars)   26
19   Median Income of Families by Race/Ethnicity,
    Selected Years, 1970–1995, (in Constant
    1995 Dollars)   27
20   Median Money Income of Households by
    State, 1984, 1990, 1994, and 1995,
    (in Constant 1995 Dollars)   28–29
21   Families with 18–24-year-olds, by Income
    Level, Race/Ethnicity, and Enrollment Status,
    October 1994   30
22   Family Income of Families with First-time,
    Full-time Freshmen, 1967, 1986, and 1996   31
23   Per Capita Personal Income, by Region and
    State, Selected Years, 1960–1995   32–33
24   State Appropriations for Higher Education
    Operating Expenses, by Region and State,
    Selected Fiscal Years, 1975–1997   34–35
25   U.S. Gross Domestic Product, Selected
    Years, 1960–1996   36
26   Education Expenditures as a Percentage of
    the Gross Domestic Product, Selected Years,
    1940–1996   37
27   Price Indexes, Selected Years, 1960–1997   38
28   U.S. Labor Force and Employment Status,
    Selected Years, 1950–1996   39
29   Labor Force, by Age, Sex, and Race/Ethnicity,
    Selected Years, 1960–2000   40
30   Civilian Employment in Selected Occupations,
    1994 and 2005   41
31   Occupation Projections, Largest Job Growth,
    1994 to 2005   42
32   Occupation Projections, Fastest Job Growth,
    1994 to 2005   43
33   Participation by Women and Minorities in
    Selected Occupation Groups, 1983 and
    1995   44
34   Employment by Broad Occupation Group,
    1983, 1995, and 2005   45
35   Unemployment Rates, by Sex and Age
    Group, Selected Years, 1950–1996   46
36   Unemployment Rates, by Race/Ethnicity,
    Selected Years, 1950–1996   47
37   Unemployment Rates for All Workers, by
    Educational Attainment, Selected Years,
    1970–1995   48
38   Unemployment Rates, by Educational
    Attainment and Race/Ethnicity, Selected
    Years, 1980–1995   49

II. Enrollment Data

	Highlights on Enrollment	53
39	Enrollment in All Levels of Education, Selected Years, 1959–2000	55
40	Elementary and Secondary School Enrollment, by Control of School, Selected Years, 1899–2000	56
41	High School Graduates and First-time Enrollment in College, Selected Years, 1960–1995	57
42	Fall Enrollment of All Students in Higher Education, by Level of Study, Selected Years, 1899–2000	58
43	Fall Enrollment of All Students in Higher Education, by Sex of Student, Selected Years, 1950–2000	59
44	Fall Enrollment of All Students in Higher Education, by Attendance Status, Selected Years, 1959–2000	60
45	Fall Enrollment of all Students in All Institutions, by Control of Institution, Selected Years, 1950–2000	61
46	Fall Enrollment of All Students in All Institutions, by Region and State, 1970–1997	62–63
47	Percentage Change in Enrollment of All Students in All Institutions, by Region and State, 1970–1995	64–65
48	Fall Enrollment in Public Institutions, by Region and State, Selected Years, 1970–1997	66–67
49	Percentage Change in Fall Enrollment in Public Institutions, by Region and State, Selected Years, 1970–1994	68–69
50	Fall Enrollment in Independent Institutions, by Region and State, Selected Years, 1970–1997	70–71
51	Percentage Change in Fall Enrollment in Independent Institutions, by Region and State, Selected Years, 1970–1994	72–73
52	Fall Enrollment, by Race/Ethnicity, and by Region and State, 1984	74–75
53	Fall Enrollment, by Race/Ethnicity, and by Region and State, 1995	76–77
54	Minorities as a Percentage of U.S. Citizens' Enrollment, by Region and State, 1984 and 1995	78–79
55	Percentage Change in Fall Enrollment, by Race/Ethnicity, and by Region and State, 1984–1995	80–81
56	Fall Enrollment of All Students in 4-year Institutions, by Sex of Student, Selected Years, 1950–2000	82
57	Fall Enrollment of All Students in 2-year Institutions, by Sex of Student, Selected Years, 1950–2000	83
58	Fall Enrollment of All Students in 4-year Institutions, by Control of Institution, Selected Years, 1950–2000	84
59	Fall Enrollment of All Students in 2-year Institutions, by Control of Institution, Selected Years, 1950–2000	85
60	Fall Enrollment in 4-year Institutions, by Attendance Status, Selected Years, 1963–2000	86
61	Fall Enrollment in 2-year Institutions, by Attendance Status, Selected Years, 1963–2000	87
62	Enrollment of Men in All Institutions, by Type of Institution, Selected Years, 1963–2000	88
63	Enrollment of Women in All Institutions, by Type of Institution, Selected Years, 1963–2000	89
64	Enrollment of Men in All Institutions, by Control of Institution, Selected Years, 1970–2000	90
65	Enrollment of Women in All Institutions, by Control of Institution, Selected Years, 1970–2000	91
66	Enrollment of Men in All Institutions, by Attendance Status, Selected Years, 1970–2000	92
67	Enrollment of Women in All Institutions, by Attendance Status, Selected Years, 1970–2000	93
68	Fall Enrollment of First-time Freshmen in All Institutions, by Sex of Student, Selected Years, 1950–2000	94
69	Fall Enrollment of First-time Freshmen in All Institutions, by Control of Institution, Selected Years, 1950–2000	95
70	Fall Enrollment of First-time Freshmen in 4-year Institutions, by Control of Institution, Selected Years, 1950–2000	96
71	Fall Enrollment of First-time Freshmen in 2-year Institutions, by Control of Institution, Selected Years, 1950–2000	97
72	First-time Freshmen in All Institutions, by Region and State, Selected Years, 1986–1997	98–99
73	Percent Change of Enrollment of First-time Freshmen, by Region and State, 1986–1990 and 1990–1994	100–101
74	First-time Student State Residents Attending College In-state, by State, 1988 and 1994	102–103
75	First-time Student State Residents Attending College Out-of-state, by State, 1988 and 1994	104–105
76	Out-of-state First-time Students, by State, 1988 and 1994	106–107
77	Full-time Equivalent (FTE) Enrollment, at All Institutions, Selected Years, 1970–2000	108

78 Full-time Equivalent (FTE) Enrollment, by Type of Institution, Selected Years, 1970–2000   109

79 Full-time Equivalent (FTE) Enrollment, at Public Institutions, Selected Years, 1970–2000   110

80 Full-time Equivalent (FTE) Enrollment, at Independent Institutions, Selected Years, 1970–2000   111

81 Graduate Enrollment, by Sex of Student, Selected Years, 1930–2000   112

82 Graduate Enrollment, by Control of Institution, Selected Years, 1930–2000   113

83 Graduate Enrollment, by Attendance Status, Selected Years, 1970–2000   114

84 Graduate Enrollment, in Science and Engineering, by Field of Study, Selected Years, 1980–1992   115

85 Graduate Enrollment, by Region and State, Selected Years, 1960–1997   116–117

III. Institutions and Finance, Faculty, Staff, and Students

Highlights on Institutions and Finance, Faculty, Staff, and Students   121–122

86 Number of Institutions of Higher Education, by Control of Institution, Selected Years, 1950–1995   123

87 Number of Institutions of Higher Education, by Type of Institutions, Selected Years, 1950–1995   124

88 Percentage Distribution of Institutions of Higher Education, by Enrollment Size, Selected Years, 1950–1994   125

89 Number of Institutions of Higher Education, by Highest Level of Offering, Selected Years, 1950–1995   126

90 Percentage Distribution of Institutions of Higher Education, by Highest Level of Offering, Selected Years, 1950–1995   127

91 Number of Institutions of Higher Education, by Type of Institution, and by Region and State, 1989–90 and 1995–96   128–129

92 Institutions of Higher Education, by Carnegie Classification Code, Selected Years, 1970–1994   130

93 Percentage Distribution of Institutions of Higher Education, by Carnegie Classification Code, Selected Years, 1970–1994   131

94 Current-fund Revenue of All Institutions of Higher Education, in Current Dollars, Selected Fiscal Years, 1930–1997   132–133

95 Percentage Distribution of Current-fund Revenues of All Institutions, by Kind of Revenue, Selected Years, 1979/80–1996/97   134

96 Current-fund Revenue of All Institutions of Higher Education, in Constant 1993–94 Dollars, Selected Years, 1979/80–1996/97   135

97 Current-fund Revenue of Public Institutions of Higher Education, in Current Dollars, Selected Fiscal Years, 1979/80–1996/97   136

98 Current-fund Revenue of Public Institutions of Higher Education, in Constant 1993–94 Dollars, Selected Fiscal Years, 1979/80–1996/97   137

99 Current-fund Revenue of Independent Institutions of Higher Education, in Current Dollars, Selected Fiscal Years, 1979/80–1996/97   138

100 Current-fund Revenue of Independent Institutions of Higher Education, in Constant 1993–94 Dollars, Selected Fiscal Years, 1979/80–1996/97   139

101 Current-fund Expenditures of All Institutions of Higher Education, in Current Dollars, Selected Fiscal Years, 1929/30–1996/97   140–141

102 Percentage Distribution of Current-fund Expenditures of All Institutions of Higher Education, Selected Fiscal Years, 1979/80–1996/97   142

103 Current-fund Expenditures of All Institutions of Higher Education, in Constant 1993–94 Dollars, Selected Fiscal Years, 1979/80–1996/97   143

104 Current-fund Expenditures of Public Institutions of Higher Education, in Current Dollars, Selected Fiscal Years, 1979/80–1996/97   144

105 Current-fund Expenditures of Public Institutions of Higher Education, in Constant Dollars, Selected Fiscal Years, 1979/80–1996/97   145

106 Current-fund Expenditures of Independent Institutions of Higher Education, in Current Dollars, Selected Fiscal Years, 1979/80–1996/97   146

107 Current-fund Expenditures of Independent Institutions, in Constant 1993-94 Dollars, Selected Fiscal Years, 1979/80–1996/97   147

108 Senior Instructional Staff, by Employment Status and Institutional Type, Selected Years, 1970–1997   148

109 Full-time Instructional Faculty, by Rank and Sex, Selected Years, 1985–1993   149

110 Faculty and Enrollment, Selected Years, 1970–1997   150

111 Full-time Instructional Faculty, by Rank, Sex, and Race/Ethnicity, 1993   151

112 Full-time Instructional Faculty, by Academic Rank, and by Region and State, Academic Year 1995–96   152–153

113 Selected Characteristics of Faculty, 1975, 1984, 1987, and 1992   154

114 Work Time Distribution of Full-time Instructional Faculty, by Type of Institution, Fall 1992   155

115 Average Faculty Salary, by Rank and Sex, Selected Years, 1974/75–1995/96   156

116 Average Faculty Compensation (Salary and Benefits), by Rank, Selected Years, 1966–1996   157

117 Percentage of Full-time Instructional Faculty with Tenure, by Rank, Sex, and Control of Institution, Selected Years, 1980/81–1994/95   158

118 Employees of Higher Education, by Primary Occupation and Employment Status, Fall 1993   159

119 Employees of Higher Education, by Primary Occupation and Race/Ethnicity, Fall 1993   160

120 Percentage Distribution of Employees of Higher Education, by Primary Occupation and Race/Ethnicity, Fall 1993   161

121 Percentage Distribution of Employees of Higher Education, by Primary Occupation and Race/Ethnicity, Fall 1993   162

122 Cost of Attendance at 4-year Institutions, in Current and Constant Dollars, 1986/87–1995/96   163

123 Aid Awarded to Postsecondary Students, in Current Dollars, Selected Academic Years, 1964–1996   164

124 Aid Awarded to Postsecondary Students, in Constant 1995 Dollars, Selected Academic Years, 1964–1996   165

125 Percentage of Undergraduates Receiving Student Aid, by Enrollment Status, Type and Control of Institution, and Source of Aid, 1992   166

126 Degree Attainment, as of Spring 1994, by 1989–90 Entering Students, by Race/Ethnicity and Degree Aspiration   167

127 National Norms for Selected Characteristics of Entering Freshmen, by Sex and Type of Institution Attended, Fall 1996   168–169

128 Selected Freshmen Characteristics, by Sex of Student, 1966, 1987, 1996   170–171

129 Percentage Distribution of Undergraduates, by Disability Status and Selected Student Characteristics, 1992–93   172

130 Federal Support for Education, Selected Years, 1965–1996   173

IV. Earned Degrees

Highlights on Earned Degrees   177–178

131 Bachelor's and Higher Degrees, by Level, Selected Years, 1950–2000   179

132 Bachelor's and Higher Degrees, by Sex of Student and Control of Institution, Selected Years, 1950–2000   180

133 Bachelor's Degrees, by Sex of Student and Control of Institution, Selected Years, 1948–2000   181

134 First-professional Degrees, by Sex of Student and Control of Institution, Selected Years, 1961–2000   182

135 Master's Degrees, by Sex of Student and Control of Institution, Selected Years, 1948–2000   183

136 Doctoral Degrees, by Sex of Student and Control of Institution, Selected Years, 1948–2000   184

137 Percentage Distribution of Bachelor's and Higher Degrees, by Sex of Student, Selected Years, 1948–2000   185

138 Percentage Distribution of Bachelor's and Higher Degrees, by Control of Institution, Selected Years, 1948–2000   186

139 Percentage of Earned Doctorates Awarded to Women, by Selected Field of Study, Selected Years, 1950–1994   187

140 Bachelor's Degrees, by Region and State, Selected Years, 1970–1994   188–189

141 First-professional Degrees, by Region and State, Selected Years, 1970–1994   190–191

142 Master's Degrees, by Region and State, Selected Years, 1970–1994   192–193

143 Doctoral Degrees, by Region and State, Selected Years, 1970–1994   194–195

144 Bachelor's Degrees, by Race/Ethnicity and Academic Area, 1993-94   196

145 First-professional Degrees, by Race/Ethnicity and Academic Area, 1993-94   197

146 Master's Degrees, by Race/Ethnicity and Academic Area, 1993-94   198

147 Doctoral Degrees, by Race/Ethnicity and Academic Area, 1993-94   199

148 Percentage Distribution of Bachelor's Degrees, by Academic Area and Race/Ethnicity, 1993–94   200

149 Percentage Distribution of Bachelor's Degrees, by Race/Ethnicity and Academic Area, 1993–94   201

150 Percentage Distribution of First-professional Degrees, by Academic Area and Race/Ethnicity, 1993–94   202

151 Percentage Distribution of First-professional Degrees, by Race/Ethnicity and Academic Area, 1993–94   203

152 Percentage Distribution of Master's Degrees, by Academic Area and Race/Ethnicity, 1993–94   204

153 Percentage Distribution of Master's Degrees, by Race/Ethnicity and Academic Area, 1993–94   205

154 Percentage Distribution of Doctoral Degrees, by Academic Area and Race/Ethnicity, 1993–94   206

155 Percentage Distribution of Doctoral Degrees, by Race/Ethnicity and Academic Area, 1993–94   207

156 Bachelor's Degrees, by Race/Ethnicity, and by Region and State, 1984–85 and 1993–94   208–209

157 Minority Bachelor's Degrees, as a Percentage of All Bachelor's Degrees, by Region and State, 1984–85 and 1993–94   210–211

158 Degrees Conferred in the Biological Sciences: Microbiology/Bacteriology, Selected Years, 1948–1996   212

159 Degrees Conferred in the Biological Sciences: Biochemistry and Biophysics, Selected Years, 1948–1996   213

160 Degrees Conferred in the Biological Sciences: Biology, Selected Years, 1948–1996   214

161 Degrees Conferred in the Biological Sciences: Botany, Selected Years, 1948–1996   215

162 Degrees Conferred in the Biological Sciences: Zoology, Selected Years, 1948–1996   216

163 Degrees Conferred in Business and Management, Selected Years, 1948–1996   217

164 Degrees Conferred in Education, Selected Years, 1948–1996   218

165 Degrees Conferred in Engineering: Chemical Engineering, Selected Years, 1950–1996   219

166 Degrees Conferred in Engineering: Civil Engineering, Selected Years, 1950–1996   220

167 Degrees Conferred in Engineering: Electrical Engineering, Selected Years, 1950–1996   221

168 Degrees Conferred in Engineering: Industrial Engineering, Selected Years, 1950–1996   222

169 Degrees Conferred in Engineering: Mechanical Engineering, Selected Years, 1950–1996   223

170 Degrees Conferred in the Humanities: English, Selected Years, 1948–1996   224

171 Degrees Conferred in the Humanities: Foreign Languages, Selected Years, 1948–1996   225

172 Degrees Conferred in the Humanities: Music, Selected Years, 1948–1996   226

173 Degrees Conferred in the Humanities: Philosophy, Selected Years, 1948–1996   227

174 Degrees Conferred in Law, Selected Years, 1948–1996   228

175 First-professional Degrees Conferred in Medicine and Dentistry, Selected Years, 1950–1996   229

176 Degrees Conferred in Nursing, Selected Years, 1948–1996   230

177 Degrees Conferred in the Physical Sciences: Chemistry, Selected Years, 1948–1996   231

178 Degrees Conferred in the Physical Sciences: Geological Sciences, Selected Years, 1948–1996   232

179 Degrees Conferred in the Physical Sciences: Mathematics, Selected Years, 1948–1996   233

180 Degrees Conferred in the Physical Sciences: Physics, Selected Years, 1948–1996   234

181 Degrees Conferred in the Social Sciences: Economics, Selected Years, 1948–1996   235

182 Degrees Conferred in the Social Sciences: History, Selected Years, 1948–1996   236

183 Degrees Conferred in the Social Sciences: Political Science, Selected Years, 1948–1996   237

184 Degrees Conferred in the Social Sciences: Psychology, Selected Years, 1948–1996   238

185 Degrees Conferred in the Social Sciences: Sociology, Selected Years, 1948–1996   239

186 Associate Degrees, by Sex of Student and Control of Institution, Selected Years, 1966–1996   240

187 Percentage Distribution of Associate Degrees, by Sex of Student and Control of Institution, Selected Years, 1966–1996   241

188 Associate Degrees, by Region and State, Selected Years, 1970–1994   242–243

Guide to Sources   245

Index   251

Introduction

This latest edition of *Fact Book on Higher Education* continues the publication's function of compiling varied data on trends related to higher education. Begun as a loose-leaf information service in 1959 by Dr. Elmer West, then director of the American Council on Education's Office of Statistical Information and Research, *Fact Book* has evolved over the years into its current form. A unique feature of the publication is that each table is accompanied by a "visual" of some sort that, in most cases, shows at a glance the direction of change over the period covered—sometimes several decades.

This edition of *Fact Book* is divided into four sections:

I. Demographic and Economic Data
II. Enrollment Data
III. Institutions and Finance, Faculty, Staff, and Students
IV. Earned Degrees

Each of the sections is preceded by a brief "Highlights" section that calls attention to some of the more important data contained in the section. A *"Guide to Sources"* section after the tabular material briefly identifies and describes some of the major data sources used in preparing the publication.

Data counts in many of the tables are shown in thousands. Largely because of this rounding, the detail may not sum to the subtotals and totals. Also, percentages and percentage changes in many cases have been calculated on the basis of the rounded numbers. Hence, they may not agree with calculations found elsewhere that were carried out using units, rather than thousands.

No new data collection has taken place. All of the data in this book come from reports published by various government agencies and nongovernmental sources. Data from governmental agencies include, especially, the U.S. Department of Education as well as the Bureau of the Census of the Department of Commerce, the Bureau of Labor Statistics of the Labor Department, and the National Science Foundation. Most of the tables contain data from published sources, although some are available only from data tapes. Data from nongovernmental sources are also presented; their provenance is identified in source notes and in most cases in the *"Guide to Sources."*

The assistance of Jill Bogard, director of the American Council on Education's (ACE) Library and Information Service, was invaluable to the preparation of this book. The ACE Library is a unique resource, and its collection—especially those publications spanning the last several decades—is a particularly fruitful resource. James J. Murray III, an ACE vice president and director of its Division of External Affairs, proposed and encouraged the preparation of this edition of *Fact Book*. Among the many contributions by the editorial staff at Oryx Press—in particular, Mary Swistara—was the great patience extended to the compiler as the book took form.

Charles J. Andersen

Highlights on the Status of Minorities in Higher Education

DEMOGRAPHIC AND ECONOMIC DATA

In 1994, 20 percent of the traditional college age population (18–24 years old) were of minority status; 15 percent were Black. Projected figures for 2000 show 21 percent minority and 15 percent Black.

As of October 1994, about 36 percent of Black high school graduates aged 18–24 years old were enrolled in college. The comparable figure for Hispanics was 33 percent; for Whites, 43 percent.

There were sizable differences in the 1995 median incomes of families according to race:

White families:	$42,646
Black families:	25,970
Hispanic families:	24,570

The 1995 median income of workers 15 years old and over varied considerably on the basis of sex and race:

White men:	$23,895
White women:	12,316
Black men:	16,006
Black women:	10,961
Hispanic men:	14,840
Hispanic women:	8,928

In 1996, the unemployment rates for Blacks and Hispanics were 10.5 percent and 9.0 percent, respectively; the rate for Whites was 4.7 percent.

In 1994, 26 percent of White families with one or more 18–24-year-olds attending college full time had incomes of $50,000 or more. The comparable figure for Black families was 8 percent, for Hispanic families, 9 percent.

Enrollment

During fall 1995, 3.5 million minority students were enrolled in higher education institutions: this represents one-quarter of the total enrollment.

Between 1984 and 1995, Blacks, as a percentage of total enrollment, increased from 8.8 percent to 10.3 percent; non-Black minorities increased from 8.2 percent to 14.2 percent.

The race/ethnicity of male first-time, full-time students in 1996 was:

White:	81 percent
Black:	9 percent
Hispanic:	6 percent
Asian/Pacific Islander:	5 percent
American Indian/Alaskan Native:	2 percent

The race/ethnicity of female first-time, full-time students in 1996 was:

White:	80 percent
Black:	10 percent
Hispanic:	5 percent
Asian/Pacific Islander:	4 percent
American Indian/Alaskan Native:	2 percent

EARNED DEGREES

Bachelor's Degrees

In academic year 1993–94, minorities earned 17 percent of the 1.2 million bachelor's degrees awarded. The distribution was as follows:

Black:	7	percent
Hispanic:	4	percent
Asian/Pacific Islander:	5	percent
American Indian/ Alaskan Native:	0.5	percent

The 1993–94 share earned by all minorities represents an increase over the share that minorities held in 1984–85 which was 11 percent.

First-professional Degrees

In academic year 1993–94, minorities earned 18 percent of the 75,000 first-professional degrees awarded. The distribution was as follows:

Black:	6	percent
Hispanic:	4	percent
Asian/Pacific Islander:	8	percent
American Indian/ Alaskan Native:	0.5	percent

The 1993–94 share earned by all minorities represents an increase over the share that minorities held in 1984–85, which was 10 percent.

Master's Degrees

In academic year 1993–94, minorities earned 13 percent of the 387,000 master's degrees awarded. The distribution was as follows:

Black:	6	percent
Hispanic:	3	percent
Asian/Pacific Islander:	4	percent
American Indian/ Alaskan Native:	0.4	percent

The 1993–94 share earned by all minorities represents a slight increase over the share that minorities held in 1984–85, which was 11 percent.

Doctoral Degrees

In academic year 1993–94, minorities earned 10 percent of the 43,000 doctoral degrees awarded. The distribution was as follows:

Black:	3	percent
Hispanic:	2	percent
Asian/Pacific Islander:	5	percent
American Indian/ Alaskan Native:	0.3	percent

The 1993–94 share earned by all minorities is essentially the same share that minorities earned in 1984–85, 10.3 percent and 9.5 percent, respectively.

Highlights on the Status of Women in Higher Education

DEMOGRAPHIC AND ECONOMIC DATA

In 1997, just over half (51 percent) of the U.S. population was women (137 million). They constituted just less than half (49 percent) of the 18–24-year-old population.

In 1995, median incomes of workers 25 years old and over varied considerably, depending on the sex and level of education attained by the worker:

Women with only a high school education had a median annual income of $20,463.

Men at the same educational level had a median annual income of $29,510.

Women with a bachelor's or higher degree had a median income of $35,259.

Men at the same educational level had a median income of $50,481.

In 1996, both men and women had unemployment rates of 5.4 percent.

Enrollment

In fall 1995, the 7.9 million women enrolled in higher education institutions comprised over half (56 percent) of the student body. Fifteen years earlier, they had accounted for 51 percent of enrollment.

Enrollment of women at four-year colleges was estimated at 4.7 million, or 54 percent of the student body.

Enrollment of women at two-year institutions was estimated at 3.1 million, or 58 percent of their total enrollment.

From 1985 to 1995, the number of women attending four-year colleges increased by 17 percent. At two-year institutions the increase was 24 percent. Increases in the enrollment of men

were considerably smaller; 3 percent and 13 percent, respectively.

Women comprised 54 percent of the 2.1 million first-time freshmen in 1995. They comprised the same share of postbaccalaureate enrollment.

Faculty and Staff

One-third (33 percent) of the full-time instructional faculty at colleges and universities was composed of women in the fall of 1993. The comparable figure for fall 1995 was 28 percent.

A smaller percentage of women than men held tenure in 1994 (50 percent versus 71 percent).

Average faculty salaries for women are less than those for men in each of the four major faculty ranks. For academic year 1995–96, the smallest percentage difference was for instructors; the average salary for women was 97 percent of that for men ($29,940 versus $30, 940).

Earned Degrees

Women earned more associate, bachelor's, and master's degrees in 1993–94 than men did.

Associate degrees: women: 322,000 men: 221,000
Bachelor's degrees: women: 637,000 men: 532,000
Master's degrees: women: 211,000 men: 176,000

Women earned fewer first-professional and doctoral degrees than men:

First-professional
  degrees: women: 31,000 men: 45,000
Doctoral degrees: women: 17,000 men: 27,000

Women earned a majority of the doctorates awarded in languages, education, anthropology, and psychology.

I

Demographic and Economic Data

Demographic and Economic Data Highlights

Population

- In 1997, the total population was estimated at 268 million. Men comprised 49 percent of the population; women 51 percent. The Black population made up 13 percent of the total population.
- Since 1990, the U.S. population increased by 8 percent.
- Of the nation's 8 major economic regions, the Southeast was the most populous, with 63.6 million residents in 1995, 24 percent of the total.
- Proportions of the population residing in other regions were:

Mideast	17 percent
Great Lakes	17 percent
Far West	17 percent
Southwest	11 percent
Plains	7 percent
New England	5 percent
Mountain	3 percent

- In 1997, the total traditional college-age population (18–24-year-olds) was estimated at 24.7 million. By the end of the century, this age group is projected to increase by 6 percent—to 26.3 million.
- During the decade of 1986 to 1996, the number of annual births increased from 3.8 million to 3.9 million.

Income

- In 1995, per capita personal income in the U.S. stood at $23,208.
- The median income for all families was $40,611.
- There were large differences in family income according to race:

White families:	$42,646
Black families:	25,970
Hispanic families:	24,570

- In 1994, 31 percent of all families in the U.S. had incomes of less than $25,000. Just over half of Black families and Hispanic families had incomes of less than $25,000.
- Median incomes for year-round full-time workers, 25 years old and over, varied on the basis of sex and level of education:

Men, with a high school education,	$29,510.
Men, with a bachelor's degree or higher,	$50,481.
Women, with a high school education,	$20,463.
Women, with a bachelor's degree or higher,	$35,259.

- The gross domestic product (GDP) of the U.S. increased by 26 percent from 1986 to 1996, growing from $5.5 trillion, as measured in constant 1992 dollars.
- Expenditures for all levels of education were 7.3 percent of the GDP in school year 1995–96; for higher education, they were 2.9 percent.

Employment

- The U.S. civilian labor force in 1996 was 134 million. This is up from 126 million in 1990.
- In 1996, 5.4 percent of the civilian labor force was unemployed, compared with 7.5 percent in 1992.
- In 1996, the unemployment rate for Blacks stood at 10.5 percent; the unemployment rates for Whites and Hispanics were 4.7 percent and 9.0 percent, respectively.
- In March 1995, the unemployment rate for workers with less than a high school diploma stood at 10 percent; for high school graduates with some college, 4.5 percent; for college graduates, 2.5 percent.

- From 1994 to 2005, the number of jobs is projected to increase by 14 percent.
- The fastest growing occupations between 1994 and 2005 are expected to be personal and home care aides.

- The occupations with the largest job growth between 1994 and 2005 are expected to be cashiers and janitors with an increase of over half a million jobs each.

U.S. Resident Population, by Sex, Race, and Age, Selected Years, 1900–2050

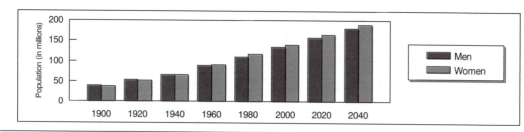

	Resident Population (in thousands)					Percentage of Total Population			
Year	Both Sexes	Men	Women	Black	65 & Over	Men	Women	Black	65 & Over
1900	75,994	38,816	37,178	8,834	--	51	49	12	--
1910	91,972	47,332	44,640	9,828	--	51	49	11	--
1920	105,710	53,900	51,810	10,463	--	51	49	10	--
1930	122,775	62,137	60,638	11,891	--	51	49	10	--
1940	131,670	66,062	65,608	12,866	9,031	50	50	10	7
1950	151,326	75,187	76,139	15,045	12,397	50	50	10	8
1960	179,323	88,331	90,992	18,872	16,675	49	51	11	9
1970	203,235	98,926	104,309	22,581	19,973	49	51	11	10
1980	226,546	110,053	116,493	26,683	25,550	49	51	12	11
1990	248,718	121,244	127,474	30,486	31,080	49	51	12	12
1991	252,138	122,951	129,187	31,110	31,763	49	51	12	13
1992	255,039	124,436	130,603	31,659	32,270	49	51	12	13
1993	257,800	125,812	131,988	32,174	32,778	49	51	12	13
1994	260,350	127,085	133,265	32,669	33,151	49	51	13	13
1995	262,755	128,314	134,441	33,141	33,522	49	51	13	13
	Middle Series Projections								
1996	265,253	129,522	135,731	33,611	33,872	49	51	13	13
1997	267,645	130,712	136,933	34,075	34,096	49	51	13	13
2000	274,634	134,181	140,453	35,454	34,710	49	51	13	13
2010	297,716	145,584	152,132	40,109	39,408	49	51	13	13
2020	322,742	158,021	164,721	45,075	53,220	49	51	14	16
2030	346,899	169,950	176,949	50,001	69,378	49	51	14	20
2040	369,980	181,261	188,719	55,094	75,233	49	51	15	20
2050	393,931	193,234	200,696	60,592	78,859	49	51	15	20

Note: Population count for 1900 is as of June 1; for 1910, as of April 15; for 1920, as of Jan. 1; for 1930 thru 1990, as of April 1; for subsequent years, as of July 1. Alaska and Hawaii excluded from 1900 thru 1940. Data for 1991 thru 1995 are estimated; for 1996 and later are middle series projections. Data for ages 65 and over for years 1940-1960 are as of July 1.
-- Not available.

Sources: 1 U.S. Bureau of the Census, Statistical Abstract of the U.S., 1996 (Washington: GPO, 1996), tbls 12, 14, 17, 18.
2 Council of Economic Advisers, Economic Report of the President, 1997 (Washington: GPO, 1997), tbl. B-32.

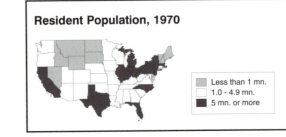

Resident Population, 1970

	Less than 1 mn.
	1.0 - 4.9 mn.
	5 mn. or more

Region and State	Resident Population (in thousands)					
	1970	1980	1990	1995	2000	2010
50 States & D.C.	**203,302**	**226,546**	**248,718**	**262,755**	**276,242**	**300,430**
New England	**11,848**	**12,348**	**13,207**	**13,312**	**13,216**	**13,755**
Connecticut	3,032	3,108	3,287	3,275	3,271	3,412
Maine	994	1,125	1,228	1,241	1,240	1,309
Massachusetts	5,689	5,737	6,016	6,074	5,950	6,097
New Hampshire	738	921	1,109	1,148	1,165	1,280
Rhode Island	950	947	1,003	990	998	1,034
Vermont	445	511	563	585	592	623
Mideast	**42,442**	**42,236**	**43,658**	**44,466**	**45,286**	**46,720**
Delaware	548	594	666	717	759	815
D.C.	757	638	607	554	537	577
Maryland	3,924	4,217	4,781	5,042	5,322	5,782
New Jersey	7,171	7,365	7,730	7,945	8,135	8,562
New York	18,241	17,558	17,991	18,136	18,237	18,546
Pennsylvania	11,801	11,864	11,883	12,072	12,296	12,438
Southeast	**43,825**	**52,659**	**59,266**	**63,573**	**67,205**	**73,678**
Alabama	3,444	3,894	4,040	4,253	4,485	4,856
Arkansas	1,923	2,286	2,351	2,484	2,578	2,782
Florida	6,791	9,746	12,938	14,166	15,313	17,372
Georgia	4,588	5,463	6,478	7,201	7,637	8,553
Kentucky	3,221	3,661	3,687	3,860	3,989	4,160
Louisiana	3,645	4,206	4,220	4,342	4,478	4,808
Mississippi	2,217	2,521	2,575	2,697	2,750	2,918
North Carolina	5,084	5,882	6,632	7,195	7,617	8,341
South Carolina	2,591	3,122	3,486	3,673	3,932	4,311
Tennessee	3,926	4,591	4,877	5,256	5,538	6,007
Virginia	4,651	5,347	6,189	6,618	7,048	7,728
West Virginia	1,744	1,940	1,793	1,828	1,840	1,842
Great Lakes	**40,262**	**41,683**	**42,009**	**43,456**	**44,806**	**46,259**
Illinois	11,110	11,427	11,431	11,830	12,168	12,652
Indiana	5,195	5,490	5,544	5,803	6,045	6,286
Michigan	8,882	9,262	9,295	9,549	9,759	10,033
Ohio	10,657	10,798	10,847	11,151	11,453	11,659
Wisconsin	4,418	4,706	4,892	5,123	5,381	5,629

Note: Data for 1970, 1980, 1990 are as of April 1; for 1995, estimates as of July 1; Data for 2000 and 2010 are series A, the preferred, projections as of July 1.

Continued on next page.

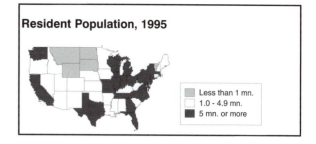

Resident Population, 1995

Less than 1 mn.
1.0 - 4.9 mn.
5 mn. or more

Region and State	Resident Population (in thousands)					
	1970	1980	1990	1995	2000	2010
Plains	**16,327**	**17,183**	**17,660**	**18,348**	**19,030**	**20,074**
Iowa	2,825	2,914	2,777	2,842	2,930	2,981
Kansas	2,249	2,364	2,478	2,565	2,722	2,922
Minnesota	3,806	4,076	4,376	4,610	4,824	5,127
Missouri	4,678	4,917	5,117	5,324	5,437	5,760
Nebraska	1,485	1,570	1,578	1,637	1,704	1,793
North Dakota	618	653	639	641	643	676
South Dakota	666	691	696	729	770	815
Southwest	**16,550**	**21,275**	**25,312**	**27,905**	**29,681**	**33,689**
Arizona	1,775	2,718	3,665	4,218	4,437	5,074
New Mexico	1,017	1,303	1,515	1,685	1,823	2,082
Oklahoma	2,559	3,025	3,146	3,278	3,382	3,683
Texas	11,199	14,229	16,986	18,724	20,039	22,850
Rocky Mountains	**5,008**	**6,552**	**7,277**	**8,211**	**8,939**	**10,002**
Colorado	2,210	2,890	3,294	3,747	4,059	4,494
Idaho	713	944	1,007	1,163	1,290	1,454
Montana	694	787	799	870	920	996
Utah	1,059	1,461	1,723	1,951	2,148	2,462
Wyoming	332	470	454	480	522	596
Far West	**27,038**	**32,600**	**40,327**	**43,482**	**48,079**	**56,253**
Alaska	303	402	550	604	699	781
California	19,971	23,668	29,758	31,589	34,888	41,085
Hawaii	770	965	1,108	1,187	1,327	1,551
Nevada	489	800	1,202	1,530	1,691	1,935
Oregon	2,092	2,633	2,842	3,141	3,404	3,876
Washington	3,413	4,132	4,867	5,431	6,070	7,025

Source: U.S. Bureau of the Census, *Statistical Abstract of the U.S., 1996* (Washington: GPO, 1996), tbls 27, 36.

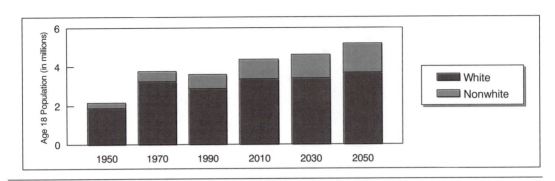

Population, Age 18 Years Old (in thousands)								
	All Races			Black & Other Races			Black		
Year	Total	Men	Women	Total	Men	Women	Total	Men	Women
1950	2,164	1,090	1,074	271	133	138	–	–	–
1960	2,612	1,323	1,289	312	155	157	288	143	145
1970	3,782	1,914	1,868	513	254	259	463	229	234
1975	4,256	2,159	2,097	641	320	321	568	283	285
1980	4,243	2,155	2,088	694	348	346	596	297	299
1985	3,679	1,872	1,808	661	333	329	542	271	271
1990	3,595	1,842	1,753	709	360	350	549	276	273
1991	3,383	1,733	1,650	683	346	337	526	265	261
1992	3,304	1,693	1,611	664	315	349	508	263	245
1993	3,346	1,712	1,633	680	343	335	516	260	256
1994	3,419	1,753	1,667	691	350	341	524	265	260
Middle Series Projections									
1995	3,509	1,795	1,714	710	358	352	547	276	272
1996	3,544	1,813	1,731	719	362	357	548	276	272
1997	3,656	1,870	1,786	755	380	375	573	289	284
1998	3,844	1,966	1,878	797	402	395	602	304	298
2000	3,937	2,013	1,924	717	412	305	604	305	299
2010	4,364	2,229	2,135	994	502	492	693	352	341
2020	4,198	2,147	2,051	1,045	530	515	711	362	349
2030	4,607	2,356	2,251	1,202	609	593	800	408	392
2040	4,914	2,512	2,402	1,342	681	661	868	443	425
2050	5,196	2,656	2,540	1,494	758	736	949	485	464

Note: Population estimates and projections as of July 1 of year indicated. Data prior to 1985 shows total population, including armed forces overseas; data for subsequent years show resident population.

-- Not available

Sources: 1 U.,S. Bureau of the Census, Current Population Reports, Series P-25 (Washington: GPO), No. 311, p. 22; No. 519, tbl. 1; No. 917, tbl. 1; No. 1095, tbl. 1; No. 1104, tbl. 2; No. 1130, tbl 2.

2 _____, Statistical Abstract of the U.S., 1994 (Washington: GPO, 1994), tbls. 15, 22.

4 Population, Ages 18–24, by Sex and Race, Selected Years, 1950–2050

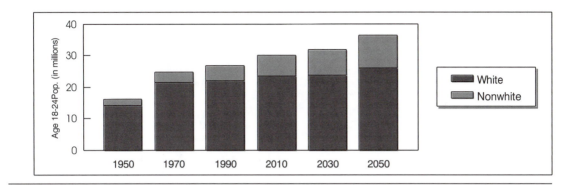

	Population, Ages 18 - 24 (in thousands)								
	All Races			Black & Other Races			Black		
Year	Total	Men	Women	Total	Men	Women	Total	Men	Women
1950	16,076	8,009	8,067	1,890	898	992	--	--	--
1960	16,127	8,093	8,034	1,959	946	1,013	1,798	863	935
1970	24,712	12,451	12,261	3,181	1,551	1,630	2,829	1,374	1,455
1975	28,005	14,137	13,868	4,015	1,964	2,051	3,510	1,711	1,799
1980	30,349	15,327	15,022	4,749	2,339	2,410	4,030	1,972	2,058
1985	28,902	14,596	14,306	4,927	2,431	2,496	3,990	1,948	2,042
1990	26,828	13,679	13,149	5,001	2,495	2,509	3,808	1,877	1,932
1991	26,385	13,456	12,929	5,005	2,496	2,507	3,778	1,865	1,912
1992	25,919	13,217	12,703	5,009	2,501	2,509	3,747	1,853	1,894
1993	26,133	13,311	12,820	5,111	2,545	2,562	3,797	1,876	1,920
1994	25,846	13,159	12,687	5,121	2,550	2,570	3,777	1,868	1,909
	Middle Series Projections								
1995	24,926	12,676	12,250	4,990	2,477	2,513	3,726	1,845	1,882
1996	24,615	12,516	12,099	4,968	2,463	2,505	3,703	1,834	1,869
1997	24,690	12,550	12,140	5,016	2,484	2,532	3,727	1,847	1,880
1998	25,160	12,787	12,373	5,190	2,601	2,589	3,805	1,887	1,918
2000	26,259	13,339	12,920	5,405	2,675	2,730	3,965	1,967	1,998
2010	30,137	15,313	14,824	6,649	3,311	3,338	4,674	2,332	2,342
2020	29,920	15,202	14,718	7,253	3,618	3,635	4,855	2,429	2,426
2030	31,825	16,170	15,655	8,238	4,115	4,123	5,370	2,691	2,679
2040	34,568	17,562	17,006	9,292	4,646	4,646	5,896	2,958	2,938
2050	36,334	18,461	17,873	10,323	5,167	5,156	6,410	3,221	3,189

Note: Population estimates and projections as of July 1 of year indicated. Data prior to 1985 shows total population, including armed forces overseas; data for subsequent years show resident population.

-- Not available

Sources: 1 U.S. Bureau of the Census, Current Population Reports, Series P-25 (Washington: GPO), No. 311, p. 22; No. 519, tbl. 1; No. 917, tbl. 1; No. 1095, tbl. 1; No. 1104, tbl. 2; No. 1130, tbl. 2.

2 _____, Statistical Abstract of the U.S., 1994 (Washington: GPO, 1994), tbl. 20.

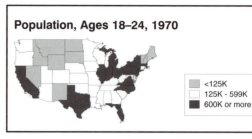

Population, Ages 18–24, 1970

	<125K
	125K - 599K
	600K or more

Region and State	Population, Ages 18- 24 (in thousands)				
	1970	1980	1990	1995	2000 Estimate
50 States & D.C.	**23,687**	**30,022**	**26,827**	**24,932**	**25,954**
New England	**1,372**	**1,631**	**1,483**	**1,158**	**1,155**
Connecticut	326	385	345	269	265
Maine	111	141	125	113	112
Massachusetts	671	784	710	536	532
New Hampshire	85	121	118	96	101
Rhode Island	124	129	121	90	89
Vermont	55	71	64	54	56
Mideast	**4,599**	**5,264**	**4,640**	**3,928**	**3,943**
Delaware	63	83	76	66	70
D.C.	110	97	83	52	52
Maryland	459	552	505	432	456
New Jersey	728	872	781	672	667
New York	1,982	2,158	1,964	1,636	1,627
Pennsylvania	1,257	1,502	1,231	1,070	1,071
Southeast	**5,323**	**6,946**	**6,440**	**6,199**	**6,332**
Alabama	403	515	448	442	441
Arkansas	211	278	239	249	252
Florida	714	1,140	1,212	1,158	1,243
Georgia	588	732	741	728	756
Kentucky	392	492	404	400	396
Louisiana	444	595	469	458	471
Mississippi	262	339	298	302	296
North Carolina	677	822	785	715	721
South Carolina	352	447	410	383	382
Tennessee	470	601	530	516	526
Virginia	615	742	722	658	673
West Virginia	195	243	182	190	175
Great Lakes	**4,578**	**5,560**	**4,491**	**4,158**	**4,209**
Illinois	1,220	1,508	1,219	1,115	1,127
Indiana	607	737	611	582	584
Michigan	1,032	1,258	1,007	918	919
Ohio	1,215	1,414	1,143	1,063	1,065
Wisconsin	504	643	511	480	514

Continued on next page.

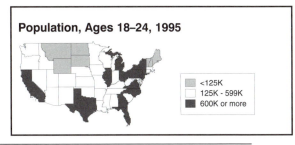

Population, Ages 18–24, 1995

<125K
125K - 599K
600K or more

Region and State	Population, Ages 18- 24 (in thousands)				
	1970	1980	1990	1995	2000 Estimate
Plains	**1,857**	**2,312**	**1,794**	**1,727**	**1,842**
Iowa	309	388	284	272	285
Kansas	274	327	255	246	267
Minnesota	433	558	442	415	455
Missouri	522	636	519	497	517
Nebraska	171	211	157	159	170
North Dakota	73	97	69	66	70
South Dakota	75	95	68	72	79
Southwest	**2,012**	**2,935**	**2,757**	**2,823**	**3,033**
Arizona	211	369	391	397	437
New Mexico	120	178	152	167	181
Oklahoma	301	402	322	329	344
Texas	1,380	1,986	1,892	1,930	2,071
Rocky Mountains	**629**	**930**	**748**	**855**	**945**
Colorado	292	418	335	350	391
Idaho	80	123	99	125	137
Montana	77	104	70	83	90
Utah	143	216	202	247	273
Wyoming	37	69	42	50	55
Far West	**3,317**	**4,444**	**4,474**	**4,084**	**4,496**
Alaska	46	60	56	62	71
California	2,447	3,252	3,420	3,000	3,277
Hawaii	109	142	122	115	120
Nevada	53	105	119	128	152
Oregon	238	331	268	281	311
Washington	424	554	489	498	566

Note: Data are for resident population. Figures for 1970 are as of April 1; for 1980, as of November.
for other years, as of July. Estimates for 2000 are based on the relationship between 1995 population
estimates for ages 18-24 and ages 15-24. They will differ from total 18-24 figures in other tables.

Sources: 1 U.S. Bureau of the Census, 1970 Census of Population PC(V2)(Washington: GPO,
1971), Reports 1 - 52.
2 _____ , Current Population Reports, Series P-25 (Washington: GPO), No. 970, tbls. 3 & 7;
No. 1111, tbl. 4; No. 1127, tbl. 4.
3 _____ , Statistical Abstract of the U.S., 1996 (Washington: GPO, 1996), tbl. 34.

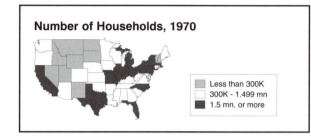

Number of Households, 1970

Less than 300K
300K - 1.499 mn
1.5 mn. or more

Region and State	Number of Households (in thousands)			
	1970	1980	1990	1994
50 States & D.C.	**63,480**	**80,390**	**91,946**	**95,946**
New England	**3,675**	**4,362**	**4,942**	**4,980**
Connecticut	933	1,094	1,230	1,222
Maine	303	395	465	474
Massachusetts	1,760	2,033	2,247	2,265
New Hampshire	255	323	411	424
Rhode Island	292	339	378	374
Vermont	132	178	211	220
Mideast	**13,440**	**15,030**	**16,176**	**16,397**
Delaware	165	207	247	264
D.C.	263	253	250	237
Maryland	1,175	1,461	1,749	1,831
New Jersey	2,218	2,549	2,795	2,845
New York	5,914	6,340	6,639	6,669
Pennsylvania	3,705	4,220	4,496	4,551
Southeast	**13,371**	**18,517**	**22,301**	**23,606**
Alabama	1,034	1,342	1,507	1,583
Arkansas	615	816	891	927
Florida	2,285	3,744	5,136	5,456
Georgia	1,369	1,872	2,367	2,581
Kentucky	984	1,263	1,380	1,440
Louisiana	1,052	1,412	1,499	1,543
Mississippi	637	827	911	949
North Carolina	1,510	2,043	2,517	2,679
South Carolina	734	1,030	1,258	1,337
Tennessee	1,213	1,619	1,854	1,966
Virginia	1,391	1,863	2,292	2,439
West Virginia	547	686	689	705
Great Lakes	**12,382**	**14,653**	**15,596**	**16,051**
Illinois	3,502	4,045	4,202	4,308
Indiana	1,609	1,927	2,065	2,161
Michigan	2,653	3,195	3,419	3,502
Ohio	3,289	3,834	4,088	4,190
Wisconsin	1,329	1,652	1,822	1,890

Note: Data prior to 1994 are as of April 1; figures for 1994 are estimates as of July 1. Totals vary from data on the following table because of differences in dates.

Continued on next page.

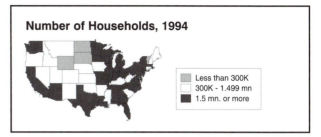

Number of Households, 1994

Legend:
- Less than 300K
- 300K - 1.499 mn
- 1.5 mn. or more

Region and State	Number of Households (in thousands)			
	1970	1980	1990	1994
Plains	**5,155**	**6,205**	**6,720**	**6,886**
Iowa	896	1,053	1,064	1,082
Kansas	727	872	945	966
Minnesota	1,154	1,445	1,648	1,711
Missouri	1,521	1,793	1,961	2,008
Nebraska	474	571	602	614
North Dakota	182	228	241	241
South Dakota	201	243	259	265
Southwest	**5,113**	**7,446**	**9,189**	**9,865**
Arizona	539	957	1,369	1,503
New Mexico	289	441	543	587
Oklahoma	851	1,119	1,206	1,236
Texas	3,434	4,929	6,071	6,539
Rocky Mountains	**1,530**	**2,284**	**2,655**	**2,924**
Colorado	691	1,061	1,282	1,417
Idaho	219	324	361	405
Montana	217	284	306	325
Utah	298	449	537	599
Wyoming	105	166	169	178
Far West	**8,814**	**11,892**	**14,367**	**15,237**
Alaska	79	131	189	208
California	6,574	8,630	10,381	10,850
Hawaii	203	294	356	381
Nevada	160	304	466	560
Oregon	692	992	1,103	1,195
Washington	1,106	1,541	1,872	2,042

Source: 1 U.S. Bureau of the Census, Current Population Reports, Series P-25, No. 710, tbl 1.
  2 ____, Statistical Abstract of the U.S., 1996 (Washington: GPO, 1996), tbl. 73.

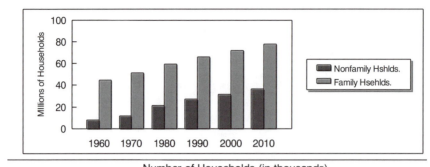

	Number of Households (in thousands)				
		Family Households			Nonfamily
			Married Couple		
Year	Total	Total	Number	Pct. of Total	Households
1960	52,800	44,905	39,254	87	7,895
1970	63,401	51,456	44,728	87	11,945
1980	80,776	59,550	49,112	82	21,226
1985	86,788	62,706	50,350	80	24,082
1990	93,347	66,090	52,317	79	27,257
1991	94,312	66,322	52,147	79	27,990
1992	95,669	67,173	52,457	78	28,496
1993	96,391	68,144	53,171	78	28,247
1994	97,107	68,490	53,171	78	28,617
1995	98,990	69,305	53,858	78	29,686
Projections					
1996	98,857	69,090	53,893	78	29,767
1997	99,965	69,761	54,319	78	30,204
1998	101,043	70,387	54,707	78	30,656
1999	102,119	71,015	55,092	78	31,104
2000	103,246	71,669	55,496	77	31,577
2005	108,819	74,733	57,371	77	34,086
2010	114,825	77895	59,308	76	36,931

Note: Data are estimates as of March of the year indicated.

Source: U.S. Bureau of the Census, Statistical Abstract of the U.S. (Washington: GPO), 1993, tbl.65; 1994, tbl. 66; 1996, tbls. 66, 67.

Year	Births (in thous.)	Birth Rate (per thous.)	Deaths (in thous.)	Death Rate (per thous.)
1910	2,777	30.1	697	14.7
1920	2,950	27.7	1,118	13.0
1930	2,618	21.3	1,327	11.3
1940	2,559	19.4	1,417	10.8
1950	3,632	24.1	1,452	9.6
1960	4,258	23.7	1,712	9.5
1970	3,731	18.4	1,921	9.5
1975	3,144	14.6	1,893	8.9
1980	3,612	15.9	1,990	8.8
1985	3,761	15.8	2,086	8.8
1986	3,757	15.6	2,105	8.8
1987	3,809	15.7	2,123	8.8
1988	3,910	16.0	2,168	8.9
1989	4,041	16.4	2,150	8.7
1990	4,158	16.7	2,148	8.6
1991	4,111	16.3	2,170	8.6
1992	4,065	15.9	2,176	8.5
1993	4,000	15.5	2,269	8.8
1994	3,979	15.3	2,286	8.8
1995	3,961	15.1	2,329	8.9
Projections				
1996	3,921	14.8	2,329	8.8
1997	3,907	14.6	2,353	8.8
1998	3,899	14.4	2,377	8.8
2000	3,899	14.2	2,425	8.8

Source: U.S. Bureau of the Census, Statistical Abstract of the U.S.
    (Washington: GPO), 1987, p. 58; 1996, tbls. 4, 90.

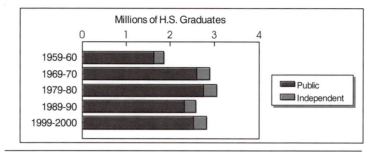

Millions of H.S. Graduates

	Public	Independent

	Number of High School Graduates (in thousands)			Annual Percentage Change (Total Grads.)
School Year	Total	Public	Independent	
1909-10	156	111	45	--
1919-20	311	231	80	--
1929-30	667	592	75	--
1939-40	1,221	1,143	78	--
1949-50	1,200	1,063	136	--
1959-60	1,858	1,627	231	--
1969-70	2,889	2,589	300	--
1979-80	3,043	2,748	295	--
1981-82	2,995	2,705	290	*-1.6*
1983-84	2,767	2,495	272	*-7.6*
1984-85	2,677	2,414	263	-3.3
1985-86	2,643	2,383	260	-1.3
1986-87	2,694	2,429	265	1.9
1987-88	2,773	2,500	273	2.9
1988-89	2,727	2,459	268	-1.7
1989-90	2,586	2,320	266	-5.2
1990-91	2,503	2,235	268	-3.2
1991-92	2,482	2,226	256	-0.8
1992-93	2,490	2,233	257	0.3
1993-94	2,479	2,221	258	-0.4
Projections				
1994-95	2,486	2,229	257	0.3
1995-96	2,552	2,287	264	2.7
1996-97	2,564	2,298	265	0.5
1999-2000	2,816	2,524	292	9.8

-- Not calculated; intervals are greater than one year. Percentages in italics are for a two-year period.

Note: For most years, private school data are estimates based on periodic surveys. Data for 1994-5 and 1995-6 for public schools are based on state estimates.

Sources: 1 NCES, Digest of Education Statistics, 1996 (Washington: GPO, 1996), tbl. 98.
2 ____, Projections of Education Statistics to 2007 (Washington: GPO, 1997), tbl. 26.

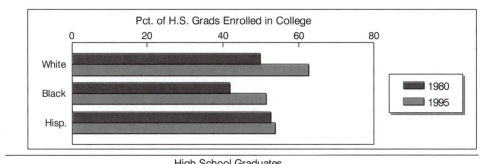

Pct. of H.S. Grads Enrolled in College

	High School Graduates					
	(Persons 16 to 24 who graduated from high school in the preceding 12 months.)					
Year	All Graduates	Male	Female	White	Black	Hispanic
	Number (in thousands)					
1960	1,679	756	923	1,565	na	na
1965	2,659	1,254	1,405	2,417	na	na
1970	2,757	1,343	1,414	2,461	na	na
1975	3,186	1,513	1,673	2,825	na	na
1980	3,089	1,500	1,589	2,682	361	129
1985	2,666	1,286	1,380	2,241	333	141
1990	2,355	1,169	1,185	1,921	341	112
1991	2,276	1,139	1,137	1,867	320	154
1992	2,398	1,216	1,182	1,900	353	199
1993	2,338	1,118	1,219	1,910	302	200
1994	2,517	1,244	1,273	2,065	318	178
1995	2,599	1,238	1,361	2,088	356	288
	Percentage Enrolled in College					
1960	45.1	54.0	37.9	45.8	na	na
1965	50.9	57.3	45.3	51.7	na	na
1970	51.8	55.2	48.5	52.0	na	na
1975	50.7	52.6	49.0	51.2	na	na
1980	49.3	46.7	51.8	49.9	41.8	52.7
1985	57.7	58.6	56.9	59.4	42.3	51.1
1990	59.9	57.8	62.0	61.5	46.3	47.3
1991	62.4	57.6	67.1	64.6	45.6	57.1
1992	61.7	59.6	63.8	63.4	47.9	54.8
1993	62.6	59.7	65.4	62.8	55.6	62.5
1994	61.9	60.6	63.2	63.6	50.9	48.9
1995	61.9	62.6	61.4	62.6	51.4	53.8

na: Not available.

Notes: Includes GED recipients. Figures may not agree with other counts of high school graduates because of varying survey procedures. Hispanic data may be subject to wide sampling errors. White and Black students include persons of Hispanic origin.

Source: NCES, Digest of Education Statistics, 1996 (Washington: GPO, 1996), tbls. 179, 180.

12 High School Completions, by Persons Aged 18–24 and by Race/Ethnicity, 1975–1994

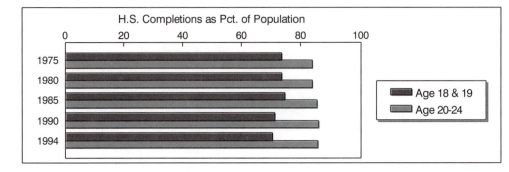

	High School Completions as Percentage of Population							
	Ages 18 & 19 Years Old				Ages 20 - 24 Years Old			
Year	Total	White	Black	Hispanic	Total	White	Black	Hispanic
1975	74	77	53	50	84	86	71	61
1980	74	76	59	46	84	85	74	57
1982	72	75	58	52	84	85	76	60
1984	73	76	63	58	85	86	79	61
1985	75	77	63	50	85	86	81	67
1986	75	77	65	55	85	85	81	62
1988	72	74	58	52	85	86	82	56
1990	71	73	61	42	86	86	84	59
1991	71	73	60	42	85	85	82	56
1992	71	74	56	51	86	87	82	60
1993	71	73	60	49	86	87	81	65
1994	70	73	57	47	86	86	85	60

Note: Hispanics may be of any race. Most year-to-year differences of data for Hispanics are not statistically significant because of the small size of the Hispanic sample.

Source: U.S. Bureau of the Census, School Enrollment - Social and Economic Characteristics of Students, CPR Series P-20 (Washington: GPO), Annually.

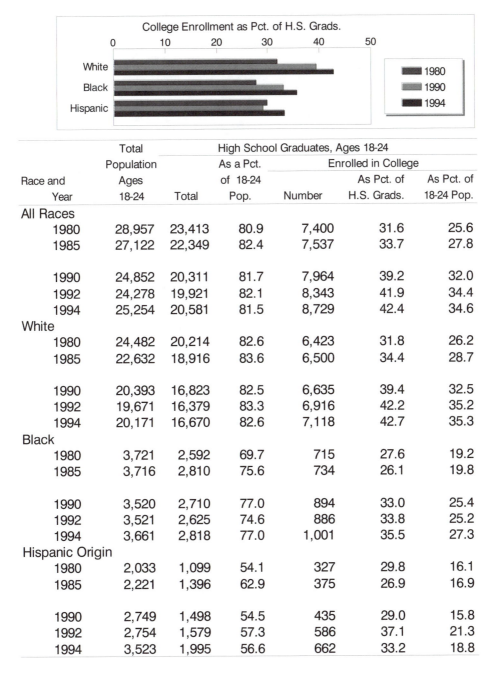

Race and Year	Total Population Ages 18-24	High School Graduates, Ages 18-24				
		Total	As a Pct. of 18-24 Pop.	Enrolled in College		
				Number	As Pct. of H.S. Grads.	As Pct. of 18-24 Pop.
All Races						
1980	28,957	23,413	80.9	7,400	31.6	25.6
1985	27,122	22,349	82.4	7,537	33.7	27.8
1990	24,852	20,311	81.7	7,964	39.2	32.0
1992	24,278	19,921	82.1	8,343	41.9	34.4
1994	25,254	20,581	81.5	8,729	42.4	34.6
White						
1980	24,482	20,214	82.6	6,423	31.8	26.2
1985	22,632	18,916	83.6	6,500	34.4	28.7
1990	20,393	16,823	82.5	6,635	39.4	32.5
1992	19,671	16,379	83.3	6,916	42.2	35.2
1994	20,171	16,670	82.6	7,118	42.7	35.3
Black						
1980	3,721	2,592	69.7	715	27.6	19.2
1985	3,716	2,810	75.6	734	26.1	19.8
1990	3,520	2,710	77.0	894	33.0	25.4
1992	3,521	2,625	74.6	886	33.8	25.2
1994	3,661	2,818	77.0	1,001	35.5	27.3
Hispanic Origin						
1980	2,033	1,099	54.1	327	29.8	16.1
1985	2,221	1,396	62.9	375	26.9	16.9
1990	2,749	1,498	54.5	435	29.0	15.8
1992	2,754	1,579	57.3	586	37.1	21.3
1994	3,523	1,995	56.6	662	33.2	18.8

Note: High school graduates include all persons who have completed 4 years or more of high school or passed the GED tests. All persons enrolled in college are counted as high school graduates. Persons of Hispanic origin may be of any race.

Source: U.S. Bureau of the Census, Current Population Reports, Series P-20 (Washington: GPO), No. 487, tbl. A-5.

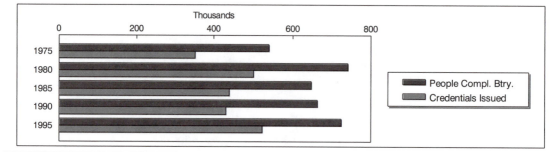

Year	Number of Official GED Test Centers	Persons Tested Average Age	Persons Tested Average Years of Schooling	Persons Tested Pct. Planning Further Study	Persons Completing GED Battery Number	Persons Completing GED Battery Pct. Meeting Score Requirements	Credentials Issued Number	Credentials Issued As Pct. of Persons Completing Test Btry.
1949-58	587	27.0	10.0	38.0	--	77.8	--	--
1960	658	29.0	10.0	31.0	--	77.0	--	--
1965	928	29.0	9.7	38.0	--	72.0	--	--
1970	1,711	29.1	9.7	40.1	--	70.8	234,726	--
1975	2,462	25.1	10.0	42.1	541,194	70.2	351,327	64.9
1980	2,753	25.1	10.0	36.6	741,601	70.8	500,203	67.4
1985	3,371	25.8	9.8	51.3	647,496	72.4	439,922	67.9
1986	3,243	26.5	9.9	54.8	674,430	72.6	451,294	66.9
1987	3,314	26.7	9.9	49.7	690,509	74.1	472,007	68.4
1988	3,450	26.7	9.9	47.5	651,247	72.3	435,318	66.8
1989	3,468	26.2	10.0	53.6	589,002	68.4	376,879	64.0
1990	3,316	26.5	9.9	56.5	662,789	69.9	431,231	65.1
1991	3,445	26.4	9.9	58.6	706,182	71.5	483,854	68.5
1992	3,401	26.6	9.9	61.4	688,582	71.4	479,252	69.6
1993	3,250	26.0	9.9	61.7	685,304	71.4	489,474	71.4
1994	3,300	25.6	9.9	65.6	712,421	73.0	510,587	71.7
1995	3,255	25.3	9.9	63.7	723,899	72.0	523,463	72.3

-- Not available.

Note: Data include persons tested in the 50 states, D.C., outlying areas, and Canada. 1949-58 data for test centers and the percentage score requirements are averages for the 10-year period; the number of people tested is the ten-year total; data for average age and years of schooling are for 1958 only. Credentials issued are high school credentials awarded based on passing the Tests of General Educational Development (GED Tests) published by the American Council on Education.

Source: American Council on Education (ACE), GED Statistical Report (Washington: ACE), 1986, p. 22; 1995, tbl. 11.

Educational Attainment of Population Aged 18 Years Old and Over, by Sex, Race/Ethnicity, and Age, 1995

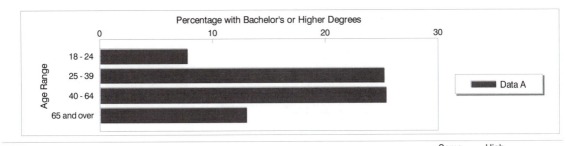

Race, Age, and Sex	Population 18 years Old & Over	Highest Degree Earned					Some College, No Degree	High School Graduate Only	Not a High School Graduate
		Docto-rate	Profes-sional	Master's	Bache-lor's	Asso-ciate			
				Number of Individuals (in thousands)					
Total population, ages 18 years old and over	191,596	1,673	2,432	8,887	27,189	12,927	38,014	64,228	36,246
Men	92,008	1,195	1,713	4,620	13,909	5,575	17,890	29,491	17,615
Women	99,588	478	719	4,267	13,280	7,352	20,124	34,738	18,631
Race									
White, non-Hispanic	145,875	1,408	2,102	7,780	23,031	10,510	29,750	50,157	21,137
Black, non-Hispanic	21,807	85	84	501	1,889	1,248	4,395	7,826	5,779
Hispanic	17,619	50	103	237	995	753	2,616	4,678	8,186
Other racial groups	6,295	130	143	369	1,274	416	1,253	1,567	1,144
Age									
18 to 24 years old	25,158	5	4	70	1,876	1,032	8,659	7,778	5,733
25 to 39 years old	63,629	402	864	2,809	11,942	5,549	12,400	21,744	7,916
40 to 64 years old	71,542	1,024	1,267	5,060	10,804	5,263	12,707	24,132	11,287
65 years old and over	31,267	242	298	948	2,566	1,083	4,249	10,575	11,306
				Percentage Distribution					
Total population, ages 18 years old and over	100.0	0.9	1.3	4.6	14.2	6.7	19.8	33.5	18.9
Men	100.0	1.3	1.9	5.0	15.1	6.1	19.4	32.1	19.1
Women	100.0	0.5	0.7	4.3	13.3	7.4	20.2	34.9	18.7
Race									
White, non-Hispanic	100.0	1.0	1.4	5.3	15.8	7.2	20.4	34.4	14.5
Black, non-Hispanic	100.0	0.4	0.4	2.3	8.7	5.7	20.2	35.9	26.5
Hispanic	100.0	0.3	0.6	1.3	5.6	4.3	14.8	26.6	46.5
Other racial groups	100.0	2.1	2.3	5.9	20.2	6.6	19.9	24.9	18.2
Age									
18 to 24 years old	100.0	0.0	0.0	0.3	7.5	4.1	34.4	30.9	22.8
25 to 39 years old	100.0	0.6	1.4	4.4	18.8	8.7	19.5	34.2	12.4
40 to 64 years old	100.0	1.4	1.8	7.1	15.1	7.4	17.8	33.7	15.8
65 years old and over	100.0	0.8	1.0	3.0	8.2	3.5	13.6	33.8	36.2

Note: Data are based on a sample survey of the civilian noninstitutional population; cells with fewer than 75,000 people are subject to wide sampling variation.

Source: NCES, Digest of Education Statistics, 1996 (Washington: GPO, 1996), tbl. 9.

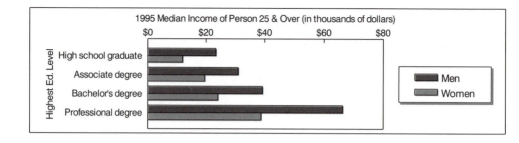

| Race and Highest Level | Median Income (in constant 1995 dollars) of - | | | |
| of School Completed | Men | | Women | |
	1993	1995	1993	1995
Total, 15 years and over	**$22,256**	**$22,562**	**$11,650**	**$12,130**
White	23,183	23,895	11,882	12,316
Black	15,403	16,006	10,028	10,961
Hispanic Origin	14,437	14,840	8,543	8,928
Total, 25 years and over	**25,950**	**26,346**	**12,903**	**13,821**
Bachelor's or higher	43,926	43,322	26,626	26,843
Bachelor's	39,523	39,040	23,679	24,065
Master's	48,090	49,076	33,105	33,509
Professional	73,487	66,257	34,532	38,588
Doctorate	58,799	57,356	45,072	39,821
Associate degree	31,362	31,027	19,349	19,450
Some college, no degree	27,762	28,004	15,281	15,552
High School graduate (includes				
equivalency)	22,973	23,365	11,695	12,046
9th to 12th grade (no diploma)	15,345	15,791	7,580	8,057
Less than 9th grade	11,491	11,723	6,834	7,096
Year-round Full-time Workers,				
25 years and over	**34,128**	**34,551**	**24,921**	**24,875**
Bachelor's or higher	50,350	50,481	36,183	35,259
Bachelor's	45,095	45,266	32,903	32,051
Master's	54,703	55,216	40,723	40,263
Professional	84,953	79,668	52,956	50,000
Doctorate	66,601	65,336	49,831	48,141
Associate degree	35,532	35,201	27,298	27,311
Some college, no degree	33,831	33,883	24,317	23,997
High School graduate (includes				
equivalency)	28,866	29,510	21,054	20,463
9th to 12th grade (no diploma)	22,941	22,185	16,227	15,825
Less than 9th grade	17,785	18,354	13,094	13,577

Note: In constant 1995 dollars.

Source: U.S. Bureau of the Census, Current Population Reports (CPR), No. P60-193 (Washington: GPO, 1996), tbl. 7.

Percentage of All Families

| | 1970 | 1994 |

Less than $25,000
$25,000-$49,999
$50,000 +

Year	Under $10,000	$10,000- $14,999	$15,000- 24,900	$25,000- $34,999	$35,000- $49,999	$50,000- $74,999	$75,000 & Over
				Percentage of Families with Incomes (in constant 1994 dollars) of			
All Families							
1970	7.9	7.0	15.8	18.8	24.1	18.3	8.0
1980	7.7	6.8	15.4	15.7	21.9	20.7	11.8
1990	7.9	6.4	14.4	14.4	19.4	20.6	16.9
1992	9.1	6.8	14.7	14.7	18.7	20.2	15.7
1994	8.7	6.9	15.0	14.3	18.0	19.9	17.2
White Families							
1970	6.7	6.5	15.0	18.9	25.0	19.3	8.6
1980	6.2	6.0	14.8	15.9	22.7	21.8	12.7
1990	6.0	5.7	13.9	14.6	20.0	21.8	17.9
1992	6.8	6.2	14.3	14.9	19.4	21.5	17.0
1994	6.8	6.2	14.6	14.5	18.5	20.9	18.5
Black Families							
1970	19.5	12.7	23.3	17.2	15.8	9.4	2.2
1980	20.0	13.5	20.8	14.6	15.4	12.0	3.7
1990	22.0	11.5	18.3	13.0	15.8	12.1	7.4
1992	25.1	11.7	18.1	13.4	14.2	11.4	6.1
1994	21.0	11.2	18.4	13.5	14.8	13.3	7.9
Hispanic Families							
1980	14.2	11.4	21.4	17.8	17.5	12.8	4.9
1990	15.3	12.6	19.5	16.2	16.9	12.4	7.1
1992	17.1	12.0	21.2	16.2	15.3	12.1	6.1
1994	17.8	12.6	21.0	14.9	14.9	11.7	7.2

Note: Income is total money income before deductions for taxes and is in constant 1994 dollars.

Beginning with 1980 based on household concept and restricted to primary families, a group of 2 or more persons related by blood, marriage, or adoption, and residing together.

Source: U.S. Bureau of the Census, Statistical Abstract of the U.S., 1996 (Washington: GPO, 1996), tbl. 717.

Median Income of Families by Race/Ethnicity, Selected Years, 1950–1995 (in Current Dollars)

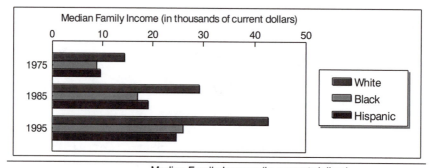

| | Median Family Income (in current dollars) | | | |
Year	All	White	Black	Hispanic	Asian, Pacific Islander
1950	$3,319	$3,445	$1,869	-	-
1960	5,620	5,835	3,230	-	-
1965	6,957	7,251	3,993	-	-
1970	9,867	10,236	6,279	-	-
1975	13,719	14,268	8,779	9,551	-
1980	21,023	21,904	12,674	14,716	-
1985	27,735	29,152	16,786	19,027	-
1986	29,458	30,809	17,604	19,995	-
1987	30,970	32,385	18,406	20,300	-
1988	32,191	33,915	19,329	21,769	36,560
1989	34,213	35,975	20,209	23,446	40,351
1990	35,353	36,915	21,423	23,431	42,246
1991	35,939	37,783	21,548	23,895	40,974
1992	36,573	38,670	21,103	23,555	42,255
1993	36,959	39,300	21,542	23,654	44,456
1994	38,782	40,884	24,698	24,318	46,122
1995	40,611	42,646	25,970	24,570	-

- Not available.

Note: In 1983 and 1987 revisions were adopted so data are not strictly comparable with prior years. Figures in the Black column prior to 1970 refer to all nonwhite families.

Sources: 1 U.S. Bureau of the Census, Current Population Reports (CPR), No. 60-101, pp. 19, 20.
2 _____, Statistical Abstract of the U.S., 1996 (Washington: GPO, 1996), tbl. 718.

Median Income of Families by Race/Ethnicity, Selected Years, 1970–1995 (in Constant 1995 Dollars)

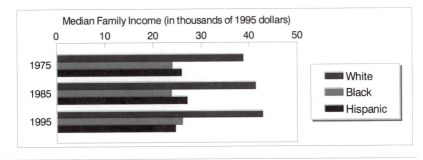

Year	All	White	Black	Hispanic	Asian, Pacific Islander
	Median Family Income (in constant 1995 dollars)				
1970	$36,410	$37,772	$23,170	-	-
1975	37,202	38,691	23,806	25,900	-
1980	38,930	40,561	23,836	27,251	-
1985	39,283	41,290	23,775	26,949	-
1986	40,962	42,840	24,479	27,803	-
1987	41,548	43,446	24,693	27,233	-
1988	41,470	43,691	24,901	28,044	47,098
1989	42,049	44,214	24,838	28,816	49,593
1990	41,223	43,044	24,980	27,321	49,260
1991	40,214	42,277	24,111	26,737	45,848
1992	39,727	42,005	22,923	25,586	45,899
1993	38,980	41,449	22,720	24,947	46,886
1994	39,881	42,043	25,398	25,007	47,429
1995	40,611	42,646	25,970	24,570	-

- Not available.

Note: In 1983 and 1987 revisions were adopted so data are not strictly comparable with prior years. Figures in the Black column prior to 1970 refer to all nonwhite families. Constant dollars are based on the Consumer Price Index.

Sources: 1 U.S. Bureau of the Census, Current Population Reports (CPR), No. P60-193 (Washington: GPO, 1996), tbls. B-1, B-4.
2 _____, Statistical Abstract of the U.S., 1996 (Washington: GPO, 1996), tbl.718

Median Money Income of Households, by State, 1984, 1990, 1994, and 1995 (in Constant 1995 Dollars)

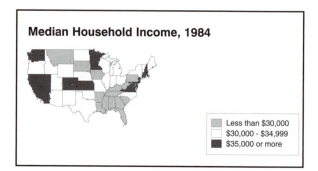

Median Household Income, 1984

Less than $30,000
$30,000 - $34,999
$35,000 or more

Region and State	Median Income of Households (in constant 1995 dollars)			
	1984	1990	1994	1995
50 States & D.C.	$32,878	$34,914	$33,178	$34,076
New England				
Connecticut	43,932	45,323	42,262	40,243
Maine	30,287	32,024	31,175	33,858
Massachusetts	39,544	42,265	41,648	38,574
New Hampshire	38,011	47,580	36,244	39,171
Rhode Island	31,701	37,275	32,833	35,359
Vermont	33,118	36,261	36,817	33,824
Mideast				
Delaware	37,871	35,918	36,890	34,928
D.C.	29,934	31,940	30,969	30,748
Maryland	43,576	45,309	40,309	41,041
New Jersey	40,742	45,165	43,478	43,924
New York	32,309	36,836	32,803	33,028
Pennsylvania	29,843	33,821	32,975	34,524
Southeast				
Alabama	25,390	27,235	27,967	25,991
Arkansas	22,991	26,569	26,290	25,814
Florida	29,021	31,116	30,124	29,745
Georgia	29,313	32,137	32,359	34,099
Kentucky	25,933	28,894	27,349	29,810
Louisiana	27,794	26,125	26,404	27,949
Mississippi	22,633	23,528	26,120	26,538
North Carolina	30,170	30,700	30,967	31,979
South Carolina	29,789	33,505	30,692	29,071
Tennessee	24,615	26,343	29,451	29,015
Virginia	38,907	40,896	38,714	36,222
West Virginia	24,705	25,812	24,232	24,880
Great Lakes				
Illinois	34,839	37,945	36,075	38,071
Indiana	33,398	31,398	28,647	33,385
Michigan	33,685	34,907	36,284	36,426
Ohio	33,917	34,996	32,758	34,941
Wisconsin	30,425	35,810	36,391	40,955

Continued on next page.

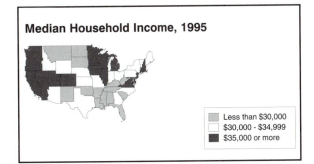

Median Household Income, 1995

Less than $30,000
$30,000 - $34,999
$35,000 or more

Region and State	Median Income of Households (in constant 1995 dollars)			
	1984	1990	1994	1995
Plains				
Iowa	$29,135	$31,819	$34,016	35,519
Kansas	36,126	34,884	29,125	30,341
Minnesota	35,843	36,689	34,597	37,933
Missouri	30,473	31,870	31,046	34,825
Nebraska	31,385	32,045	32,695	32,929
North Dakota	30,467	29,459	29,079	29,089
South Dakota	28,469	28,651	30,576	29,578
Southwest				
Arizona	31,426	34,076	32,180	30,863
New Mexico	30,260	29,197	27,667	25,991
Oklahoma	31,020	28,433	27,756	26,311
Texas	33,772	32,915	31,627	32,039
Rocky Mountains				
Colorado	37,845	35,836	38,905	40,706
Idaho	30,938	29,506	32,430	32,676
Montana	28,656	27,256	28,414	27,757
Utah	33,820	35,147	36,728	36,480
Wyoming	34,933	34,352	34,079	31,529
Far West				
Alaska	47,460	45,823	46,653	47,954
California	37,091	38,817	36,332	37,009
Hawaii	42,356	45,383	43,453	42,851
Nevada	37,808	37,340	36,888	36,084
Oregon	31,388	34,143	32,347	36,374
Washington	36,695	37,444	34,483	35,568

Note: CPI-U-X1 used as deflator. Tabulations by state are considered less reliable than national estimates and should be used with caution. In 1987 and 1994 data collection and processing procedures were changed from previous methods, so data are not directly comparable to earlier figures.

Sources: 1 U.S. Bureau of the Census, Statistical Abstract of the U.S., 1996 (Washington: GPO, 1996), tbl. 716.

2 _____, Current Population Reports, P60-193, Money Income in the U. S.: 1995 (Washington: GPO, 1996), tbl. C.

21 Families with 18–24-year-olds, by Income Level, Race/Ethnicity, and Enrollment Status, October 1994

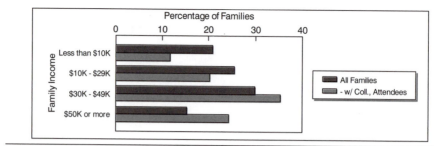

Race/ethnicity and Income Level	All Families w/ 18-24 yr-olds	Percentage of Families with - 18-24-yr-olds NOT Attending College Full-time	One or More 18-24-yr-old Attending College Full-time
All Races			
All income levels	100	100	100
Less than $10,000	21	27	12
$10,000 - $19,000	12	14	9
$20,000 - $29,000	14	15	11
$30,000 - $39,000	11	10	12
$40,000 - $49,000	19	16	24
$50,000 and over	15	9	24
Not reported	8	8	8
White			
All income levels	100	100	100
Less than $10,000	17	23	9
$10,000 - $19,000	11	14	8
$20,000 - $29,000	14	16	11
$30,000 - $39,000	12	11	12
$40,000 - $49,000	21	18	25
$50,000 and over	17	10	26
Not reported	8	9	8
Black			
All income levels	100	100	100
Less than $10,000	38	43	26
$10,000 - $19,000	14	14	14
$20,000 - $29,000	14	13	18
$30,000 - $39,000	8	7	9
$40,000 - $49,000	12	10	16
$50,000 and over	5	4	8
Not reported	9	9	9
Hispanic			
All income levels	100	100	100
Less than $10,000	45	48	36
$10,000 - $19,000	18	18	15
$20,000 - $29,000	10	11	9
$30,000 - $39,000	6	5	10
$40,000 - $49,000	9	7	14
$50,000 and over	4	3	9
Not reported	8	8	7

Note: Data describe primary families in the civilian noninstitutional population. Excludes families in which the only members aged 18-24 are householders or are married, spouse present. Hispanics may be of any race.

Source: U.S. Bureau of the Census, Current Population Reports (CPR), No. P20-487 (Washington: GPO, 1996), tbl. 16.

Family Income of Families with First-time, Full-time Freshmen, 1967, 1986, and 1996

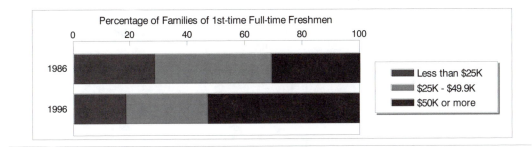

Percentage of Families of 1st-time Full-time Freshmen

Annual Income Level	All Families	Families with First-time, Full-time Freshmen (Percentage)			
		All Institutions	Two-year Colleges	Four-year Colleges	Universities
1967					
Less than $10,000	66.1	40.8	48.3	40.0	33.6
$10,000 - $14,999	22.6	21.4	19.8	21.5	23.1
$15,000 - $24,999	9.3	12.0	8.0	12.5	15.8
$25,000 and over	2.1	6.0	2.5	6.5	9.1
No idea	-	19.8	21.5	19.5	18.4
1986					
Less than $10,000	12.4	7.6	10.8	7.0	4.2
$10,000 - $14,999	9.7	6.4	8.5	6.1	4.0
$15,000 - $24,999	19.5	14.4	18.4	13.6	10.2
$25,000 - $34,999	18.1	18.6	21.8	18.1	15.0
$35,000 - $49,999	19.6	22.1	21.7	22.4	22.0
$50,000 and over	20.7	30.9	18.8	32.8	44.6
1996					
Less than $10,000	7.5	5.2	8.0	4.7	3.0
$10,000 - $14,999	6.5	4.0	5.7	3.7	2.7
$15,000 - $24,999	14.4	9.2	12.3	8.7	6.9
$25,000 - $34,999	14.1	11.0	13.4	10.9	9.0
$35,000 - $49,999	18.5	17.4	20.1	17.2	14.7
$50,000 and over	39.0	53.0	40.7	54.7	63.7

Notes: Dollar figures are in current, not constant, dollars. "All Families" data are Census Bureau figures for total money income as of March. Most recent data are for 1995. Freshman family data for 1996 for ranges $25,000 - $34,999 and $35,000 - $49,999 include estimates from the $30,000 - $39,999 range shown in the source.
Freshman data are from surveys in which students were asked to estimate their family's income.

Sources: 1 U.S. Bureau of the Census, Current Population Reports, Series P-60 (Washington: GPO) No. 99, tbl 2; No. 157, tbl. 2; No. 193, tbl. 5.
2 Robert J. Panos, Alexander W. Astin, and John A. Creager, National Norms for Entering College Freshmen - Fall 1967 (Washington: American Council on Education, 1967), p. 33.
3 Alexander Astin, et. al., The American Freshman, National Norms (Los Angeles: Graduate School of Education, UCLA), Fall 1986, p. 48; Fall 1996, p. 14.

Per Capita Personal Income, by Region and State, Selected Years, 1960–1995

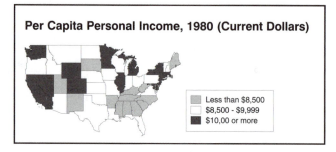

Per Capita Personal Income, 1980 (Current Dollars)

Less than $8,500
$8,500 - $9,999
$10,00 or more

Region and State	Per Capita Personal Income (Current Dollars)				
	1960	1970	1980	1990	1995
50 States & D.C.	**$2,222.0**	**$3,966.0**	**$9,919.0**	**$19,142.0**	**$23,208.0**
New England	**2,435**	**4,300**	**10,542**	**22,715**	**27,388**
Connecticut	2,838	4,917	12,110	26,375	31,776
Maine	1,862	3,302	8,224	17,167	20,105
Massachusetts	2,461	4,340	10,612	23,203	28,021
New Hampshire	2,135	3,737	9,789	20,671	25,587
Rhode Island	2,217	3,959	9,516	19,691	23,844
Vermont	1,847	3,468	8,578	17,691	21,231
Mideast	**2,573**	**4,471**	**10,662**	**22,366**	**26,844**
Delaware	2,785	4,524	10,241	21,696	26,273
D.C.	2,983	5,079	12,279	25,628	33,452
Maryland	2,341	4,309	10,809	22,483	26,333
New Jersey	2,727	4,701	11,579	24,925	29,848
New York	2,740	4,712	10,718	23,132	27,678
Pennsylvania	2,269	3,971	9,893	19,365	23,558
Southeast	**1,629**	**3,257**	**8,483**	**16,840**	**20,970**
Alabama	1,519	2,948	7,704	15,225	19,181
Arkansas	1,390	2,878	7,470	14,032	18,101
Florida	1,947	3,738	9,765	19,106	23,061
Georgia	1,651	3,354	8,350	17,378	21,741
Kentucky	1,586	3,112	8,018	15,088	18,849
Louisiana	1,668	3,090	8,682	14,761	18,981
Mississippi	1,222	2,626	6,927	12,710	16,683
North Carolina	1,592	3,252	7,998	16,664	21,103
South Carolina	1,397	2,990	7,587	15,421	18,998
Tennessee	1,576	3,119	8,027	16,295	21,038
Virginia	1,864	3,712	9,718	19,996	23,974
West Virginia	1,621	3,061	7,916	14,177	17,687
Great Lakes	**2,392**	**4,135**	**10,079**	**18,726**	**23,396**
Illinois	2,646	4,507	10,840	20,494	25,225
Indiana	2,178	3,772	9,248	17,174	21,433
Michigan	2,357	4,180	10,165	18,710	23,915
Ohio	2,345	4,020	9,723	18,125	22,514
Wisconsin	2,188	3,812	9,846	17,720	22,261

Continued on next page.

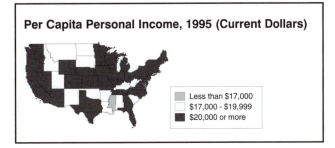

Per Capita Personal Income, 1995 (Current Dollars)

Less than $17,000
$17,000 - $19,999
$20,000 or more

Region and State	Per Capita Personal Income (Current Dollars)				
	1960	1970	1980	1990	1995
Plains	**$2,056**	**$3,751**	**$9,533**	**$17,849**	**$21,992**
Iowa	1,983	3,751	9,538	16,959	20,921
Kansas	2,160	3,853	9,941	17,988	21,841
Minnesota	2,075	3,859	10,062	19,374	23,971
Missouri	2,112	3,781	9,296	17,656	21,819
Nebraska	2,110	3,789	9,272	17,624	21,477
North Dakota	1,704	3,086	8,539	15,324	18,625
South Dakota	1,784	3,123	8,218	15,538	19,576
Southwest	**1,927**	**3,546**	**9,558**	**16,752**	**20,608**
Arizona	2,012	3,665	9,161	16,542	20,489
New Mexico	1,843	3,077	8,174	14,441	18,206
Oklahoma	1,876	3,387	9,395	15,584	18,580
Texas	1,936	3,606	9,795	17,219	21,206
Rocky Mountains	**2,099**	**3,590**	**9,568**	**16,900**	**21,107**
Colorado	2,252	3,855	10,597	19,224	23,961
Idaho	1,850	3,290	8,570	15,317	18,906
Montana	2,035	3,500	8,924	15,042	18,445
Utah	1,979	3,227	7,953	14,204	18,232
Wyoming	2,247	3,815	11,339	17,061	20,684
Far West	**2,618**	**4,374**	**11,336**	**20,773**	**23,882**
Alaska	2,809	4,644	13,830	21,047	24,002
California	2,706	4,493	11,603	21,287	24,073
Hawaii	2,368	4,623	10,616	21,333	24,590
Nevada	2,799	4,563	11,421	20,124	24,390
Oregon	2,220	3,719	9,864	17,437	21,611
Washington	2,360	4,053	10,727	19,583	23,774

Note: Data for 1990 and 1995 have been revised from previous estimates.

Source: U.S. Department of Commerce, Bureau of Economic Analysis, Survey of Current Business
(Washington: GPO), April 1969, p. 26; August 1976, p. 17; August 1987, p. 45; October 1996, p. 63.

State Appropriations for Higher Education, 1984–85

	Less than $200 mn.
	$200 mn. - $699 mn.
	$700 mn. or more

Region and State	Appropriations of State Tax Funds for Operating Expenses of Higher Education (In millions of current dollars)				Pct. Change 1994/95-96/97 (In Current Dollars)
	1974-75	1984-85	1994-95	1996-97	
50 States	**$11,278.9**	**$28,644.3**	**$42,821.0**	**$46,507.6**	**9**
New England	**474.9**	**1,216.5**	**1,839.7**	**1,833.4**	**-0**
Connecticut	135.2	302.9	500.3	538.8	8
Maine	43.9	91.3	173.0	182.6	6
Massachusetts	209.6	641.8	902.9	844.3	-6
New Hampshire	19.1	42.6	85.3	83.0	-3
Rhode Island	47.0	96.1	125.0	130.0	4
Vermont	20.1	41.8	53.2	54.7	3
Mideast	**2,269.2**	**4,612.9**	**6,872.4**	**6,853.4**	**-0**
Delaware	37.2	84.9	137.4	148.5	8
Maryland	209.0	487.7	788.2	850.0	8
New Jersey	289.5	695.0	1,259.3	1,397.3	11
New York	1,159.9	2,356.4	3,106.5	2,805.4	-10
Pennsylvania	573.6	988.9	1,581.0	1,652.2	5
Southeast	**2,452.8**	**6,570.0**	**10,629.3**	**11,673.1**	**10**
Alabama	177.1	551.0	1,016.1	962.4	-5
Arkansas	82.4	249.0	418.7	472.5	13
Florida	412.3	1,027.0	1,695.7	2,016.9	19
Georgia	237.4	611.9	1,119.9	1,302.6	16
Kentucky	169.6	400.5	657.6	706.7	7
Louisiana	185.5	550.7	589.6	645.9	10
Mississippi	130.7	338.9	628.6	669.0	6
North Carolina	349.3	960.3	1,723.3	1,852.0	7
South Carolina	202.8	451.0	634.5	698.5	10
Tennessee	174.3	495.7	864.5	934.5	8
Virginia	242.4	713.7	976.9	1,071.9	10
West Virginia	89.0	220.3	303.9	340.2	12
Great Lakes	**2,106.3**	**4,330.5**	**6,964.6**	**7,641.8**	**10**
Illinois	623.9	1,182.2	1,894.5	2,132.5	13
Indiana	247.1	551.2	923.5	1,030.6	12
Michigan	524.2	1,005.1	1,607.6	1,756.8	9
Ohio	386.0	974.0	1,559.7	1,754.9	13
Wisconsin	325.1	618.0	979.3	967.0	-1

Continued on next page.

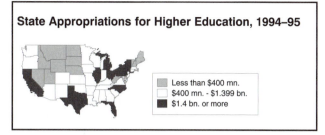

State Appropriations for Higher Education, 1994–95

Less than $400 mn.
$400 mn. - $1.399 bn.
$1.4 bn. or more

Region and State	Appropriations of State Tax Funds for Operating Expenses of Higher Education (In millions of dollars)				Pct. Change 1994/95-96/97 (In Current Dollars)
	1974-75	1984-85	1994-95	1996-97	
Plains	**$884.7**	**$2,158.8**	**$3,473.6**	**$3,781.0**	**9**
Iowa	165.2	393.0	641.2	711.2	11
Kansas	126.5	335.9	502.4	531.0	6
Minnesota	245.8	643.2	1,030.8	1,091.6	6
Missouri	197.9	400.9	672.8	775.1	15
Nebraska	85.4	213.3	369.6	401.8	9
North Dakota	31.7	110.5	143.9	151.9	6
South Dakota	32.2	62.0	112.9	118.4	5
Southwest	**853.5**	**3,358.6**	**4,753.2**	**5,011.7**	**5**
Arizona	152.5	376.2	665.5	731.8	10
New Mexico	61.4	250.0	437.5	487.4	11
Oklahoma	106.0	367.6	540.9	616.7	14
Texas	533.6	2,364.8	3,109.3	3,175.8	2
Rocky Mountains	**353.0**	**948.2**	**1,410.0**	**1,585.8**	**12**
Colorado	167.2	383.7	543.7	619.1	14
Idaho	50.2	112.2	226.9	247.7	9
Montana	35.6	107.4	113.2	126.4	12
Utah	75.7	235.8	397.5	457.5	15
Wyoming	24.3	109.1	128.7	135.1	5
Far West	**1,884.5**	**5,448.8**	**6,878.1**	**8,127.5**	**18**
Alaska	36.1	233.0	171.5	169.4	-1
California	1,365.9	4,080.0	4,748.7	5,817.0	22
Hawaii	70.7	185.1	386.0	351.1	-9
Nevada	29.7	78.6	194.4	234.3	21
Oregon	129.9	281.5	434.7	480.7	11
Washington	252.2	590.6	942.8	1,075.0	14

Sources: 1 M.M Chambers, Appropriations of State Tax Funds for Operating Expenses of Higher Education, 1984-85
(Washington: National Association of State Universities and Land-grant Colleges, 1984), tbl. 1.
2 Edward R. Hines, et al., State Higher Education Appropriations (Denver, CO: State Higher Education
Executive Officers [SHEEO]), 1994-95, tbl. 6; 1996-97, tbl. 6.

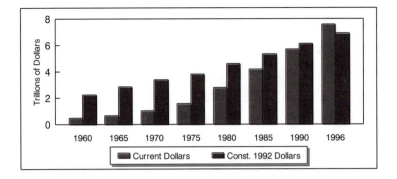

	Gross Domestic Product (In billions of dollars)	
Year	Current Dollars	Constant 1992 Dollars
1960	$526.6	$2,261.7
1965	719.1	2,874.8
1970	1,035.6	3,388.2
1975	1,630.6	3,865.1
1980	2,784.2	4,611.9
1982	3,242.1	4,623.6
1984	3,902.4	5,138.2
1985	4,180.7	5,329.5
1986	4,422.2	5,489.9
1987	4,692.3	5,648.4
1988	5,049.6	5,862.9
1989	5,438.7	6,060.4
1990	5,743.8	6,138.7
1991	5,916.7	6,079.0
1992	6,244.4	6,244.4
1993	6,553.0	6,386.4
1994	6,935.7	6,608.7
1995	7,253.8	6,742.9
1996	7,576.1	6,906.8

Note: Gross domestic product (GDP) chain-type price index was used to calculate constant dollar figures.

Sources: 1 Council of Economic Advisers, Economic Report of the President (Washington: GPO, 1997), tbls. B-1, B-2. 2 U. S. Deptartment of Commerce, Bureau of Economic Analysis, Survey of Current Business, July 1977, p. D-2.

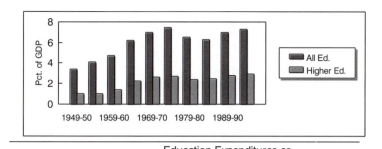

School Year	All Education	Education Expenditures as Percentage of the Gross Domestic Product		
		Higher Education		
		Total	Public	Independent
1939-40	3.6	0.8	0.4	0.4
1949-50	3.4	1.0	0.5	0.5
1959-60	4.7	1.4	0.8	0.6
1969-70	7.0	2.6	1.7	0.9
1979-80	6.5	2.4	1.6	0.8
1980-81	6.6	2.5	1.7	0.9
1981-82	6.3	2.5	1.6	0.9
1982-83	6.5	2.6	1.7	0.9
1983-84	6.5	2.5	1.7	0.9
1984-85	6.3	2.5	1.6	0.9
1985-86	6.4	2.6	1.7	0.9
1986-87	6.6	2.6	1.7	1.0
1987-88	6.7	2.7	1.7	1.0
1988-89	6.9	2.7	1.7	1.0
1989-90	7.0	2.8	1.8	1.0
1990-91	7.2	2.9	1.8	1.0
1991-92	7.3	2.9	1.8	1.1
1992-93	7.3	2.9	1.8	1.1
1993-94	7.3	2.9	1.8	1.1
1994-95	7.3	2.9	1.8	1.1
1995-96	7.3	2.9	1.8	1.1

Note: Expenditure data are reported on a school year basis. Includes current expenditures, interest, and capital outlay.

Sources: 1 U.S Bureau of the Census, Historical Statistics of the U.S.: Colonial Times to 1972 (Washington: GPO, 1975), pp. 373, 375.
2 NCES, Digest of Education Statistics, 1996 (Washington: GPO, 1996), tbls. 30, 31.

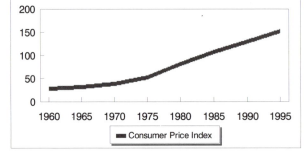

Year	Consumer Price Index (1982-84=100)	Producer Price Index (1982=100)	Higher Ed. Price Index (1983 =100)
1960	29.6	33.4	--
1965	31.5	34.1	29.8
1970	38.8	39.3	39.5
1975	53.8	58.2	54.3
1980	82.4	88.0	77.5
1982	96.5	100.0	93.9
1984	103.9	103.7	104.8
1985	107.6	104.7	110.7
1986	109.6	103.2	116.2
1987	113.6	105.4	120.7
1988	118.3	108.0	126.8
1989	124.0	113.6	132.6
1990	130.7	119.2	140.7
1991	136.2	121.7	148.1
1992	140.3	123.2	153.2
1993	144.5	124.7	157.9
1994	148.2	125.5	163.2
1995	152.4	127.9	--
1996	156.9	131.3	--
1997	*161.3*	*133.6*	--

Note: The "higher education index" is an index for current operations that measures
the effects of price changes on goods and services purchased by colleges
and universities; it excludes sponsored research. The index refers to the fiscal year
ending in the year indicated. Figures in italics are estimates based on recent trends.
-- Not available.

Sources: 1 NCES, Digest of Education Statistics, 1996 (Washington: GPO, 1996), tbl. 37.
2 Joint Economic Comittee, Economic Indicators, February 1997; tbls. 22, 23.

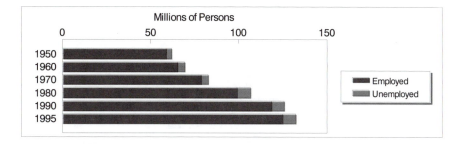

Year	Civilian Non-institutional Population Age 16 & Over	Civilian Labor Force				
		Total	Percent of Population	Number Employed	Unemployed Number	Percent of Civilian Labor Force
1950	105.0	62.2	59.2	58.9	3.3	5.3
1960	117.2	69.6	59.4	65.8	3.9	5.6
1970	137.1	82.8	60.4	78.7	4.1	4.9
1975	152.3	93.8	61.6	85.8	7.9	8.3
1980	167.7	106.9	63.7	99.3	7.6	7.1
1981	170.1	108.7	63.9	100.4	8.3	7.6
1982	172.3	110.2	64.0	99.5	10.7	9.7
1983	174.2	111.6	64.1	100.8	10.7	9.6
1984	176.4	113.5	64.3	105.0	8.5	7.5
1985	178.2	115.5	64.8	107.2	8.3	7.2
1986	180.6	117.8	65.2	109.6	8.2	7.0
1987	182.8	119.9	65.6	112.4	7.4	6.2
1988	184.6	121.7	65.9	115.0	6.7	5.5
1989	186.4	123.9	66.5	117.3	6.5	5.3
1990	189.2	125.8	66.5	118.8	7.0	5.6
1991	190.9	126.3	66.2	117.7	8.6	6.8
1992	192.8	128.1	66.4	118.5	9.6	7.5
1993	194.8	129.2	66.3	120.3	8.9	6.9
1994	196.8	131.1	66.6	123.1	8.0	6.1
1995	198.6	132.3	66.6	124.9	7.4	5.6
1996	200.6	133.9	66.6	126.7	7.2	5.4

Note: All figures except percentages are in millions.

Sources: 1 U.S. Bureau of the Census, Statistical Abstract of the U.S. (Washington: GPO) 1994, tbl. 614; 1996, tbl. 614.
2 Joint Economic Committee of the 105th Congress, Economic Indicators, June 1997 (Washington: GPO, 1997), p. 11.

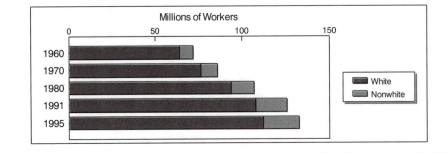

	Annual Average Labor Force (in thousands)					
Year	1960	1970	1980	1991	1995	2000 Projections
All Races						
Both Sexes	72,104	85,903	106,821	125,304	132,304	140,000
Age 16 - 24	12,720	19,916	25,741	20,628	21,453	22,300
Age 25 - 54	46,596	51,487	66,301	89,423	95,172	99,600
Age 55 and over	12,788	14,500	14,777	15,252	15,679	18,000
Men	48,933	54,343	62,088	68,411	71,360	74,200
Age 16 - 24	8,101	11,773	14,213	10,858	11,374	11,800
Age 25 - 54	31,962	33,279	38,833	48,863	51,280	52,700
Age 55 and over	8,870	9,291	9,042	8,689	8,705	9,600
Women	23,171	31,560	44,733	56,893	60,944	65,800
Age 16 - 24	4,619	8,143	11,528	9,770	10,078	10,500
Age 25 - 54	14,634	18,208	27,468	40,560	43,891	46,900
Age 55 and over	3,918	5,209	5,735	6,563	6,974	8,400
Nonwhite						
Both Sexes	7,894	9,526	13,026	17,818	20,354	22,300
Age 16 - 24	1,481	2,361	3,100	3,087	3,642	-
Age 25 - 54	5,263	5,845	8,329	12,945	14,931	-
Age 54 and over	1,150	1,320	1,429	1,783	1,781	-
Men	4,814	5,507	6,955	9,079	10,214	11,100
Age 16 - 24	930	1,378	1,812	1,616	1,851	-
Age 25 - 54	3,149	3,332	4,364	6,527	7,467	-
Age 54 and over	735	797	784	934	896	-
Women	3,080	4,019	6,071	8,739	10,140	11,200
Age 16 - 24	551	983	1,288	1,471	1,790	-
Age 25 - 54	2,114	2,513	3,965	6,418	7,464	-
Age 54 and over	415	523	645	849	886	-

- Not available.

Note: Data beginning in 1991 and again in1995 are not strictly comparable with data for earlier years. Projections are for the "middle growth level" projections for the civilian labor force.

Sources: 1 U.S. Dept. of Labor, Employment and Training Report of the President (Washington: GPO), 1976, tbls.E-2, E-4; 1982, tbl. E-2.
2 U.S. Bureau of Labor Statistics, Employment and Earnings (Washington: GPO), Jan. 1988, p. 160.
3 U.S. Bureau of the Census, Statistical Abstract of the U.S. (Washington: GPO), 1992, tbl. 608; 1996, tbl. 628.

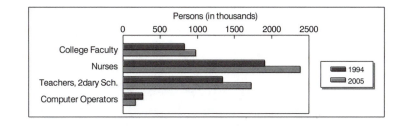

Persons (in thousands)

Occupation Group & Occupation	Employment 1994	Employment Projection for 2005	1994-2005 Percentage Change
All occupations	127,014	144,708	14
Administrative, Managerial, & Administrative Support			
Accountants & auditors	962	1,083	13
Computer operators (except peripheral equipment)	259	162	-38
Education administrators	393	459	17
Lawyers	656	839	28
Personnel, training and labor relations specialists	307	374	22
Health & Life Sciences			
Dentists	164	173	5
Physicians	539	659	22
Physician assistants	56	69	23
Registered nurses	1,906	2,379	25
Veterinarians & veterinary inspectors	56	62	11
Physical and Life Sciences			
Chemists	97	115	19
Computer systems analysts	483	928	92
Engineers	1,327	1,573	19
Geologists, geophysicists, & oceanographers	46	54	17
Life scientists	186	230	24
Mathematical scientists, actuaries, & statisticians	45	48	6
Teaching professions			
College & university faculty	823	972	18
Librarians	148	159	7
Teachers, preschool & kindergarten	462	602	30
Teachers, elementary school	1,419	1,639	16
Teachers, secondary school	1,340	1,726	29
Social Sciences			
Economists	48	59	25
Psychologists	144	177	23
Social workers	557	744	34

Note: Projections are for the moderate growth series.

Source: U.S. Bureau of Labor Statistics, Monthly Labor Review (Washington: GPO), November 1995, pp. 64 - 68.

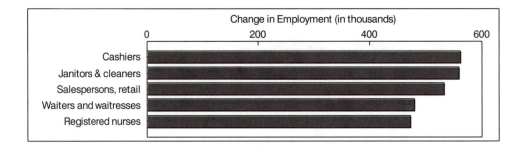

| Occupation | Employment (in thousands) | | Change in Employment 1994-2005 | |
	1994	Projected 2005	Number (in thous.)	Percentage
Cashiers	3,005	3,567	562	18.7
Janitors & cleaners	3,043	3,602	559	18.4
Salespersons, retail	3,842	4,374	532	13.8
Waiters and waitresses	1,847	2,326	479	25.9
Registered nurses	1,906	2,379	473	24.8
General managers and top executives	3,046	3,512	466	15.3
Systems analysts	483	928	445	92.1
Home health aides	420	848	428	102.0
Guards	867	1,282	415	47.9
Nursing aides, orderlies & attendants	1,265	1,652	387	30.6
Teachers, secondary school	1,340	1,726	386	28.8
Marketing and sales workers supervisors	2,293	2,673	380	16.6
Teacher aides & educational ass'ts.	932	1,296	364	39.0
Receptionists & information clerks	1,019	1,337	318	31.2
Truck drivers, light & heavy	2,565	2,837	272	10.6
Secretaries, except legal & medical	2,842	3,109	267	9.4
Clerical supervisors & managers	1,340	1,600	260	19.5
Child care workers	757	1,005	248	32.8
Maintenance repairers, general utility	1,273	1,505	232	18.2
Teachers, elementary	1,419	1,639	220	15.5
Personal & home care aides	179	391	212	118.7
Teachers, special education	388	593	205	53.0
Licensed practical nurses	702	899	197	28.0
Food service & lodging managers	579	771	192	33.2
Food preparation workers	1,190	1,378	188	15.7

Note: Data show the 25 occupations with the greatest job growth from 1994 to 2005 according to moderate trend assumptions. Janitors & cleaners category includes maids & housekeepers.

Source: U.S. Bureau of the Census, Statistical Abstract of the U.S., 1996 (Washington: GPO, 1996), tbl. 638.

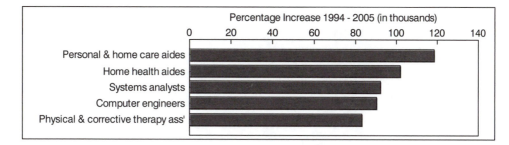

	Employment (in thousands)		Change in Employment 1994-2005	
Occupation	1994	Projected 2005	Number (in thous.)	Percentage
Personal & home care aides	179	391	212	118.7
Home health aides	420	848	428	102.0
Systems analysts	483	928	445	92.1
Computer engineers	195	372	177	90.4
Physical & corrective therapy ass'ts & aides	78	142	64	83.1
Electronic pagination systems workers	18	33	15	82.8
Occupational therapy ass'ts & aides	16	29	13	82.1
Physical therapists	102	183	81	80.0
Residential counselors	165	290	125	76.5
Human services workers	168	293	125	74.5
Occupational therapists	54	93	39	72.2
Manicurists	38	64	26	69.5
Medical assistants	206	327	121	59.0
Paralegals	110	175	65	58.3
Medical records technicians	81	126	45	55.8
Teachers, special education	388	593	205	53.0
Amusement & recreation attendants	267	406	139	52.0
Corrections officers	310	468	158	50.9
Operations research analysts	44	67	23	50.0
Guards	867	1,282	415	47.9
Speech-language pathologists & audiologists	85	125	40	46.0
Detectives, except public	55	79	24	44.3
Surgical technologists	46	65	19	42.5
Dental hygienists	127	180	53	42.1
Dental assistants	190	269	79	41.9

Note: Data show the 25 occupations with the fastest job growth from 1994 to 2005 according to moderate trend assumptions.

Source: U.S. Bureau of the Census, Statistical Abstract of the U.S., 1996 (Washington: GPO, 1996), tbl. 639.

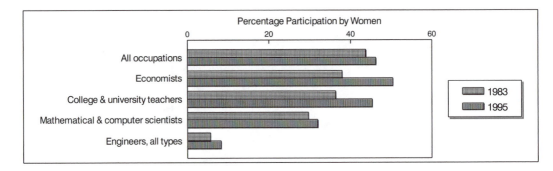

Percentage Participation by Women

All occupations		1983 / 1995
Economists		
College & university teachers		
Mathematical & computer scientists		
Engineers, all types		

	Percent of Employed Civilians					
	Women		Black		Hispanic	
Occupation Group	1983	1995	1983	1995	1983	1995
All occupations	43.7	46.1	9.3	10.6	5.3	8.9
Administrative, Managerial & Administrative Support						
Accountants & auditors	38.7	52.1	5.5	8.4	3.3	4.4
Computer operators	63.7	60.5	12.1	15.7	6.0	8.9
Administrators, education & related fields	41.4	58.7	11.3	11.2	2.4	4.7
Lawyers	15.3	26.4	2.6	3.6	0.9	3.2
Personnel & labor relations mgrs.	43.9	58.5	4.9	15.9	2.6	3.4
Health & Life Sciences						
Dentists	6.7	13.4	2.4	1.9	1.0	2.6
Pharmacists	26.7	36.2	3.8	4.3	2.6	1.8
Physicians	15.8	24.4	3.2	4.9	4.5	4.3
Physician assistants	36.3	53.2	7.7	7.6	4.4	5.7
Registered nurses	95.8	93.1	6.7	8.4	1.8	2.6
Physical & Life Sciences						
Chemists, except biochemists	23.3	31.9	4.3	4.6	1.2	3.7
Electrical & electronic engineers	6.1	8.7	3.4	5.8	3.1	3.7
Engineers, all types	5.8	8.4	2.7	4.7	2.2	3.3
Geologists & geodesists	18.0	15.0	1.1	0.5	2.6	0.6
Biological & life scientists	40.8	31.8	2.4	5.2	1.8	4.3
Mathematical & computer scientists	29.6	32.0	5.4	7.2	2.6	2.8
Teaching Professions						
College & university teachers	36.3	45.2	4.4	6.2	1.8	3.6
Librarians	87.3	83.9	7.9	7.6	1.8	1.3
Teachers, preschool & kindergarten	98.2	98.2	11.8	13.9	3.4	6.9
Teachers, elementary school	83.3	84.1	11.1	10.1	3.1	4.3
Teachers, secondary school	51.8	57.0	7.2	7.5	2.3	4.1
Social Sciences						
Economists	37.9	50.3	6.3	5.0	2.7	7.9
Psychologists	57.1	59.2	8.6	10.2	1.1	3.4
Social workers	64.3	37.9	18.2	23.7	6.3	7.8

Note: Data for the two years are not fully comparable because of occupational and industrial classification changes introduced for the 1990 census. Data describe civilian noninstitutional population ages 16 years old and over.

Source: U.S. Bureau of the Census, Statistical Abstract of the U.S., 1996 (Washington: GPO, 1996), tbl. 637.

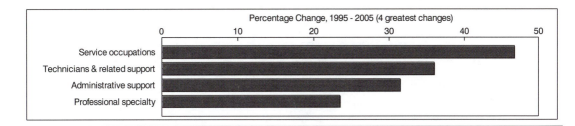

Occupation Group	1983 Number (in thous.)	1983 Per-centage	1995 Number (in thous.)	1995 Per-centage	2005 (projected) Number (in thous.)	2005 (projected) Per-centage	Percentage Change 1995 - 2005
Total, all occupations	100,834	100.0	124,900	100.0	144,708	100.0	15.9
Executive, administrative, & managerial occupations	10,772	10.7	17,186	13.8	15,071	10.4	-12.3
Professional specialty occupations	12,820	12.7	18,132	14.5	22,387	15.5	23.5
Technicians & related support occupations	3,053	3.0	3,909	3.1	5,316	3.7	36.0
Sales occupations	11,818	11.7	15,119	12.1	16,502	11.4	9.1
Administrative support occupations, including clerical	16,395	16.3	18,389	14.7	24,172	16.7	31.4
Service occupations	13,857	13.7	16,930	13.6	24,832	17.2	46.7
Farming, forestry, & fishing, & related occupations	3,700	3.7	3,642	2.9	3,650	2.5	0.2
Precision production, craft, & repair occupations	12,328	12.2	13,524	10.8	14,880	10.3	10.0
Operators, fabricators & laborers	16,091	16.0	18,068	14.5	17,898	12.4	-0.9

Note: Figures for 2005 are for the moderate growth scenario.

Source: 1 U.S. Bureau of Labor Statistics, Monthly Labor Review (Washington: GPO), November 1995, p. 7.
2 Bureau of the Census, Statistical Abstract of the U.S., 1996 (Washington: GPO, 1996), tbl. 637.

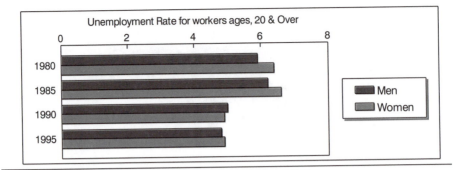

Unemployment Rate for workers ages, 20 & Over

	Civilian Unemployment Rate					
	Men			Women		
Year	All 16 Years and Over)	16 - 19 Years Old	20 Years and Over	All 16 Years and Over)	16 - 19 Years Old	20 Years and Over
1950	5.1	12.7	4.7	5.7	11.4	5.1
1960	5.4	15.3	4.7	5.9	13.9	5.1
1965	4.0	14.1	3.2	5.5	15.7	4.5
1970	4.4	15.0	3.5	5.9	15.6	4.8
1975	7.9	20.1	6.8	9.3	19.7	8.0
1980	6.9	18.3	5.9	7.4	17.2	6.4
1985	7.0	19.5	6.2	7.4	17.6	6.6
1986	6.9	19.0	6.1	7.1	17.6	6.2
1987	6.2	17.8	5.4	6.2	15.9	5.4
1988	5.5	16.0	4.8	5.6	14.4	4.9
1989	5.2	15.9	4.5	5.4	14.0	4.7
1990	5.7	16.3	5.0	5.5	14.7	4.9
1991	7.2	19.8	6.4	6.4	17.5	5.7
1992	7.9	21.5	7.1	7.0	18.6	6.3
1993	7.2	20.4	6.4	6.6	17.5	5.9
1994	6.2	19.0	5.4	6.0	16.2	5.4
1995	5.6	18.4	4.8	5.6	16.1	4.9
1996	5.4	18.1	4.6	5.4	15.2	4.8

Note: Data beginning in 1970, 1986, 1990 and 1994 are not strictly comparable with previous years' data because of adjustments made in connection with the decennial censuses and revisions in the survey methodology of the Current Population Survey.

Source: Council of Economic Advisers, Economic Report of the President, 1997 (Washington: GPO, 1997), tbl. B-40.

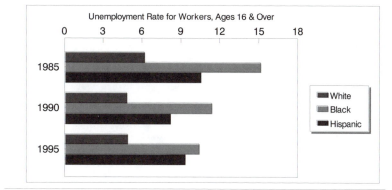

	Civilian Unemployment Rate			
Year	All Workers	White	Black	Hispanic
1950	5.3	4.9	9.0	-
1960	5.5	4.9	10.2	-
1965	4.5	4.1	8.1	-
1970	4.9	4.5	8.2	-
1975	8.5	7.8	14.8	-
1980	7.1	6.3	14.3	10.1
1985	7.2	6.2	15.1	10.5
1986	7.0	6.0	14.5	10.6
1987	6.2	5.3	13.0	8.8
1988	5.5	4.7	11.7	8.2
1989	5.3	4.5	11.4	8.0
1990	5.6	4.8	11.4	8.2
1991	6.8	6.1	12.5	10.0
1992	7.5	6.6	14.2	11.6
1993	6.9	6.1	13.0	10.8
1994	6.1	5.3	11.5	9.9
1995	5.6	4.9	10.4	9.3
1996	5.4	4.7	10.5	9.0

Note: Figures show annual unemployment rates (percentages) of the labor force.
 Prior to 1975, figures in the "Black" column show unemployment rates for all
 non-white workers. See Note on table 35 for caveats concerning data comparability.
 - Not available.

Sources: 1 Economic Report of the President, 1997 (Washington: GPO, 1997), tbl. B-40.
 2 U.S. Dep't. of Labor, Employment and Earnings (Washington: GPO), Dec. 1996, tbl. A-4.
 3 U.S. Bureau of the Census, Statistical Abstract of the U.S. (Washington: GPO),
 1993, tbl. 652; 1996, tbl. 644.

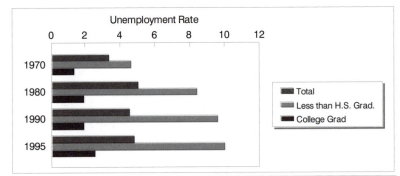

Year (as of March)	Total	Less than 4 yrs. High School	4 years of High School Only	College	
				1 - 3 Years	4 or More Years
1970	3.3	4.6	2.9	2.9	1.3
1975	6.9	10.7	6.9	5.5	2.5
1980	5.0	8.4	5.1	4.3	1.9
1985	6.1	11.4	6.9	4.7	2.4
1986	6.1	11.6	6.9	4.7	2.3
1987	5.7	11.1	6.3	4.5	2.3
1988	4.7	9.4	5.4	3.7	1.7
1989	4.4	8.9	4.8	3.4	2.2
1990	4.5	9.6	4.9	3.7	1.9
1991	6.1	12.3	6.7	5.0	2.9
	Total	Less than High School Diploma	H.S. Grad. but No Coll. Degree	Less than Bachelor's Degree	College Graduate
1992	6.7	13.5	7.7	5.9	2.9
1993	6.4	13.0	7.3	5.5	3.2
1994	5.8	12.6	6.7	5.0	2.9
1995	4.8	10.0	5.2	4.5	2.5

Note: Rates are as of March and pertain to civilian noninstitutional population 25 to 64 years old.
Thus, these figures will differ from rates in other tables that show annual averages. Data prior to 1992
are not strictly comparable to earlier rates because of changes in the method of reporting
educational attainment. Also, data for 1994 and later are not strictly comparable to earlier rates.

Source: U.S. Bureau of the Census, Statistical Abstract of the U.S., 1996 (Washington: GPO, 1996),
tbls. 648, 649.

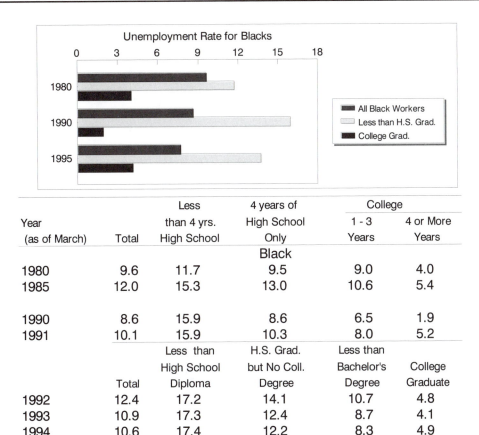

Year (as of March)	Total	Less than 4 yrs. High School	4 years of High School Only	College 1 - 3 Years	4 or More Years
			Black		
1980	9.6	11.7	9.5	9.0	4.0
1985	12.0	15.3	13.0	10.6	5.4
1990	8.6	15.9	8.6	6.5	1.9
1991	10.1	15.9	10.3	8.0	5.2

Year	Total	Less than High School Diploma	H.S. Grad. but No Coll. Degree	Less than Bachelor's Degree	College Graduate
1992	12.4	17.2	14.1	10.7	4.8
1993	10.9	17.3	12.4	8.7	4.1
1994	10.6	17.4	12.2	8.3	4.9
1995	7.7	13.7	8.4	6.3	4.1
			Hispanic		
1992	9.8	13.6	9.6	5.9	4.2
1993	10.3	14.5	9.1	7.0	5.2
1994	9.7	13.4	8.3	7.2	5.2
1995	8.0	10.9	8.1	5.2	3.7

Note: Rates are as of March and pertain to civilian noninstitutional population 25 to 64 years old. Thus, these figures will differ from rates in other tables that show annual averages. Data prior to 1992 are not strictly comparable to earlier rates because of changes in the method of reporting educational attainment. Also, data for 1994 and later are not strictly comparable to earlier rates. Hispanics may be of any race.

Source: U.S. Bureau of the Census, Statistical Abstract of the U.S., 1996 (Washington: GPO, 1996), tbls. 648, 649.

II

Enrollment Data

Highlights on Enrollment

- In fall 1995, college enrollment was 14.3 million. This was up from 1990, when 13.8 million students were enrolled. However, projections call for a slight drop in enrollment for 1996 to 13.9 million.
- Women represent 56 percent of 1995 enrollments. Women have constituted more than half of the student body since 1979.
- About 57 percent of all students attended college full-time; 43 percent were part-timers.
- Enrollment at public institutions in 1995 was 11.1 million (78 percent); at independent institutions, 3.2 million (22 percent).
- Regional enrollment figures for fall 1995 were:

  3.0 million in the Southeast
  2.4 million in the Great Lakes
  2.4 million in the Mideast
  2.4 million in the Far West
  1.5 million in the Southwest
  1.1 million in the Plains
  0.8 million in New England
  0.5 million in the Rocky Mountains

- In 1995, there were 3.5 million students identified as members of racial/ethnic minorities. They constituted one-quarter of the entire student body. Composition of this group by race/ethnicity was:

  Black: 42 percent
  Hispanic: 31 percent
  Asian/Pacific Islander: 23 percent
  American Indian/
    Alaskan Native: 4 percent

- Less than 5 percent of the student population was identified as "Alien, non-U.S. citizen."
- It is estimated that there were 2.1 million first-time, full-time freshmen enrolled in fall 1995. This is down slightly from 1990 when the figure was 2.3 million.

Enrollment in Four-year Institutions

- Fall 1995 enrollment at four-year colleges stood at 8.5 million; a little more than half the students were women (54 percent).
- Public institutions enrolled two-thirds of all four-year college students.
- Full-time students at four-year colleges accounted for 69 percent of their enrollment.
- Undergraduates represented 77 percent of the student population at these institutions.

Enrollment in Two-year Institutions

- Fall 1996 enrollment at two-year colleges stood at 5.4 million; more than half the students were women (58 percent).
- Public institutions enrolled almost all (96 percent) of all two-year college students.
- Part-time students are in the majority at two-year colleges, accounting for 64 percent of their enrollment.

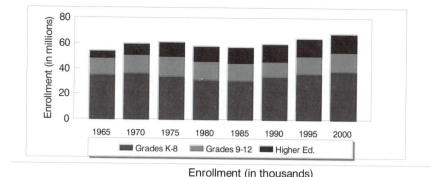

| | | Elementary & Secondary Schools | | | |
Year	Total	All Grades	Kindergarten & Grades 1-8	Grades 9-12	Higher Education
1959	44,497	40,857	31,551	9,306	3,640
1965	54,394	48,473	35,463	13,010	5,921
1970	59,838	51,257	36,610	14,647	8,581
1975	61,004	49,819	34,215	15,604	11,185
1980	58,305	46,208	31,639	14,570	12,097
1982	57,591	45,166	31,361	13,805	12,426
1984	57,150	44,908	31,205	13,704	12,242
1985	57,226	44,979	31,229	13,750	12,247
1986	57,709	45,205	31,536	13,669	12,504
1987	58,254	45,488	32,165	13,323	12,767
1988	58,485	45,430	32,537	12,893	13,055
1989	59,436	45,898	33,314	12,583	13,539
1990	60,267	46,448	33,973	12,475	13,819
1991	61,605	47,246	34,580	12,666	14,359
1992	62,686	48,198	35,300	12,898	14,487
1993	63,241	48,936	35,784	13,152	14,305
1994	63,984	49,705	36,254	13,450	14,279
Projections					
1995	64,572	50,600	36,792	13,808	13,913
1996	65,400	51,483	37,316	14,167	13,917
1997	66,996	52,217	37,759	14,457	14,085
2000	68,265	53,465	38,490	14,976	14,800

Enrollment (in thousands)

Note: Data include enrollment at public and independent institutions. Data for private schools are estimates. Data for 1994 are preliminary; for 1995, public elementary and secondary enrollment are estimates.

Sources: 1 NCES, Digest of Education Statistics, 1996 (Washington: GPO, 1996), tbl 3.
            2 _____, Projections of Education Statistics to 2007 (Washington: GPO, 1997), tbls 1, 3.

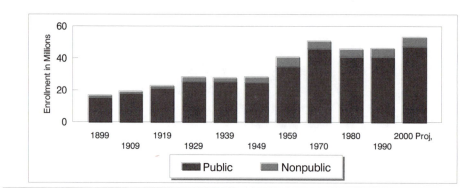

	Elementary and Secondary Regular Day School Enrollment (in thousands)					
	Public Schools			Nonpublic Schools		
Year	All Schools	All Grades	Kindergarten & Grades 1-8	Grades 9-12	All Grades	Kindergarten & Grades 1-8	Grades 9-12
1899-1900	16,855	15,503	14,984	519	1,352	1,241	111
1909-10	19,372	17,814	16,899	915	1,558	1,441	117
1919-20	23,278	21,578	19,378	2,200	1,699	1,486	214
1929-30	28,329	25,678	21,279	4,399	2,651	2,310	341
1939-40	28,045	25,434	18,832	6,601	2,611	2,153	458
1949-50	28,492	25,111	19,387	5,725	3,380	2,708	672
Fall 1959	40,857	35,182	26,911	8,271	5,675	4,640	1,035
1970	51,257	45,894	32,558	13,336	5,363	4,052	1,311
1980	46,208	40,877	27,647	13,231	5,331	3,992	1,339
1985	44,979	39,422	27,034	12,388	5,557	4,195	1,362
1986	45,205	39,753	27,420	12,333	5,452	4,116	1,336
1988	45,430	40,189	28,501	11,687	5,241	4,036	1,206
1990	46,448	41,217	29,878	11,338	5,232	4,095	1,137
1991	47,246	42,047	30,506	11,541	5,199	4,074	1,125
1992	48,198	42,823	31,088	11,735	5,375	4,212	1,163
1993	48,936	43,465	31,504	11,961	5,471	4,280	1,191
1994	49,705	44,109	31,894	12,214	5,596	4,360	1,236
Projections						
1995	50,600	44,912	32,365	12,548	5,688	4,427	1,260
1996	51,484	45,700	32,826	12,874	5,784	4,490	1,293
1997	52,217	46,353	33,216	13,138	5,863	4,544	1,320
2000	53,465	47,467	33,858	13,609	5,998	4,631	1,367

Note: Beginning in 1980, data include estimates for an expanded universe of nonpublic schools.

Sources: 1 NCES, Digest of Education Statistics, 1996 (Washington: GPO, 1996), tbl 3.
　　　　　2 NCES, Projections of Education Statistics to 2007 (Washington: GPO, 1997), tbl. 1.

High School Graduates and First-time Enrollment in College, Selected Years, 1960–1995

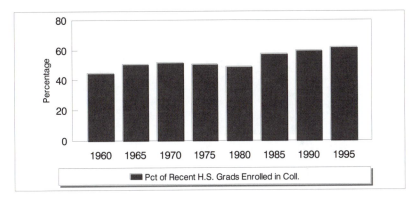

Pct of Recent H.S. Grads Enrolled in Coll.

Year	High School Graduates (in thousands)	Total First-time Enrollment in College (in thousands)	Recent High School Graduates Enrolled in College		
			Number (in thousands)	As a Percentage of H. S. Grads	First-time Enrlt.
1960	1,679	923	758	45	82
1965	2,659	1,442	1,354	51	94
1970	2,757	2,063	1,427	52	69
1975	3,186	2,515	1,615	51	64
1980	3,089	2,588	1,524	49	59
1982	3,100	2,505	1,568	51	63
1984	3,012	2,357	1,662	55	71
1985	2,666	2,292	1,539	58	67
1986	2,786	2,219	1,499	54	68
1987	2,647	2,246	1,503	57	67
1988	2,673	2,379	1,575	59	66
1989	2,454	2,341	1,463	60	62
1990	2,355	2,257	1,410	60	62
1991	2,276	2,278	1,420	62	62
1992	2,398	2,184	1,479	62	68
1993	2,338	2,161	1,464	63	68
1994	2,517	2,133	1,559	62	73
1995	2,599	2,120	1,610	62	76

Note: High school graduates are individuals age 16-24 who graduated from high school during the preceding 12 months. College enrollment is as of October of each year. Recent H.S. graduates enrolled are those who graduated from high school during the preceding 12 months. Data for 1994 and later are estimates.

Source: NCES, Digest of Education Statistics, 1996 (Washington: GPO, 1996), tbls. 177, 179.

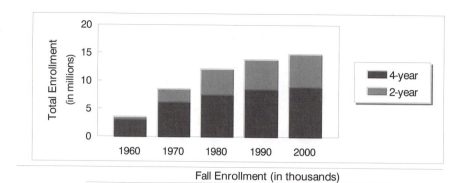

	Fall Enrollment (in thousands)				
		Undergraduate & First-professional			
Year	Total	Total	4-year Institutions	2-year Institutions	Graduate
1899-1900	238	232	232	-	6
1909-10	355	346	346	-	9
1919-20	571	555	547	8	16
1929-30	1,101	1,054	998	56	47
1939-40	1,494	1,389	1,239	150	106
1949-50	2,659	2,422	2,178	244	237
1960	3,583	3,227	2,775	451	356
1970	8,580	7,549	5,230	2,319	1,031
1980	12,096	10,753	6,227	4,526	1,343
1985	12,247	10,871	6,340	4,531	1,376
1990	13,818	12,232	6,992	5,240	1,586
1991	14,359	12,720	7,068	5,652	1,639
1992	14,488	12,819	7,097	5,722	1,669
1993	14,304	12,616	7,050	5,566	1,688
1994	14,279	12,558	7,028	5,530	1,721
1995	14,262	12,530	7,037	5,493	1,732
Projections					
1996	13,917	12,253	6,819	5,434	1,663
1997	14,085	12,413	6,910	5,503	1,672
2000	14,800	13,106	7,350	5,756	1,694

Note: Fall enrollment in thousands. Prior to 1970, enrollment in 2-year branches of 4-year institutions was included in the 4-year institution totals. Data for 1970 and later include degee-credit and non-degree-credit enrollment.

Sources: 1 USOE, Statistics of Higher Education, 1957-58, Faculty, Students, and Degrees, chap. 4, sec. 1, Biennial Survey of Education (Washington: GPO, 1962), pp. 7, 11.
2 NCES, Digest of Education Statistics, 1996 (Washington: GPO, 1996), tbls. 170, 183-185.
3 NCES, Projections of Education Statistics to 2007 (Washington: GPO, 1997), tbls. 4, 5, 14, 17, 20.

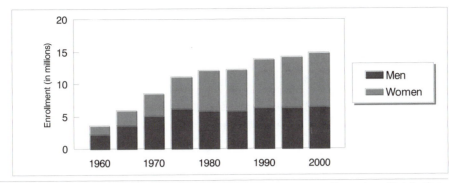

	Enrollment (in thousands)			Percentage Distribution	
Year	Total	Men	Women	Men	Women
1950	2,281.3	1,560.4	720.9	68	32
1960	3,610.0	2,270.6	1,339.4	63	37
1965	5,920.9	3,630.0	2,290.8	61	39
1970	8,580.9	5,043.6	3,537.2	59	41
1975	11,184.9	6,149.0	5,035.9	55	45
1980	12,096.9	5,874.4	6,222.5	49	51
1982	12,425.8	6,031.4	6,394.4	49	51
1984	12,241.9	5,863.6	6,378.4	48	52
1985	12,247.1	5,818.5	6,428.6	48	52
1986	12,503.5	5,884.5	6,619.0	47	53
1987	12,766.6	5,932.1	6,834.6	46	54
1988	13,055.3	6,001.9	7,053.4	46	54
1989	13,538.6	6,190.0	7,348.5	46	54
1990	13,818.6	6,283.9	7,534.7	45	55
1991	14,359.0	6,501.8	7,857.1	45	55
1992	14,487.4	6,524.0	7,963.4	45	55
1993	14,304.8	6,427.5	7,877.4	45	55
1994	14,278.8	6,371.9	7,906.9	45	55
1995	14,262.0	6,343.0	7,919.0	44	56
Projections					
1996	13,917.0	6,154.0	7,763.0	44	56
1997	14,085.0	6,205.0	7,880.0	44	56
2000	14,800.0	6,459.0	8,341.0	44	56

Note: Data for 1960 include outlying parts; other data are degree-credit and non-degree-credit enrollment for 50 states and D.C. Data for 1996 and later are projections.

Sources: 1 USOE, Opening Fall Enrollment in Higher Education, 1960: Analytic Report (Washington: GPO, 1991), p. 10.
2 NCES, Digest of Education Statistics, 1996 (Washington: GPO, 1996), tbl. 169.
3 _____, Projections of Education Statistics to 2007 (Washington: GPO, 1997), tbl. 3.

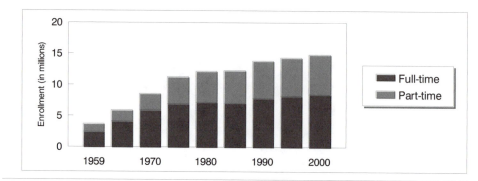

Year	Enrollment (in thousands)			Percentage Distribution	
	Total	Full-time	Part-time	Full-time	Part-time
1959	3,639.8	2,421.0	1,218.8	67	33
1965	5,920.8	4,095.7	1,825.1	69	31
1970	8,580.9	5,816.3	2,764.6	68	32
1975	11,184.9	6,841.3	4,343.5	61	39
1980	12,096.9	7,098.0	4,998.9	59	41
1982	12,425.8	7,220.6	5,205.2	58	42
1984	12,242.0	7,098.4	5,143.6	58	42
1985	12,247.1	7,075.2	5,171.8	58	42
1986	12,503.5	7,119.6	5,384.0	57	43
1987	12,766.7	7,231.1	5,535.6	57	43
1988	13,055.3	7,436.8	5,618.6	57	43
1989	13,538.5	7,661.0	5,877.6	57	43
1990	13,818.6	7,821.0	5,997.7	57	43
1991	14,359.0	8,115.3	6,243.6	57	43
1992	14,487.4	8,162.1	6,325.2	56	44
1993	14,304.8	8,127.6	6,177.2	57	43
1994	14,278.8	8,137.8	6,141.0	57	43
1995	14,262.0	8,128.0	6,134.0	57	43
Projections					
1996	13,917.0	7,798.0	6,119.0	56	44
1997	14,085.0	7,911.0	6,174.0	56	44
2000	14,800.0	8,469.0	6,331.0	57	43

Note: Data for 1959 include outlying parts; other data are degree-credit and non-degree-credit enrollment for 50 states and D.C. Full/part-time distribution for 1995 is estimated.

Sources: 1 USOE, Opening Fall Enrollment in Higher Education, 1960: Analytic Report (Washington: GPO, 1961), p. 10.
2 NCES, Digest of Education Statistics, 1996 (Washington: GPO, 1996), tbl 169.
3 _____, Projections of Education Statistics to 2007 (Washington: GPO, 1997), tbl 3.

Fall Enrollment of All Students in All Institutions, by Control of Institution, Selected Years, 1950–2000

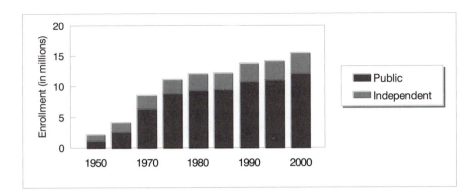

Year	Enrollment (in thousands)			Percentage	
	Total	Public	Independent	Public	Independent
1950	2,281.3	1,139.7	1,141.6	50	50
1961	4,145.0	2,561.4	1,583.6	62	38
1970	8,580.9	6,428.1	2,152.8	75	25
1975	11,184.9	8,834.5	2,350.4	79	21
1980	12,096.9	9,457.4	2,639.5	78	22
1982	12,425.8	9,696.1	2,729.7	78	22
1984	12,242.0	9,477.4	2,764.6	77	23
1985	12,247.1	9,479.3	2,767.8	77	23
1986	12,503.5	9,713.9	2,789.6	78	22
1987	12,766.7	9,973.3	2,793.4	78	22
1988	13,055.3	10,161.4	2,893.9	78	22
1989	13,538.6	10,578.0	2,960.6	78	22
1990	13,818.6	10,844.7	2,973.9	78	22
1991	14,359.0	11,309.6	3,049.4	79	21
1992	14,487.4	11,384.6	3,102.8	79	21
1993	14,304.8	11,189.1	3,115.7	78	22
1994	14,278.8	11,133.7	3,145.1	78	22
1995	14,262.0	11,092.0	3,169.0	78	22
	Projections				
1996	13,917.0	10,894.0	3,023.0	78	22
1997	14,085.0	11,028.0	3,057.0	78	22
2000	14,800.0	11,583.0	3,217.0	78	22

Note: Data for 1950 are degree-credit enrollment only; other data are degree-credit and non-degree-credit enrollment for 50 states and D.C. Data for 1996 and later are projections.

Sources: 1 NCES, Digest of Education Statistics, 1996 (Washington: GPO, 1996), tbl 169.
2 _____, Projections of Education Statistics to 2007 (Washington: GPO, 1997), tbl 3.

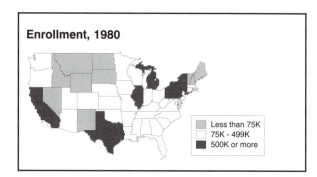

Enrollment, 1980

Less than 75K
75K - 499K
500K or more

Region & State	Enrollment (in thousands)					
	1970	1980	1990	1994	1995	1997 Est.
50 States & D.C.	**8,580.9**	**12,097.0**	**13,818.6**	**14,278.8**	**14,261.8**	**14,085**
New England	**560.1**	**765.6**	**817.8**	**806.1**	**801.5**	**791**
Connecticut	124.7	159.6	168.6	160.0	157.7	157
Maine	34.1	43.3	57.2	56.7	56.5	56
Massachusetts	303.8	418.4	417.8	416.5	413.8	408
New Hampshire	29.4	46.8	59.5	62.8	64.3	62
Rhode Island	45.9	66.9	78.3	74.7	74.1	73
Vermont	22.2	30.6	36.4	35.4	35.1	35
Mideast	**1,685.7**	**2,166.6**	**2,358.6**	**2,392.6**	**2,381.1**	**2,353**
Delaware	25.3	32.9	42.0	44.2	44.3	44
D.C.	77.2	86.7	80.2	77.7	77.3	76
Maryland	149.6	225.5	259.7	266.2	266.3	263
New Jersey	216.1	321.6	324.3	335.5	333.8	331
New York	806.5	992.2	1,048.3	1,057.8	1,041.6	1,039
Pennsylvania	411.0	507.7	604.1	611.2	617.8	600
Southeast	**1,402.8**	**2,230.7**	**2,812.3**	**3,002.9**	**3,015.3**	**2,965**
Alabama	103.9	164.3	218.6	229.5	225.6	227
Arkansas	52.0	77.6	90.4	96.3	98.2	95
Florida	235.5	411.9	588.1	634.2	637.3	626
Georgia	126.5	184.2	251.8	308.6	314.7	304
Kentucky	98.6	143.1	177.9	182.6	178.9	180
Louisiana	120.7	160.1	186.8	203.6	203.9	201
Mississippi	74.0	102.4	122.9	120.9	122.7	120
North Carolina	171.9	287.5	352.1	369.4	372.0	365
South Carolina	69.5	132.5	159.3	173.0	174.1	171
Tennessee	135.1	204.6	226.2	243.0	246.0	240
Virginia	151.9	280.5	353.4	354.1	355.9	350
West Virginia	63.2	82.0	84.8	87.7	86.0	87
Great Lakes	**1,615.9**	**2,169.8**	**2,441.3**	**2,428.2**	**2,396.3**	**2,396**
Illinois	452.1	644.2	729.2	731.4	717.9	721
Indiana	192.7	247.3	284.8	292.3	289.6	288
Michigan	392.7	520.1	569.8	551.3	548.3	545
Ohio	376.3	489.1	557.7	549.3	540.3	542
Wisconsin	202.1	269.1	299.8	303.9	300.2	300

Continued on next page.

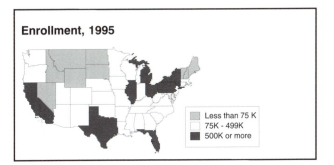

Enrollment, 1995

Less than 75 K
75K - 499K
500K or more

Region & State	Enrollment (in thousands)					
	1970	1980	1990	1994	1995	1997 Est.
Plains	**685.1**	**874.5**	**1,062.8**	**1,120.2**	**1,116.5**	**1,105**
Iowa	108.9	140.4	170.5	172.5	173.8	170
Kansas	102.5	136.6	163.7	170.6	177.6	169
Minnesota	160.8	206.7	253.8	289.3	280.8	285
Missouri	183.9	234.4	289.9	293.8	291.5	289
Nebraska	66.9	89.5	112.8	116.0	115.7	115
North Dakota	31.5	34.1	37.9	40.2	40.4	40
South Dakota	30.6	32.8	34.2	37.8	36.7	37
Southwest	**706.5**	**1,122.7**	**1,424.5**	**1,516.5**	**1,509.6**	**1,499**
Arizona	109.6	202.7	264.1	274.9	274.0	272
New Mexico	44.5	58.3	85.8	101.9	102.4	101
Oklahoma	110.2	160.3	173.2	185.2	180.7	183
Texas	442.2	701.4	901.4	954.5	952.5	943
Rocky Mountains	**285.0**	**356.2**	**467.5**	**518.7**	**522.5**	**512**
Colorado	123.4	162.9	227.1	241.3	242.7	238
Idaho	34.6	43.0	51.9	60.4	59.6	60
Montana	30.1	35.2	35.9	40.1	42.7	40
Utah	81.7	94.0	121.3	146.2	147.3	144
Wyoming	15.2	21.1	31.3	30.7	30.2	30
Far West	**1,622.7**	**2,361.1**	**2,385.7**	**2,442.1**	**2,430.2**	**2,413**
Alaska	9.5	21.3	29.8	28.8	29.3	29
California	1,257.2	1,791.0	1,808.7	1,835.8	1,817.0	1,814
Hawaii	36.6	47.2	56.4	64.3	63.2	63
Nevada	13.7	40.5	61.7	64.1	67.8	63
Oregon	122.2	157.5	165.7	164.4	167.1	162
Washington	183.5	303.6	263.4	284.7	285.8	281
U.S. Service Schools	**17.1**	**49.8**	**48.1**	**51.4**	**88.5**	**51**
Outlying Parts	**67.2**	**137.7**	**164.6**	**170.7**	**na**	**na**

Note: Figures are in thousands. Estimates for 1997 were calculated by applying each state's share of 1995 enrollment to 1997 projections, for public and independent sectors separately. The results were then summed to provide an estimate of each state's total enrollment.

Sources: 1 NCES, Digest of Education Statistics (Washington: GPO), 1992, tbl. 177; 1996, tbl. 186.
    2 _____, Projections of Education Statistics to 2007 (Washington: GPO, 1997), tbl. 3.
    3 _____, unpublished tabulations from the 1995 IPEDS Fall Enrollment Surveys.

Percentage Change, 1980–1990

Less than 10 pct.
10 - 24 pct. increase
Increase greater than 25 pct.

Region & State	10-year Percentage Change		5-year Pct. Change
	1970 to 1980	1980 to 1990	(1990-1995)
50 States & D.C.	**41.0**	**14.2**	**3.2**
New England	**36.7**	**6.8**	**-2.0**
Connecticut	28.0	5.6	-6.5
Maine	27.0	32.1	-1.2
Massachusetts	37.7	-0.1	-1.0
New Hampshire	59.2	27.1	8.1
Rhode Island	45.8	17.0	-5.4
Vermont	37.8	19.0	-3.6
Mideast	**28.5**	**8.9**	**1.0**
Delaware	30.0	27.7	5.5
D.C.	12.3	-7.5	-3.6
Maryland	50.7	15.2	2.5
New Jersey	48.8	0.8	2.9
New York	23.0	5.7	-0.6
Pennsylvania	23.5	19.0	2.3
Southeast	**59.0**	**26.1**	**7.2**
Alabama	58.1	33.0	3.2
Arkansas	49.2	16.5	8.6
Florida	74.9	42.8	8.4
Georgia	45.6	36.7	25.0
Kentucky	45.1	24.3	0.6
Louisiana	32.6	16.7	9.2
Mississippi	38.4	20.0	-0.2
North Carolina	67.2	22.5	5.7
South Carolina	90.6	20.2	9.3
Tennessee	51.4	10.6	8.8
Virginia	84.7	26.0	0.7
West Virginia	29.7	3.4	1.4
Great Lakes	**34.3**	**12.5**	**-1.8**
Illinois	42.5	13.2	-1.5
Indiana	28.3	15.2	1.7
Michigan	32.4	9.6	-3.8
Ohio	30.0	14.0	-3.1
Wisconsin	33.2	11.4	0.1

Continued on next page.

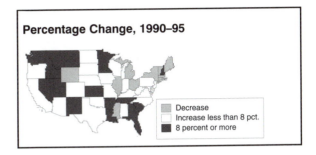

Percentage Change, 1990–95

Decrease
Increase less than 8 pct.
8 percent or more

| Region & State | 10-year Percentage Change | | 5-year Pct. Change |
	1970 to 1980	1980 to 1990	(1990-1995)
Plains	**27.6**	**21.5**	**5.1**
Iowa	28.9	21.4	1.9
Kansas	33.3	19.8	8.5
Minnesota	28.5	22.8	10.6
Missouri	27.5	23.7	0.6
Nebraska	33.8	26.0	2.6
North Dakota	8.3	11.1	6.6
South Dakota	7.2	4.3	7.3
Southwest	**58.9**	**26.9**	**6.0**
Arizona	84.9	30.3	3.7
New Mexico	31.0	47.2	19.3
Oklahoma	45.5	8.0	4.3
Texas	58.6	28.5	5.7
Rocky Mountains	**25.0**	**31.2**	**11.8**
Colorado	32.0	39.4	6.9
Idaho	24.3	20.7	14.8
Montana	16.9	2.0	18.9
Utah	15.1	29.0	21.4
Wyoming	38.8	48.3	-3.5
Far West	**45.5**	**1.0**	**1.9**
Alaska	124.2	39.9	-1.7
California	42.5	1.0	0.5
Hawaii	29.0	19.5	12.1
Nevada	195.6	52.3	9.9
Oregon	28.9	5.2	0.8
Washington	65.4	-13.2	8.5
U.S. Service Schools	**191.2**	**-3.4**	**84.0**
Outlying Parts	**104.9**	**19.5**	**na**

Source: Calculated from data in preceding table.

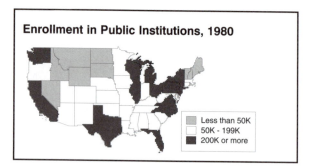

Enrollment in Public Institutions, 1980

Less than 50K
50K - 199K
200K or more

Region & State	Enrollment in Public Institutions (in thousands)				
	1970	1980	1990	1994	1997 Est.
50 States & D.C.	**6,428.1**	**9,457.4**	**10,844.7**	**11,133.7**	**11,028**
New England	**268.9**	**390.7**	**432.6**	**416.4**	**412**
Connecticut	73.4	97.8	109.6	102.5	102
Maine	25.4	31.9	41.5	39.2	39
Massachusetts	116.1	183.8	186.0	179.8	178
New Hampshire	16.0	24.1	32.2	35.0	35
Rhode Island	25.5	35.1	42.4	39.4	39
Vermont	12.5	18.0	20.9	20.5	20
Mideast	**980.2**	**1,340.1**	**1,489.7**	**1,490.4**	**1,476**
Delaware	21.2	28.3	34.3	36.3	36
D.C.	12.2	13.9	12.6	11.0	11
Maryland	119.0	195.1	220.8	223.7	222
New Jersey	145.4	247.0	261.6	272.4	270
New York	449.4	563.3	616.9	604.4	599
Pennsylvania	233.0	292.5	343.5	342.6	339
Southeast	**1,110.7**	**1,837.0**	**2,331.3**	**2,511.9**	**2,488**
Alabama	87.9	143.7	195.9	206.5	205
Arkansas	43.6	66.1	78.6	85.6	85
Florida	189.5	334.3	489.1	528.0	523
Georgia	101.9	140.2	196.4	243.9	242
Kentucky	77.2	114.9	147.1	151.6	150
Louisiana	101.1	136.7	158.3	175.1	173
Mississippi	65.0	90.7	109.0	108.4	107
North Carolina	123.8	228.2	285.4	303.6	301
South Carolina	47.1	107.7	131.1	148.5	147
Tennessee	98.9	156.8	175.0	191.4	190
Virginia	123.3	246.5	291.3	293.2	290
West Virginia	51.4	71.2	74.1	76.1	75
Great Lakes	**1,243.3**	**1,751.6**	**1,943.8**	**1,908.9**	**1,891**
Illinois	315.6	491.3	551.3	546.0	541
Indiana	136.7	189.2	224.0	228.3	226
Michigan	339.6	454.1	487.4	466.8	462
Ohio	281.0	381.8	427.6	417.6	414
Wisconsin	170.4	235.2	253.5	250.2	248

Continued on next page.

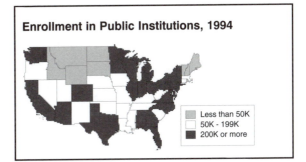

Enrollment in Public Institutions, 1994

Less than 50K
50K - 199K
200K or more

Region & State	Enrollment in Public Institutions (in thousands)				
	1970	1980	1990	1994	1997 Est.
Plains	**525.3**	**676.6**	**822.1**	**857.2**	**849**
Iowa	68.4	97.5	117.8	122.0	121
Kansas	88.2	122.0	149.1	152.8	151
Minnesota	130.6	162.4	199.2	227.0	225
Missouri	132.5	165.2	200.1	191.9	190
Nebraska	51.5	73.5	94.6	95.9	95
North Dakota	30.2	31.7	34.7	36.6	36
South Dakota	23.9	24.3	26.6	31.0	31
Southwest	**605.0**	**999.9**	**1,285.0**	**1,354.0**	**1,341**
Arizona	107.3	194.0	248.2	252.2	250
New Mexico	40.8	55.1	83.4	97.1	96
Oklahoma	91.4	137.2	151.1	161.7	160
Texas	365.5	613.6	802.3	843.0	835
Rocky Mountains	**227.8**	**292.0**	**390.6**	**432.2**	**428**
Colorado	108.6	145.6	200.7	209.7	208
Idaho	27.1	34.5	41.3	49.0	49
Montana	27.3	31.2	31.9	34.9	35
Utah	49.6	59.6	86.1	108.6	108
Wyoming	15.2	21.1	30.6	30.0	30
Far West	**1,449.9**	**2,120.1**	**2,101.4**	**2,111.1**	**2,091**
Alaska	8.6	20.6	27.8	27.6	27
California	1,123.5	1,599.8	1,594.7	1,582.8	1,568
Hawaii	33.0	43.3	45.7	51.6	51
Nevada	13.6	40.3	61.2	63.3	63
Oregon	108.5	140.1	144.4	141.0	140
Washington	162.7	276.0	227.6	244.8	242
U.S. Service Schools	**17.1**	**49.8**	**48.1**	**51.5**	**51**
Outlying Parts	**46.7**	**60.7**	**66.2**	**70.9**	**na**

Note: Estimates calculated by applying each state's percentage of the 1994 total enrollment to the projected total for 1997 enrollment at public institutions.

Sources: 1 NCES, Digest of Education Statistics, 1996 (Washington: GPO, 1996), tbl. 187.
2 _____, Projections of Education Statistics to 20007 (Washington: GPO, 1997), tbl. 3.

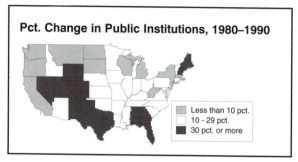

Pct. Change in Public Institutions, 1980–1990

Less than 10 pct.
10 - 29 pct.
30 pct. or more

Region & State	10-year Percentage Change		4-year Pct. Change
	1970 to 1980	1980 to 1990	(1990-1994)
50 States & D.C.	**47.1**	**14.7**	**2.7**
New England	**45.3**	**10.7**	**-3.7**
Connecticut	33.2	12.1	-6.5
Maine	25.6	30.1	-5.5
Massachusetts	58.3	1.2	-3.3
New Hampshire	50.6	33.6	8.7
Rhode Island	37.6	20.8	-7.1
Vermont	44.0	16.1	-1.9
Mideast	**36.7**	**11.2**	**nc**
Delaware	33.5	21.2	5.8
D.C.	13.9	-9.4	-12.7
Maryland	63.9	13.2	1.3
New Jersey	69.9	5.9	4.1
New York	25.3	9.5	-2.0
Pennsylvania	25.5	17.4	-0.3
Southeast	**65.4**	**26.9**	**7.7**
Alabama	63.5	36.3	5.4
Arkansas	51.6	18.9	8.9
Florida	76.4	46.3	8.0
Georgia	37.6	40.1	24.2
Kentucky	48.8	28.0	3.1
Louisiana	35.2	15.8	10.6
Mississippi	39.5	20.2	-0.6
North Carolina	84.3	25.1	6.4
South Carolina	128.7	21.7	13.3
Tennessee	58.5	11.6	9.4
Virginia	99.9	18.2	0.7
West Virginia	38.5	4.1	2.7
Great Lakes	**40.9**	**11.0**	**-1.8**
Illinois	55.7	12.2	-1.0
Indiana	38.4	18.4	1.9
Michigan	33.7	7.3	-4.2
Ohio	35.9	12.0	-2.3
Wisconsin	38.0	7.8	-1.3

Continued on next page.

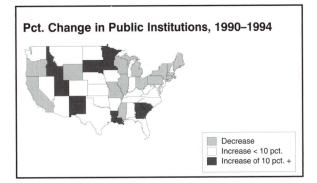

Pct. Change in Public Institutions, 1990–1994

Decrease
Increase < 10 pct.
Increase of 10 pct. +

Region & State	10-year Percentage Change		4-year Pct. Change
	1970 to 1980	1980 to 1990	(1990-1994)
Plains	**28.8**	**21.5**	**4.3**
Iowa	42.5	20.8	3.6
Kansas	38.3	22.2	2.5
Minnesota	24.3	22.7	14.0
Missouri	24.7	21.1	-4.1
Nebraska	42.7	28.7	1.4
North Dakota	5.0	9.5	5.5
South Dakota	1.7	9.5	16.5
Southwest	**65.3**	**28.5**	**5.4**
Arizona	80.8	27.9	1.6
New Mexico	35.0	51.4	16.4
Oklahoma	50.1	10.1	7.0
Texas	67.9	30.8	5.1
Rocky Mountains	**28.2**	**33.8**	**10.7**
Colorado	34.1	37.8	4.5
Idaho	27.3	19.7	18.6
Montana	14.3	2.2	9.4
Utah	20.2	44.5	26.1
Wyoming	38.8	45.0	-2.0
Far West	**46.2**	**-0.9**	**0.5**
Alaska	139.5	35.0	-0.7
California	42.4	-0.3	-0.7
Hawaii	31.2	5.5	12.9
Nevada	196.3	51.9	3.4
Oregon	29.1	3.1	-2.4
Washington	69.6	-17.5	7.6
U.S. Service Schools	**191.2**	**-3.4**	**7.1**
Outlying Parts	**30.0**	**9.1**	**7.1**

nc: Change of less than one-tenth of one percent.

Source: Calculated from data in preceding table.

Fall Enrollment in Independent Institutions, by Region and State, Selected Years, 1970–1997

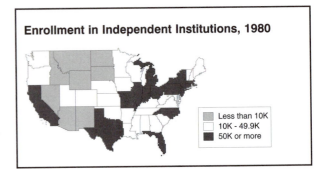

Enrollment in Independent Institutions, 1980

Less than 10K
10K - 49.9K
50K or more

Region & State	Enrollment in Independent Institutions (in thousands)				
	1970	1980	1990	1994	1997 Estimate
50 States & D.C.	**2,152.8**	**2,639.5**	**2,973.9**	**3,145.1**	**3,057**
New England	**291.2**	**375.0**	**385.2**	**389.8**	**379**
Connecticut	51.3	61.8	59.0	57.5	56
Maine	8.7	11.4	15.7	17.5	17
Massachusetts	187.7	234.7	231.8	236.7	230
New Hampshire	13.4	22.7	27.3	27.9	27
Rhode Island	20.4	31.8	35.9	35.3	34
Vermont	9.7	12.6	15.5	14.9	14
Mideast	**705.5**	**826.7**	**869.0**	**902.2**	**877**
Delaware	4.1	4.6	7.8	7.9	8
D.C.	65.0	72.8	67.6	66.7	65
Maryland	30.6	30.5	38.9	42.5	41
New Jersey	70.7	74.6	62.7	63.1	61
New York	357.0	429.0	431.4	453.4	441
Pennsylvania	178.1	215.2	260.6	268.6	261
Southeast	**292.4**	**393.5**	**481.1**	**491.0**	**477**
Alabama	16.1	20.6	22.7	23.0	22
Arkansas	8.4	11.5	11.8	10.7	10
Florida	46.1	77.5	99.0	106.2	103
Georgia	24.6	44.0	55.4	64.7	63
Kentucky	21.4	28.2	30.8	31.0	30
Louisiana	19.6	23.4	28.6	28.5	28
Mississippi	9.0	11.7	13.8	12.5	12
North Carolina	48.2	59.4	66.7	65.7	64
South Carolina	22.4	24.8	28.2	24.6	24
Tennessee	36.2	47.7	51.2	51.5	50
Virginia	28.6	34.0	62.2	61.0	59
West Virginia	11.8	10.7	10.7	11.6	11
Great Lakes	**372.4**	**418.3**	**497.5**	**519.3**	**505**
Illinois	136.5	153.0	177.9	185.5	180
Indiana	55.9	58.0	60.9	64.0	62
Michigan	53.1	66.0	82.4	84.5	82
Ohio	95.2	107.4	130.1	131.7	128
Wisconsin	31.7	33.9	46.2	53.6	52

Continued on next page.

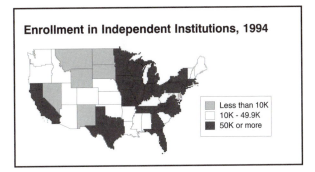

Enrollment in Independent Institutions, 1994

Less than 10K
10K - 49.9K
50K or more

Region & State	Enrollment in Independent Institutions (in thousands)				
	1970	1980	1990	1994	1997 Estimate
Plains	**159.9**	**197.9**	**240.7**	**262.9**	**256**
Iowa	40.5	43.0	52.7	50.4	49
Kansas	14.3	14.6	14.6	17.8	17
Minnesota	30.2	44.3	54.6	62.3	61
Missouri	51.4	69.2	89.8	102.0	99
Nebraska	15.5	16.0	18.2	20.1	20
North Dakota	1.3	2.4	3.2	3.5	3
South Dakota	6.7	8.4	7.6	6.8	7
Southwest	**101.4**	**122.8**	**139.2**	**162.4**	**158**
Arizona	2.3	8.7	15.9	22.7	22
New Mexico	3.7	3.2	2.1	4.8	5
Oklahoma	18.7	23.1	22.1	23.4	23
Texas	76.7	87.8	99.1	111.5	108
Rocky Mountains	**57.2**	**64.2**	**77.0**	**86.5**	**84**
Colorado	14.8	17.3	26.5	31.6	31
Idaho	7.5	8.5	10.6	11.4	11
Montana	2.8	4.0	4.0	5.2	5
Utah	32.1	34.4	35.2	37.6	37
Wyoming	0.0	<.1	0.7	0.7	1
Far West	**172.8**	**241.0**	**284.3**	**331.0**	**322**
Alaska	0.9	0.7	2.0	1.2	1
California	133.7	191.2	214.0	253.0	246
Hawaii	3.6	3.9	10.7	12.7	12
Nevada	0.1	0.2	0.5	0.8	1
Oregon	13.7	17.4	21.3	23.4	23
Washington	20.8	27.6	35.8	39.9	39
Outlying Parts	**20.6**	**77.1**	**98.4**	**99.8**	**na**

Note: Estimates calculated by applying each state's percentage of the 1994 total enrollment to the projected total for 1997 enrollment at independent institutions.

Sources: 1 NCES, Digest of Education Statistics, 1996 (Washington: GPO, 1996), tbl. 188.
   2 _____, Projections of Education Statistics to 20007 (Washington: GPO, 1997), tbl. 3.

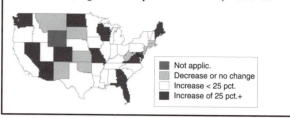

Percent Change at Independent Insts., 1980–90

Not applic.
Decrease or no change
Increase < 25 pct.
Increase of 25 pct.+

Region & State	10-year Percentage Change		4-year Pct. Change
	1970 to 1980	1980 to 1990	(1990-1994)
50 States & D.C.	**22.6**	**12.7**	**5.8**
New England	**28.8**	**2.7**	**1.2**
Connecticut	20.5	-4.5	-2.5
Maine	31.0	37.7	11.5
Massachusetts	25.0	-1.2	2.1
New Hampshire	69.4	20.3	2.2
Rhode Island	55.9	12.9	-1.7
Vermont	29.9	23.0	-3.9
Mideast	**17.2**	**5.1**	**3.8**
Delaware	12.2	69.6	1.3
D.C.	12.0	-7.1	-1.3
Maryland	-0.3	27.5	9.3
New Jersey	5.5	-16.0	0.6
New York	20.2	0.6	5.1
Pennsylvania	20.8	21.1	3.1
Southeast	**34.6**	**22.3**	**2.1**
Alabama	28.0	10.2	1.3
Arkansas	36.9	2.6	-9.3
Florida	68.1	27.7	7.3
Georgia	78.9	25.9	16.8
Kentucky	31.8	9.2	0.6
Louisiana	19.4	22.2	-0.3
Mississippi	30.0	17.9	-9.4
North Carolina	23.2	12.3	-1.5
South Carolina	10.7	13.7	-12.8
Tennessee	31.8	7.3	0.6
Virginia	18.9	82.9	-1.9
West Virginia	-9.3	0.0	8.4
Great Lakes	**12.3**	**18.9**	**4.4**
Illinois	12.1	16.3	4.3
Indiana	3.8	5.0	5.1
Michigan	24.3	24.8	2.5
Ohio	12.8	21.1	1.2
Wisconsin	6.9	36.3	16.0

Continued on next page.

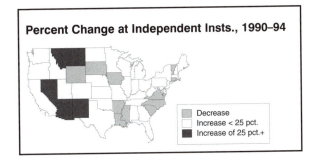

Percent Change at Independent Insts., 1990–94

Decrease
Increase < 25 pct.
Increase of 25 pct.+

Region & State	10-year Percentage Change		4-year Pct. Change (1990-1994)
	1970 to 1980	1980 to 1990	
Plains	**23.8**	**21.6**	**9.2**
Iowa	6.2	22.6	-4.4
Kansas	2.1	0.0	21.9
Minnesota	46.7	23.3	14.1
Missouri	34.6	29.8	13.6
Nebraska	3.2	13.8	10.4
North Dakota	84.6	33.3	9.4
South Dakota	25.4	-9.5	-10.5
Southwest	**21.1**	**13.4**	**16.7**
Arizona	278.3	82.8	42.8
New Mexico	-13.5	-34.4	128.6
Oklahoma	23.5	-4.3	5.9
Texas	14.5	12.9	12.5
Rocky Mountains	**12.2**	**19.9**	**12.3**
Colorado	16.9	53.2	19.2
Idaho	13.3	24.7	7.5
Montana	42.9	0.0	30.0
Utah	7.2	2.3	6.8
Wyoming	na	na	0.0
Far West	**39.5**	**18.0**	**16.4**
Alaska	-22.2	185.7	-40.0
California	43.0	11.9	18.2
Hawaii	8.3	174.4	18.7
Nevada	100.0	150.0	60.0
Oregon	27.0	22.4	9.9
Washington	32.7	29.7	11.5
Outlying Parts	**274.3**	**27.6**	**1.4**

na: Not calculated because of enrollment of less than 100 in 1970 and 1980.

Source: Calculated from data on preceding pages.

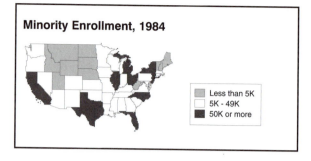

Minority Enrollment, 1984

Less than 5K
5K - 49K
50K or more

Region and State	Enrollment (in thousands)							
	Total	White Non-Hispanic	Total Minority	Black Non-Hispanic	Hispanic	Asian/ Pacific Islander	American Indian/ Alaskan Native	Non-resident Alien
50 States & D.C.	**12,235.0**	**9,815.2**	**2,085.0**	**1,076.1**	**535.3**	**389.8**	**83.8**	**334.8**
New England	**786.1**	**711.4**	**52.0**	**25.1**	**12.5**	**12.5**	**1.9**	**22.7**
Connecticut	161.6	144.4	13.2	7.2	3.2	2.3	0.5	4.0
Maine	52.7	51.7	0.8	0.3	0.1	0.2	0.2	0.2
Massachusetts	418.9	371.0	32.0	14.8	7.6	8.7	0.9	15.9
New Hampshire	53.0	50.8	1.3	0.6	0.4	0.2	0.1	0.8
Rhode Island	69.1	63.8	4.0	2.0	1.0	0.9	0.1	1.3
Vermont	30.8	29.7	0.7	0.2	0.2	0.2	0.1	0.5
Mideast	**2,187.2**	**1,735.8**	**391.9**	**241.6**	**87.8**	**55.2**	**7.3**	**59.5**
Delaware	33.5	28.9	4.0	3.3	0.3	0.4	*	0.5
D.C.	79.8	42.1	27.2	23.4	1.8	1.9	0.1	10.4
Maryland	233.9	179.6	49.3	38.1	3.2	7.4	0.6	5.0
New Jersey	305.3	243.8	54.2	28.5	16.8	8.0	0.9	7.4
New York	1,007.6	772.8	208.2	112.4	61.0	30.0	4.8	26.6
Pennsylvania	527.0	468.6	48.9	35.8	4.6	7.6	0.9	9.6
Southeast	**2,321.5**	**1,820.5**	**446.0**	**358.6**	**57.5**	**23.5**	**6.4**	**55.0**
Alabama	171.6	129.6	38.3	36.5	0.6	0.9	0.3	3.7
Arkansas	78.6	63.9	12.9	11.7	0.3	0.6	0.3	1.8
Florida	443.8	337.3	91.6	40.4	44.6	5.6	1.0	15.0
Georgia	196.3	150.3	41.1	36.9	1.8	2.1	0.3	5.0
Kentucky	143.6	129.5	12.2	10.7	0.5	0.7	0.3	1.8
Louisiana	180.0	125.7	45.7	40.5	3.1	1.7	0.4	8.6
Mississippi	104.3	71.9	31.0	29.9	0.3	0.6	0.2	1.3
North Carolina	309.2	241.4	62.6	55.6	1.7	3.0	2.3	5.2
South Carolina	131.2	101.4	27.6	26.0	0.7	0.7	0.2	2.1
Tennessee	201.2	165.9	30.7	28.3	0.9	1.2	0.3	4.5
Virginia	282.8	229.8	48.1	38.9	2.7	5.9	0.6	4.8
West Virginia	79.0	73.8	4.1	3.1	0.3	0.6	0.1	1.2
Great Lakes	**2,206.1**	**1,882.3**	**275.5**	**194.7**	**36.3**	**36.2**	**8.3**	**48.3**
Illinois	662.1	525.5	124.5	82.9	20.4	19.2	2.0	12.1
Indiana	249.9	222.9	20.1	13.7	3.2	2.6	0.6	7.0
Michigan	505.3	430.3	62.9	47.8	6.2	6.2	2.7	12.1
Ohio	517.9	454.9	51.2	41.1	3.8	5.0	1.3	11.8
Wisconsin	270.8	248.8	16.7	9.1	2.7	3.3	1.6	5.3

Continued on next page.

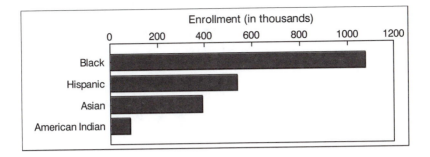

Region and State	Enrollment (in thousands)							
	Total	White Non-Hispanic	Total Minority	Black Non-Hispanic	Hispanic	Asian/ Pacific Islander	American Indian/ Alaskan Native	Non-resident Alien
Plains	**917.4**	**834.1**	**60.4**	**34.7**	**8.0**	**9.8**	**7.9**	**23.0**
Iowa	153.1	141.4	6.4	3.2	1.1	1.6	0.5	5.3
Kansas	141.9	125.7	12.0	6.5	2.3	1.4	1.8	4.3
Minnesota	215.6	202.6	8.2	2.7	1.1	3.1	1.3	4.8
Missouri	239.4	209.7	24.8	19.1	2.2	2.8	0.7	5.0
Nebraska	97.4	90.6	4.8	2.6	0.9	0.7	0.6	2.0
North Dakota	37.6	34.8	1.9	0.3	0.1	0.1	1.4	0.9
South Dakota	32.5	29.3	2.3	0.3	0.3	0.1	1.6	0.7
Southwest	**1,239.2**	**925.1**	**271.1**	**88.3**	**140.6**	**23.6**	**18.6**	**43.0**
Arizona	209.1	169.5	34.7	6.0	18.0	3.7	7.0	5.0
New Mexico	66.9	43.5	21.8	1.5	16.5	0.6	3.2	1.5
Oklahoma	167.9	140.2	20.3	10.2	1.9	2.4	5.8	7.3
Texas	795.3	571.9	194.2	70.7	104.1	16.8	2.6	29.3
Rocky Mountains	**368.1**	**330.0**	**27.0**	**5.4**	**11.5**	**5.4**	**4.7**	**11.2**
Colorado	164.4	142.3	17.3	4.1	8.8	3.0	1.4	4.9
Idaho	43.3	40.6	1.9	0.3	0.6	0.6	0.4	0.7
Montana	37.1	34.0	2.4	0.2	0.2	0.2	1.8	0.8
Utah	99.9	91.4	4.5	0.6	1.5	1.5	0.9	4.1
Wyoming	23.4	21.8	0.9	0.2	0.4	0.1	0.2	0.8
Far West	**2,156.5**	**1,530.6**	**554.2**	**122.1**	**180.5**	**223.0**	**28.6**	**71.7**
Alaska	27.0	22.3	3.9	1.0	0.4	0.5	2.0	0.8
California	1,662.1	1,126.0	478.9	111.1	173.0	173.4	21.4	57.3
Hawaii	51.9	14.6	34.2	1.1	0.8	32.2	0.1	3.1
Nevada	43.0	37.3	5.3	1.7	1.3	1.1	1.2	0.6
Oregon	141.8	127.6	10.0	1.8	1.8	5.2	1.2	4.2
Washington	230.7	202.8	22.1	5.4	3.2	10.7	2.8	5.7
U.S. Service Schools	**52.8**	**45.3**	**7.2**	**5.8**	**0.7**	**0.6**	**0.1**	**0.4**

Note: Totals may differ slightly from those shown elsewhere due to adjustments made for institutions not reporting racial/ethnic data and for separate tabulation of U.S. Service Schools.

Source: CES, Higher Education General Information Survey, Fall Enrollment and Compliance Report, 1984, tabulations.

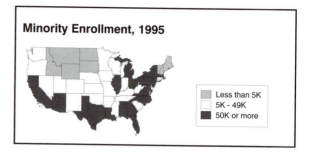

Minority Enrollment, 1995

Less than 5K
5K - 49K
50K or more

Region and State	Total	White Non-Hispanic	Total Minority	Black Non-Hispanic	Hispanic	Asian/ Pacific Islander	American Indian/ Alaskan Native	Non-resident Alien
50 States & D.C.	**14,261.8**	**10,311.2**	**3,496.2**	**1,473.7**	**1,093.8**	**797.4**	**131.3**	**454.4**
New England	**801.7**	**656.5**	**110.2**	**40.4**	**30.4**	**35.3**	**4.1**	**35.0**
Connecticut	157.6	126.3	25.7	11.9	7.7	5.6	0.5	5.6
Maine	56.6	53.2	2.8	0.6	0.4	0.9	0.9	0.6
Massachusetts	413.8	322.1	67.4	23.1	18.1	24.5	1.7	24.3
New Hampshire	64.5	59.9	3.4	1.1	1.0	1.0	0.3	1.2
Rhode Island	74.1	62.8	8.8	3.2	2.7	2.6	0.3	2.5
Vermont	35.1	32.2	2.1	0.5	0.5	0.7	0.4	0.8
Mideast	**2,381.1**	**1,688.0**	**602.0**	**314.4**	**152.0**	**128.0**	**7.6**	**91.1**
Delaware	44.3	35.3	8.1	6.0	0.8	1.1	0.2	0.9
D.C.	77.1	37.3	31.8	24.4	3.0	4.2	0.2	8.0
Maryland	266.4	177.6	79.5	57.6	6.2	14.6	1.1	9.3
New Jersey	333.8	230.3	92.1	39.3	30.8	21.1	0.9	11.4
New York	1,041.5	690.9	306.1	135.8	100.0	66.5	3.8	44.5
Pennsylvania	618.0	516.6	84.4	51.3	11.2	20.5	1.4	17.0
Southeast	**3,015.6**	**2,209.3**	**737.5**	**537.4**	**116.6**	**68.7**	**14.8**	**68.8**
Alabama	225.6	163.4	57.6	52.3	1.7	2.3	1.3	4.6
Arkansas	98.2	78.7	17.1	14.4	0.7	1.1	0.9	2.4
Florida	637.3	426.4	191.3	83.4	86.1	18.9	2.9	19.6
Georgia	314.6	215.5	91.0	77.4	4.7	8.1	0.8	8.1
Kentucky	179.0	159.8	16.1	12.1	1.2	2.1	0.7	3.1
Louisiana	203.9	135.1	62.8	53.0	4.6	4.1	1.1	6.0
Mississippi	122.8	82.7	38.1	35.9	0.7	1.1	0.4	2.0
North Carolina	372.0	277.8	88.5	73.2	4.4	7.1	3.8	5.7
South Carolina	174.2	127.9	43.4	39.1	1.6	2.2	0.5	2.9
Tennessee	246.1	198.3	42.9	36.2	2.3	3.6	0.8	4.9
Virginia	355.9	264.4	83.7	57.0	8.1	17.2	1.4	7.8
West Virginia	86.0	79.3	5.0	3.4	0.5	0.9	0.2	1.7
Great Lakes	**2,396.5**	**1,917.8**	**412.2**	**232.2**	**90.2**	**77.3**	**12.5**	**66.5**
Illinois	717.8	509.0	190.8	90.7	58.2	39.5	2.4	18.0
Indiana	289.7	250.5	30.6	18.0	6.3	5.2	1.1	8.6
Michigan	548.3	440.0	91.3	59.9	11.6	15.3	4.5	17.0
Ohio	540.3	452.8	71.5	50.9	7.8	10.8	2.0	16.0
Wisconsin	300.4	265.5	28.0	12.7	6.3	6.5	2.5	6.9

Continued on next page.

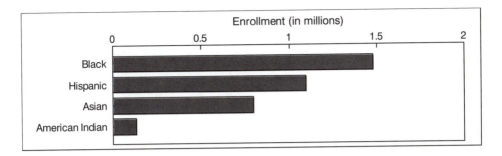

Enrollment (in millions)

Enrollment (in thousands)							
Region and State	Total	White Non-Hispanic	Total Minority	Black Non-Hispanic	Hispanic	Asian/ Pacific Islander	American Indian/ Alaskan Native	Non-resident Alien
Plains	**1,116.8**	**973.1**	**111.7**	**51.8**	**20.1**	**26.7**	**13.1**	**32.0**
Iowa	173.8	154.4	12.4	4.9	2.8	4.0	0.7	7.0
Kansas	177.6	149.7	21.9	9.4	5.9	4.0	2.6	6.0
Minnesota	280.8	250.1	24.3	8.0	4.0	9.5	2.8	6.4
Missouri	291.6	246.1	38.1	25.5	4.7	6.4	1.5	7.4
Nebraska	115.8	104.4	8.8	3.4	2.3	2.2	0.9	2.6
North Dakota	40.4	35.9	2.9	0.3	0.2	0.3	2.1	1.6
South Dakota	36.8	32.5	3.3	0.3	0.2	0.3	2.5	1.0
Southwest	**1,509.6**	**984.7**	**481.5**	**118.2**	**270.4**	**56.7**	**36.2**	**43.4**
Arizona	274.1	200.1	66.7	8.8	38.7	8.6	10.6	7.3
New Mexico	102.4	57.2	43.4	2.6	32.1	1.7	7.0	1.8
Oklahoma	180.6	137.3	35.2	13.1	4.2	4.1	13.8	8.1
Texas	952.5	590.1	336.2	93.7	195.4	42.3	4.8	26.2
Rocky Mountains	**522.3**	**446.5**	**62.2**	**10.1**	**29.8**	**12.6**	**9.7**	**13.6**
Colorado	242.6	195.0	42.0	8.4	22.5	8.1	3.0	5.6
Idaho	59.6	54.5	3.8	0.4	1.7	0.9	0.8	1.3
Montana	42.6	36.9	4.7	0.1	0.5	0.3	3.8	1.0
Utah	147.3	132.6	9.4	0.9	3.8	3.1	1.6	5.3
Wyoming	30.2	27.5	2.3	0.3	1.3	0.2	0.5	0.4
Far West	**2,430.6**	**1,364.7**	**962.4**	**157.7**	**381.7**	**389.8**	**33.2**	**103.5**
Alaska	29.4	23.2	5.6	1.0	0.8	0.9	2.9	0.6
California	1,817.0	905.1	832.1	138.2	357.9	314.9	21.1	79.8
Hawaii	63.3	16.8	40.7	1.2	1.4	37.8	0.3	5.8
Nevada	67.8	52.0	13.9	3.7	5.1	4.0	1.1	1.9
Oregon	167.2	139.2	21.6	3.0	6.3	9.7	2.6	6.4
Washington	285.9	228.4	48.5	10.6	10.2	22.5	5.2	9.0
U.S. Service Schools	**88.4**	**70.5**	**17.4**	**11.7**	**3.1**	**2.2**	**0.4**	**0.5**

Note: Totals may differ slightly from those shown elsewhere due to adjustments made for institutions not reporting racial/ethnic data and for separate tabulation of U.S. Service Schools.

Source: NCES, Enrollment in Higher Education: Fall 1995 (Washington: GPO, 1997), Appendix D.

Minorities as a Percentage of U.S. Citizens' Enrollment, by Region and State, 1984 and 1995

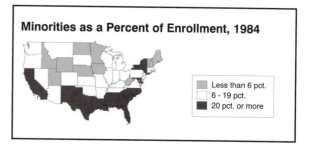

Minorities as a Percent of Enrollment, 1984

Less than 6 pct.
6 - 19 pct.
20 pct. or more

Region and State	Percentage of Enrollment of U.S. Citizens Represented by-					
	All Minorities		Black Students		Hispanic Students	
	1984	1995	1984	1995	1984	1995
50 States & D.C.	**17.5**	**25.3**	**9.0**	**10.7**	**4.5**	**7.9**
New England	**6.8**	**14.4**	**3.3**	**5.3**	**1.6**	**4.0**
Connecticut	8.4	16.9	4.6	7.8	2.0	5.1
Maine	1.5	5.0	0.6	1.1	0.2	0.7
Massachusetts	7.9	17.3	3.7	5.9	1.9	4.6
New Hampshire	2.5	5.4	1.1	1.7	0.8	1.6
Rhode Island	5.9	12.3	2.9	4.5	1.5	3.8
Vermont	2.3	6.1	0.7	1.5	0.7	1.5
Mideast	**18.4**	**26.3**	**11.4**	**13.7**	**4.1**	**6.6**
Delaware	12.1	18.7	10.0	13.8	0.9	1.8
D.C.	39.2	46.0	33.7	35.3	2.6	4.3
Maryland	21.5	30.9	16.6	22.4	1.4	2.4
New Jersey	18.2	28.6	9.6	12.2	5.6	9.6
New York	21.2	30.7	11.5	13.6	6.2	10.0
Pennsylvania	9.5	14.0	6.9	8.5	0.9	1.9
Southeast	**19.7**	**25.0**	**15.8**	**18.2**	**2.5**	**4.0**
Alabama	22.8	26.1	21.7	23.7	0.4	0.8
Arkansas	16.8	17.8	15.2	15.0	0.4	0.7
Florida	21.4	31.0	9.4	13.5	10.4	13.9
Georgia	21.5	29.7	19.3	25.3	0.9	1.5
Kentucky	8.6	9.2	7.5	6.9	0.4	0.7
Louisiana	26.7	31.7	23.6	26.8	1.8	2.3
Mississippi	30.1	31.5	29.0	29.7	0.3	0.6
North Carolina	20.6	24.2	18.3	20.0	0.6	1.2
South Carolina	21.4	25.3	20.1	22.8	0.5	0.9
Tennessee	15.6	17.8	14.4	15.0	0.5	1.0
Virginia	17.3	24.0	14.0	16.4	1.0	2.3
West Virginia	5.3	5.9	4.0	4.0	0.4	0.6
Great Lakes	**12.8**	**17.7**	**9.0**	**10.0**	**1.7**	**3.9**
Illinois	19.2	27.3	12.8	13.0	3.1	8.3
Indiana	8.3	10.9	5.6	6.4	1.3	2.2
Michigan	12.8	17.2	9.7	11.3	1.3	2.2
Ohio	10.1	13.6	8.1	9.7	0.8	1.5
Wisconsin	6.3	9.5	3.4	4.3	1.0	2.1

Continued on next page.

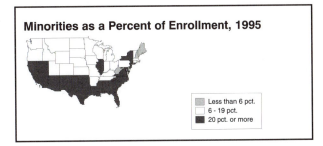

Minorities as a Percent of Enrollment, 1995

Less than 6 pct.
6 - 19 pct.
20 pct. or more

Region and State	All Minorities		Black Students		Hispanic Students	
	1984	1995	1984	1995	1984	1995
Plains	**6.8**	**10.3**	**3.9**	**4.8**	**0.9**	**1.9**
Iowa	4.3	7.4	2.2	2.9	0.7	1.7
Kansas	8.7	12.8	4.7	5.5	1.7	3.4
Minnesota	3.9	8.9	1.3	2.9	0.5	1.5
Missouri	10.6	13.4	8.1	9.0	0.9	1.7
Nebraska	5.0	7.8	2.7	3.0	0.9	2.0
North Dakota	5.2	7.5	0.8	0.8	0.3	0.5
South Dakota	7.2	9.2	0.9	0.8	0.9	0.6
Southwest	**22.7**	**32.8**	**7.4**	**8.1**	**11.8**	**18.4**
Arizona	17.0	25.0	2.9	3.3	8.8	14.5
New Mexico	33.3	43.1	2.3	2.6	25.2	31.9
Oklahoma	12.6	20.4	6.4	7.6	1.2	2.4
Texas	25.4	36.3	9.2	10.1	13.6	21.1
Rocky Mountains	**7.6**	**12.2**	**1.5**	**2.0**	**3.2**	**5.9**
Colorado	10.8	17.7	2.6	3.5	5.5	9.5
Idaho	4.5	6.5	0.7	0.7	1.4	2.9
Montana	6.6	11.3	0.6	0.2	0.6	1.2
Utah	4.7	6.6	0.6	0.6	1.6	2.7
Wyoming	4.0	7.7	0.9	1.0	1.8	4.4
Far West	**26.6**	**41.4**	**5.9**	**6.8**	**8.7**	**16.4**
Alaska	14.9	19.4	3.8	3.5	1.5	2.8
California	29.8	47.9	6.9	8.0	10.8	20.6
Hawaii	70.1	70.8	2.3	2.1	1.6	2.4
Nevada	12.5	21.1	4.0	5.6	3.1	7.7
Oregon	7.3	13.4	1.3	1.9	1.3	3.9
Washington	9.8	17.5	2.4	3.8	1.4	3.7
U.S. Service Schools	**13.7**	**19.8**	**11.1**	**13.3**	**1.3**	**3.5**

Note: Calculated from data in the two preceding tables.

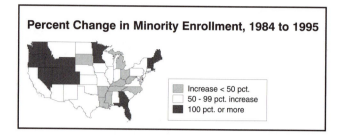

Percent Change in Minority Enrollment, 1984 to 1995

	Increase < 50 pct.
	50 - 99 pct. increase
	100 pct. or more

Region and State	Percentage Change in Enrollment, 1984 to 1995						
	Total	White Non-Hispanic	Total Minority	Black Non-Hispanic	Hispanic	Asian/ Pacific Islander	Non-resident Alien
50 States & D.C.	**16.6**	**5.1**	**67.7**	**36.9**	**104.3**	**104.6**	**35.7**
New England	**2.0**	**-7.7**	**111.9**	**61.0**	**143.2**	**182.4**	**54.2**
Connecticut	-2.5	-12.5	94.7	65.3	140.6	143.5	40.0
Maine	7.4	2.9	250.0	100.0	300.0	350.0	200.0
Massachusetts	-1.2	-13.2	110.6	56.1	138.2	181.6	52.8
New Hampshire	21.7	17.9	161.5	83.3	150.0	400.0	50.0
Rhode Island	7.2	-1.6	120.0	60.0	170.0	188.9	92.3
Vermont	14.0	8.4	200.0	150.0	150.0	250.0	60.0
Mideast	**8.9**	**-2.8**	**53.6**	**30.1**	**73.1**	**131.9**	**53.1**
Delaware	32.2	22.1	102.5	81.8	166.7	175.0	80.0
D.C.	-3.4	-11.4	17.0	4.3	66.7	122.1	-23.1
Maryland	13.9	-1.1	61.3	51.2	93.8	97.3	86.0
New Jersey	9.3	-5.5	69.9	37.9	83.3	163.8	54.1
New York	3.4	-10.6	47.0	20.8	63.9	121.7	67.3
Pennsylvania	17.3	10.2	72.6	43.3	143.5	169.7	77.1
Southeast	**29.9**	**21.4**	**65.4**	**49.9**	**102.8**	**192.3**	**25.1**
Alabama	31.5	26.1	50.4	43.3	183.3	155.6	24.3
Arkansas	24.9	23.2	32.6	23.1	133.3	83.3	33.3
Florida	43.6	26.4	108.8	106.4	93.0	237.5	30.7
Georgia	60.3	43.4	121.4	109.8	161.1	285.7	62.0
Kentucky	24.7	23.4	32.0	13.1	140.0	200.0	72.2
Louisiana	13.3	7.5	37.4	30.9	48.4	141.2	-30.2
Mississippi	17.7	15.0	22.9	20.1	133.3	83.3	53.8
North Carolina	20.3	15.1	41.4	31.7	158.8	136.7	9.6
South Carolina	32.8	26.1	57.2	50.4	128.6	214.3	38.1
Tennessee	22.3	19.5	39.7	27.9	155.6	200.0	8.9
Virginia	25.8	15.1	74.0	46.5	200.0	191.5	62.5
West Virginia	8.9	7.5	22.0	9.7	66.7	50.0	41.7
Great Lakes	**8.6**	**1.9**	**49.6**	**19.3**	**148.5**	**113.5**	**37.7**
Illinois	8.4	-3.1	53.3	9.4	185.3	105.7	48.8
Indiana	15.9	12.4	52.2	31.4	96.9	100.0	22.9
Michigan	8.5	2.3	45.2	25.3	87.1	146.8	40.5
Ohio	4.3	-0.5	39.6	23.8	105.3	116.0	35.6
Wisconsin	10.9	6.7	67.7	39.6	133.3	97.0	30.2

Continued on next page.

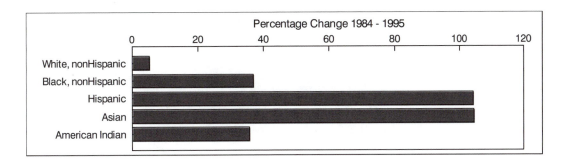

Percentage Change 1984 - 1995

White, nonHispanic	
Black, nonHispanic	
Hispanic	
Asian	
American Indian	

Region and State	Percentage Change in Enrollment, 1984 to 1995						
	Total	White Non-Hispanic	Total Minority	Black Non-Hispanic	Hispanic	Asian/ Pacific Islander	Non-resident Alien
Plains	**21.7**	**16.7**	**84.9**	**49.3**	**151.3**	**172.4**	**39.1**
Iowa	13.5	9.2	93.8	53.1	154.5	150.0	32.1
Kansas	25.2	19.1	82.5	44.6	156.5	185.7	39.5
Minnesota	30.2	23.4	196.3	196.3	263.6	206.5	33.3
Missouri	21.8	17.4	53.6	33.5	113.6	128.6	48.0
Nebraska	18.9	15.2	83.3	30.8	155.6	214.3	30.0
North Dakota	7.4	3.2	52.6	0.0	100.0	200.0	77.8
South Dakota	13.2	10.9	43.5	0.0	-33.3	200.0	42.9
Southwest	**21.8**	**6.4**	**77.6**	**33.9**	**92.3**	**140.3**	**0.9**
Arizona	31.1	18.1	92.2	46.7	115.0	132.4	46.0
New Mexico	53.1	31.5	99.1	73.3	94.5	183.3	20.0
Oklahoma	7.6	-2.1	73.4	28.4	121.1	70.8	11.0
Texas	19.8	3.2	73.1	32.5	87.7	151.8	-10.6
Rocky Mountains	**41.9**	**35.3**	**130.4**	**87.0**	**159.1**	**133.3**	**21.4**
Colorado	47.6	37.0	142.8	104.9	155.7	170.0	14.3
Idaho	37.6	34.2	100.0	33.3	183.3	50.0	85.7
Montana	14.8	8.5	95.8	-50.0	150.0	50.0	25.0
Utah	47.4	45.1	108.9	50.0	153.3	106.7	29.3
Wyoming	29.1	26.1	155.6	50.0	225.0	100.0	-50.0
Far West	**12.7**	**-10.8**	**73.7**	**29.2**	**111.5**	**74.8**	**44.4**
Alaska	8.9	4.0	43.6	0.0	100.0	80.0	-25.0
California	9.3	-19.6	73.8	24.4	106.9	81.6	39.3
Hawaii	22.0	15.1	19.0	9.1	75.0	17.4	87.1
Nevada	57.7	39.4	162.3	117.6	292.3	263.6	216.7
Oregon	17.9	9.1	116.0	66.7	250.0	86.5	52.4
Washington	23.9	12.6	119.5	96.3	218.8	110.3	57.9
U.S. Service Schools	**67.4**	**55.6**	**141.7**	**101.7**	**342.9**	**266.7**	**25.0**

Source: Calculated from data in tables 52 and 53.

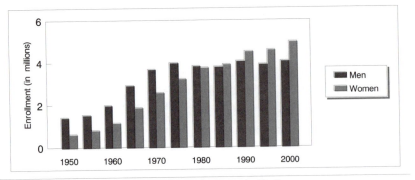

Fall Enrollment in 4-year Institutions

Year	Number of Students (in thousands)			Percentage	
	Total	Men	Women	Men	Women
1950	2,079.0	1,429.3	649.7	69	31
1960	3,156.4	1,987.3	1,169.0	63	37
1970	6,261.5	3,669.0	2,592.5	59	41
1975	7,214.7	3,983.7	3,231.1	55	45
1980	7,570.6	3,827.3	3,743.2	51	49
1982	7,654.0	3,861.2	3,792.8	50	50
1984	7,711.2	3,847.0	3,864.2	50	50
1985	7,716.0	3,816.2	3,899.8	49	51
1986	7,824.0	3,823.6	4,000.4	49	51
1987	7,990.4	3,859.2	4,131.2	48	52
1988	8,180.2	3,912.2	4,268.0	48	52
1989	8,387.8	3,973.3	4,414.5	47	53
1990	8,578.6	4,051.2	4,527.5	47	53
1991	8,707.1	4,099.9	4,607.1	47	53
1992	8,765.0	4,110.7	4,654.2	47	53
1993	8,738.9	4,082.0	4,656.9	47	53
1994	8,749.1	4,048.7	4,700.4	46	54
Projections					
1995	8,505.0	3,923.0	4,582.0	46	54
1996	8,483.0	3,886.0	4,597.0	46	54
1997	8,583.0	3,909.0	4,674.0	46	54
2000	9,045.0	4,061.0	4,983.0	45	55

Note: For years prior to 1970, data are for enrollment of bachelor's and higher degree credit only. For years prior to 1970 data are for aggregate U.S. (50 states, D.C., and outlying parts). For 1980 and later data are enrollment for degree credit and non-degree-credit enrollment. Data for 1995 and later are projections.

For Sources, see table 58.

Fall Enrollment of All Students in 2-year Institutions, by Sex of Student, Selected Years, 1950–2000

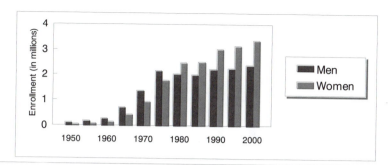

Fall Enrollment in 2-year Institutions

Year	Number of Students (in thousands)			Percentage	
	Total	Men	Women	Men	Women
1950	217.6	140.0	77.6	64	36
1960	453.6	283.3	170.3	62	38
1970	2,319.4	1,374.7	944.7	59	41
1975	3,970.1	2,165.4	1,804.8	55	45
1980	4,526.3	2,047.0	2,479.3	45	55
1982	4,771.7	2,170.2	2,601.5	45	55
1984	4,530.8	2,016.6	2,514.1	45	55
1985	4,531.1	2,002.2	2,528.8	44	56
1986	4,679.5	2,061.0	2,618.6	44	56
1987	4,776.2	2,072.9	2,703.4	43	57
1988	4,875.2	2,089.7	2,785.5	43	57
1989	5,150.9	2,216.8	2,934.1	43	57
1990	5,240.1	2,232.8	3,007.3	43	57
1991	5,651.9	2,401.9	3,250.0	42	58
1992	5,722.4	2,413.3	3,309.1	42	58
1993	5,565.9	2,345.4	3,220.4	42	58
1994	5,529.7	2,323.2	3,206.5	42	58
			Projections		
1995	5,408.0	2,263.0	3,146.0	42	58
1996	5,434.0	2,269.0	3,166.0	42	58
1997	5,503.0	2,296.0	3,207.0	42	58
2000	5,756.0	2,398.0	3,358.0	42	58

Note: For years prior to 1970, data are for enrollment of bachelor's and higher degree credit only. For years prior to 1970 data are for aggregate U.S. (50 states, D.C., and outlying parts). For 1980 and later data are enrollment for degree credit and non-degree-credit enrollment as reported by institutions of higher education in 50 states and D.C. Data for 1995 and later are projections.

For Sources, see next page.

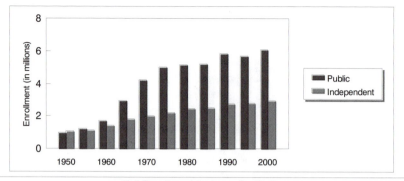

	Fall Enrollment in 4-year Institutions				
	Number of Students (in thousands)			Percentage	
Year	Total	Public	Independent	Public	Independent
1950	2,079.0	986.4	1,092.6	47	53
1960	3,156.4	1,742.1	1,414.3	55	45
1970	6,261.5	4,232.7	2,028.8	68	32
1975	7,214.7	4,998.1	2,216.6	69	31
1980	7,570.6	5,128.6	2,442.0	68	32
1982	7,654.1	5,176.4	2,477.6	68	32
1984	7,711.2	5,198.3	2,512.9	67	33
1985	7,716.0	5,209.5	2,506.4	68	32
1986	7,824.0	5,300.2	2,523.8	68	32
1987	7,990.4	5,432.2	2,558.2	68	32
1988	8,180.2	5,545.9	2,634.3	68	32
1989	8,387.7	5,694.3	2,693.4	68	32
1990	8,578.6	5,848.2	2,730.3	68	32
1991	8,707.1	5,904.7	2,802.3	68	32
1992	8,765.0	5,900.0	2,865.0	67	33
1993	8,738.9	5,851.8	2,887.2	67	33
1994	8,749.1	5,825.2	2,923.9	67	33
	Projections				
1995	8,505.0	5,702.0	2,802.0	67	33
1996	8,483.0	5,689.0	2,794.0	67	33
1997	8,582.0	5,757.0	2,825.0	67	33
2000	9,045.0	6,074.0	2,970.0	67	33

For Notes, see previous page.

Sources: 1 1950 & 1960: NCES, Oppening Fall Enrollment series (Washington: GPO).
2 NCES, Digest of Education Statistics (Washington: GPO), 1990, tbl 163; 1995, tbl. 173; 1996, tbl. 175.
3 NCES, Projections of Statistics to 2007 (Washington: GPO, 1997), tbl.4.

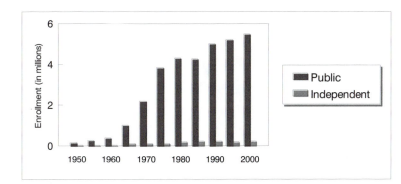

Fall Enrollment in 2-year Institutions				
	Number of Students (in thousands)		Percentage	
Year	Total	Public	Independent	Public	Independent
1950	217.6	168.0	49.5	77	23
1960	453.6	393.6	60.1	87	13
1970	2,319.4	2,195.4	124.0	95	5
1975	3,970.1	3,836.4	133.8	97	3
1980	4,526.3	4,328.8	197.5	96	4
1982	4,771.7	4,519.7	252.1	95	5
1984	4,530.8	4,279.1	251.7	94	6
1985	4,531.1	4,269.7	261.3	94	6
1986	4,679.5	4,413.7	265.9	94	6
1987	4,776.2	4,541.1	235.2	95	5
1988	4,875.2	4,615.5	259.6	95	5
1989	5,150.9	4,883.7	267.2	95	5
1990	5,240.1	4,996.5	243.6	95	5
1991	5,651.9	5,404.8	247.1	96	4
1992	5,722.4	5,484.6	237.8	96	4
1993	5,565.9	5,337.3	228.5	96	4
1994	5,529.7	5,308.5	221.2	96	4
Projections					
1995	5,408.0	5,180.0	228.0	96	4
1996	5,434.0	5,205.0	229.0	96	4
1997	5,503.0	5,270.0	233.0	96	4
2000	5,756.0	5,509.0	247.0	96	4

For Notes, see table 57.

Sources: 1 1950 & 1960: NCES, Opening Fall Enrollment series (Washington: GPO).
   2 NCES, Digest of Education Statistics (Washington: GPO), 1990, tbl 163; 1996, tbl 175.
   3 NCES, Projections of Statistics to 2007 (Washington: GPO, 1997), tbl. 5.

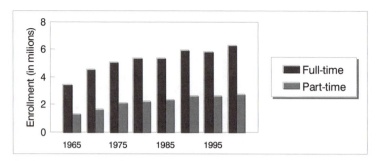

	Enrollment in 4-year Institutions (in thousands)			Percentage	
Year	Total	Full-time	Part-time	Full-time	Part-time
1963	3,900.7	2,760.7	1,140.0	71	29
1965	4,725.0	3,439.6	1,285.4	73	27
1970	6,261.5	4,587.4	1674.1	73	27
1975	7,214.7	5,080.3	2,134.5	70	30
1980	7,570.6	5,344.2	2,226.4	71	29
1982	7,654.1	5,380.8	2,273.3	70	30
1984	7,711.2	5,394.6	2,316.6	70	30
1985	7,716.0	5,384.6	2,331.4	70	30
1986	7,824.0	5,423.3	2,400.7	69	31
1987	7,990.4	5,522.4	2,468.0	69	31
1988	8,180.2	5,693.2	2,487.0	70	30
1989	8,387.7	5,805.2	2,582.4	69	31
1990	8,578.6	5,937.0	2,641.5	69	31
1991	8,707.1	6,040.8	2,666.3	69	31
1992	8,765.0	6,082.1	2,682.9	69	31
1993	8,738.9	6,084.3	2,654.6	70	30
1994	8,749.1	6,106.1	2,643.0	70	30
		Projections			
1995	8,505.0	5,863.0	2,642.0	69	31
1996	8,483.0	5,821.0	2,662.0	69	31
1997	8,582.0	5,897.0	2,686.0	69	31
2000	9,045.0	6,305.0	2,740.0	70	30

Note: For years prior to 1970, data are for enrollment of bachelor's and higher degree credit only for aggregate U.S. (50 states, D.C., and outlying parts). Data for later years are degree-credit and non-degree-credit enrollment for 50 states and D.C. Data for 1995 and later are projections.

Sources: 1 1963 & 1965: NCES, Opening Fall Enrollment series (Washington: GPO).

2 _____, Digest of Education Statistics (Washington: GPO), 1990, tbl. 163; 1996, tbl. 175.

3 _____, Projections of Education Statistics to 2007 (Washington: GPO, 1997), tbl. 4.

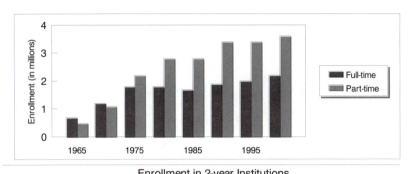

Enrollment in 2-year Institutions					
	Number (in thousands)			Percentage	
Year	Total	Full-time	Part-time	Full-time	Part-time
1963	850.4	442.2	408.2	52	48
1965	1,173.0	692.1	480.9	59	41
1970	2,319.4	1,228.9	1090.5	53	47
1975	3,970.1	1,761.1	2,209.0	44	56
1980	4,526.3	1,753.8	2,772.5	39	61
1982	4,771.7	1,839.8	2,931.9	39	61
1984	4,530.8	1,703.8	2,827.0	38	62
1985	4,531.1	1,690.6	2,840.5	37	63
1986	4,679.5	1,696.3	2,983.3	36	64
1987	4,776.2	1,708.7	3,067.6	36	64
1988	4,875.2	1,743.6	3,131.6	36	64
1989	5,150.9	1,855.7	3,295.2	36	64
1990	5,240.1	1,884.0	3,356.1	36	64
1991	5,651.9	2,074.5	3,577.4	37	63
1992	5,722.4	2,080.0	3,642.4	36	64
1993	5,565.9	2,043.3	3,522.5	37	63
1994	5,529.7	2,031.7	3,498.0	37	63
Projections					
1995	5,408.0	1,965.0	3,443.0	36	64
1996	5,434.0	1,977.0	3,457.0	36	64
1997	5,503.0	2,014.0	3,489.0	37	63
2000	5,756.0	2,164.0	3,592.0	38	62

Note: For years prior to 1970, data for 2-year branches of 4-year institutions are included with 4-year institutions. Data prior to 1970 are estimates. Data for 1995 and later are projections.

Sources: 1 NCES, Digest of Education Statistics (Washington: GPO), 1990, tbls. 158, 163; 1996, tbl.175.

2 _____, Projections of Education Statistics to 2007 (Washington: GPO, 1997), tbl. 5.

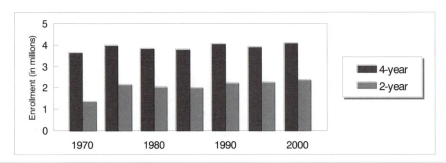

	Number of Men (in thousands)			Percentage	
Year	Total	4-year Institutions	2-year Institutions	4-year Institutions	2-year Institutions
1963	2,789.6	2,401.3	388.3	86	14
1965	3,396.5	2,873.0	523.5	85	15
1970	5,043.6	3,669.0	1,374.7	73	27
1975	6,149.0	3,983.7	2,165.4	65	35
1980	5,874.4	3,827.3	2,047.0	65	35
1982	6,031.4	3,861.2	2,170.2	64	36
1984	5,863.6	3,847.0	2,016.6	66	34
1985	5,818.5	3,816.2	2,002.2	66	34
1986	5,884.5	3,823.6	2,061.0	65	35
1987	5,932.1	3,859.2	2,072.9	65	35
1988	6,001.9	3,912.2	2,089.7	65	35
1989	6,190.0	3,973.3	2,216.8	64	36
1990	6,283.9	4,051.2	2,232.8	64	36
1991	6,501.8	4,100.0	2,401.9	63	37
1992	6,524.0	4,110.7	2,413.3	63	37
1993	6,427.5	4,082.0	2,345.4	64	36
1994	6,371.9	4,048.7	2,323.2	64	36
Projections					
1995	6,186.0	3,923.0	2,263.0	63	37
1996	6,155.0	3,886.0	2,269.0	63	37
1997	6,205.0	3,909.0	2,296.0	63	37
2000	6,459.0	4,061.0	2,398.0	63	37

Note: For years prior to 1970, data for 2-year branches of 4-year institutions are included with 4-year institutions. Data prior to 1970 are estimates. Data for 1995 and later are projections Data prior to 1970 include outlying parts.

Sources: 1 1963 - 1965: NCES, Opening Fall Enrollment series (Washington:GPO).
2 _____, Digest of Education Statistics (Washington: GPO), 1990, tbl. 163; 1996, tbl.175.
3 _____, Projections of Education Statistics to 2007 (Washington: GPO, 1997), tbls. 4, 5.

Enrollment of Women in All Institutions, by Type of Institution
Selected Years, 1963–2000

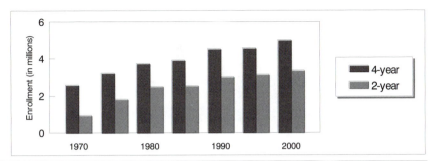

Year	Number of Women (in thousands)			Percentage	
	Total	4-year Institutions	2-year Institutions	4-year Institutions	2-year Institutions
1963	1,739.0	1,499.5	239.5	86	14
1965	2,173.7	1,852.0	321.7	85	15
1970	3,537.2	2,592.5	944.7	73	27
1975	5,035.9	3,231.2	1,804.8	64	36
1980	6,222.5	3,743.3	2,479.3	60	40
1982	6,394.4	3,792.8	2,601.5	59	41
1984	6,378.4	3,864.2	2,514.2	61	39
1985	6,428.6	3,899.9	2,528.8	61	39
1986	6,619.0	4,000.4	2,618.7	60	40
1987	6,834.6	4,131.2	2,703.4	60	40
1988	7,053.4	4,267.9	2,785.4	61	39
1989	7,348.5	4,414.3	2,934.0	60	40
1990	7,534.7	4,527.4	3,007.3	60	40
1991	7,857.1	4,607.1	3,249.9	59	41
1992	7,963.4	4,654.3	3,309.1	58	42
1993	7,877.4	4,656.9	3,220.4	59	41
1994	7,906.9	4,700.4	3,206.6	59	41
Projections					
1995	7,727.0	4,582.0	3,146.0	59	41
1996	7,763.0	4,597.0	3,166.0	59	41
1997	7,880.0	4,674.0	3,207.0	59	41
2000	8,341.0	4,983.0	3,358.0	60	40

Note: For years prior to 1970, data for 2-year branches of 4-year institutions are included with 4-year institutions. Data prior to 1970 are estimates. Data for 1995 and later are projections. Data prior to 1970 include outlying parts.

Sources: 1 1962-1965: NCES, Opening Fall Enrollment series (Washington: GPO).
2 _____, Digest of Education Statistics (Washington: GPO), 1990, tbl. 163; 1996, tbl. 175.
3 _____, Projections of Education Statistics to 2007 (Washington: GPO, 1997), tbls. 4, 5.

64

Enrollment of Men in All Institutions, by Control of Institution, Selected Years, 1970–2000

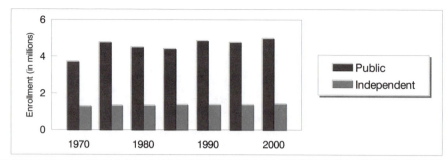

	Number of Men (in thousands)			Percentage	
Year	Total	Public Institutions	Independent Institutions	Public Institutions	Independent Institutions
1970	5,043.6	3,732.8	1,310.8	74	26
1975	6,149.1	4,804.7	1,344.4	78	22
1980	5,874.4	4,522.7	1,351.7	77	23
1982	6,031.4	4,632.9	1,398.5	77	23
1984	5,863.6	4,474.5	1,389.0	76	24
1985	5,818.5	4,437.7	1,380.9	76	24
1986	5,884.5	4,505.6	1,379.0	77	23
1987	5,932.1	4,573.5	1,358.7	77	23
1988	6,001.9	4,608.9	1,393.0	77	23
1989	6,190.0	4,776.4	1,413.6	77	23
1990	6,283.9	4,875.0	1,408.8	78	22
1991	6,501.8	5,066.4	1,435.4	78	22
1992	6,524.0	5,074.4	1,449.5	78	22
1993	6,427.4	4,984.5	1,442.9	78	22
1994	6,371.9	4,930.1	1,441.9	77	23
Projections					
1995	6,186.0	4,795.0	1,392.0	78	23
1996	6,154.0	4,777.0	1,377.0	78	22
1997	6,205.0	4,820.0	1,384.0	78	22
2000	6,459.0	5,025.0	1,434.0	78	22

Sources: 1 NCES, Digest of Education Statistics (Washington: GPO), 1990, tbl. 163; 1996, tbl. 175.
2 ____, Projections of Education Statistics to 2007 (Washington: GPO, 1997), tbls 10-13.

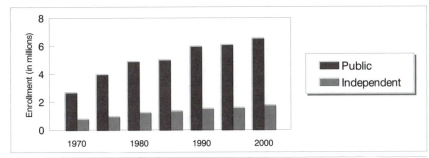

Year	Number of Women (in thousands)			Percentage	
	Total	Public Institutions	Independent Institutions	Public Institutions	Independent Institutions
1970	3,537.2	2,695.2	842.0	76	24
1975	5,035.9	4,029.9	1,006.1	80	20
1980	6,222.5	4,934.8	1,287.8	79	21
1982	6,394.4	5,063.1	1,331.2	79	21
1984	6,378.4	5,002.9	1,375.5	78	22
1985	6,428.6	5,041.8	1,386.9	78	22
1986	6,619.0	5,208.3	1,410.8	79	21
1987	6,834.6	5,399.8	1,434.8	79	21
1988	7,053.4	5,552.4	1,500.9	79	21
1989	7,348.5	5,801.5	1,546.8	79	21
1990	7,534.7	5,969.7	1,565.0	79	21
1991	7,857.1	6,243.1	1,613.9	79	21
1992	7,963.4	6,310.2	1,653.2	79	21
1993	7,877.4	6,204.5	1,672.8	79	21
1994	7,906.9	6,203.7	1,703.3	78	22
Projections					
1995	7,727.0	6,089.0	1,638.0	79	21
1996	7,763.0	6,118.0	1,645.0	79	21
1997	7,880.0	6,208.0	1,673.0	79	21
2000	8,341.0	6,558.0	1,783.0	79	21

Sources: 1 NCES, Digest of Education Statistics (Washington: GPO), 1990, tbl. 163; 1996, tbl. 175.
 2 _____, Projections of Education Statistics to 2007 (Washington: GPO, 1997), tbls 10-13.

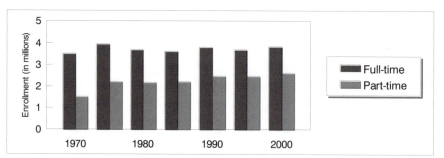

Year	Number of Men (in thousands)			Percentage	
	Total	Full-time	Part-time	Full-time	Part-time
1970	5,043.6	3,504.1	1,539.5	69	31
1975	6,149.0	3,926.8	2,222.3	64	36
1980	5,874.4	3,689.2	2,185.2	63	37
1982	6,031.4	3,752.9	2,278.5	62	38
1984	5,863.6	3,647.5	2,216.0	62	38
1985	5,818.5	3,607.9	2,210.7	62	38
1986	5,884.5	3,599.1	2,285.5	61	39
1987	5,932.1	3,611.0	2,321.2	61	39
1988	6,001.9	3,661.8	2,340.1	61	39
1989	6,190.0	3,740.3	2,449.7	60	40
1990	6283.9	3,807.8	2,476.0	61	39
1991	6,501.8	3,929.3	2,572.5	60	40
1992	6,524.0	3,926.8	2,597.1	60	40
1993	6,427.5	3,890.5	2,536.9	61	39
1994	6,371.9	3,855.2	2,516.8	61	39
		Projections			
1995	6,186.0	3,695.0	2,491.0	60	40
1996	6,154.0	3,637.0	2,517.0	59	41
1997	6,205.0	3,654.0	2,551.0	59	41
2000	6,459.0	3,829.0	2,630.0	59	41

Sources: 1 NCES, Digest of Education Statistics (Washington: GPO), 1990, tbl. 163; 1996, tbl. 175.

2 ____, Projections of Education Statistics to 2007 (Washington: GPO, 1996), tbl. 9.

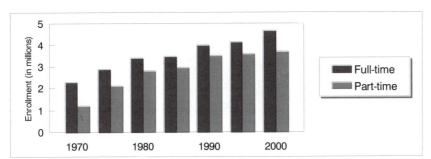

| Year | Number of Women (in thousands) | | | Percentage | |
	Total	Full-time	Part-time	Full-time	Part-time
1970	3,537.2	2,312.2	1,225.1	65	35
1975	5,035.9	2,914.6	2,121.3	58	42
1980	6,222.5	3,408.7	2,813.8	55	45
1982	6,394.4	3,467.7	2,926.7	54	46
1984	6,378.4	3,450.9	2,927.5	54	46
1985	6,428.6	3,467.5	2,961.1	54	46
1986	6,619.0	3,520.5	3,098.5	53	47
1987	6,834.6	3,620.2	3,214.4	53	47
1988	7,053.4	3,775.0	3,278.5	54	46
1989	7,348.5	3,920.7	3,427.8	53	47
1990	7,534.7	4,013.2	3,521.5	53	47
1991	7,857.1	4,186.0	3,671.2	53	47
1992	7,963.4	4,235.2	3,728.2	53	47
1993	7,877.4	4,237.0	3,640.3	54	46
1994	7,906.9	4,282.6	3,624.3	54	46
Projections					
1995	7,727.0	4,133.0	3,595.0	53	47
1996	7,763.0	4,160.0	3,602.0	54	46
1997	7,880.0	4,257.0	3,623.0	54	46
2000	8,341.0	4,640.0	3,701.0	56	44

Sources: 1 NCES, Digest of Education Statistics (Washington: GPO), 1990, tbl. 163; 1996, tbl. 175.

2 ____, Projections of Education Statistics to 2007 (Washington: GPO, 1997), tbl. 9.

Fall Enrollment of First-time Freshmen in All Institutions, by Sex of Student, Selected Years, 1950–2000

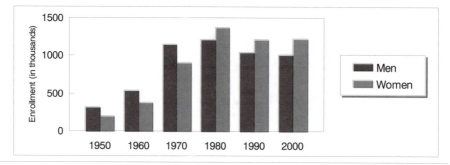

Year	Number (in thousands)			Percentage	
	Total	Men	Women	Men	Women
1950	517	320	197	62	38
1955	670	416	254	62	38
1960	923	540	384	59	42
1965	1,442	829	613	57	43
1970	2,063	1,152	911	56	44
1975	2,515	1,328	1,187	53	47
1980	2,588	1,219	1,369	47	53
1982	2,505	1,199	1,306	48	52
1984	2,357	1,112	1,245	47	53
1985	2,292	1,076	1,216	47	53
1986	2,219	1,047	1,173	47	53
1987	2,246	1,047	1,200	47	53
1988	2,379	1,100	1,279	46	54
1989	2,341	1,095	1,246	47	53
1990	2,257	1,045	1,211	46	54
1991	2,278	1,068	1,209	47	53
1992	2,184	1,013	1,171	46	54
1993	2,161	1,008	1,153	47	53
1994	2,133	985	1,149	46	54
Projections					
1995	2,084	957	1,127	46	54
1996	2,086	954	1,132	46	54
1997	2,113	963	1,150	46	54
2000	2,234	1,011	1,223	45	55

NOTE: Data for 1950 are for 1st-time students; other years are for first-time freshmen. Prior to 1970, data exclude students in occupational programs not creditable to a baccalaureate. Figures for 1995 and later are based on the 1994 share of undergraduate enrollments that first-time freshmen represented and on projections for undergraduate enrollments. Calculations were made for men and women separately.

Sources: 1 USOE, Opening Enrollment in Higher Education, 1960 Analytic Report (Washington: GPO, 1961), p. 11.

2 NCES, Digest of Education Statistics, 1996 (Washington: GPO, 1996), tbls.177, 183.

3 ____, Projections of Education Statistics to 2007 (Washington: GPO, 1997), tbl. 14.

Fall Enrollment of First-time Freshmen in All Institutions, by Control of Institution, Selected Years, 1950–2000

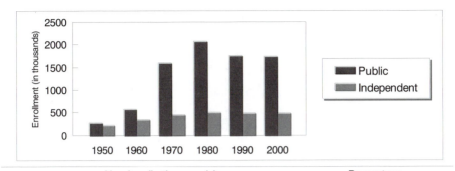

Year	Number (in thousands)			Percentage	
	Total	Public	Independent	Public	Independent
1950	517	286	231	55	45
1955	670	400	270	60	40
1960	923	578	345	63	37
1965	1,442	990	452	69	31
1970	2,063	1,608	455	78	22
1975	2,515	2,056	459	82	18
1980	2,588	2,079	509	80	20
1982	2,505	1,985	520	79	21
1984	2,357	1,844	513	78	22
1985	2,292	1,777	515	78	22
1986	2,219	1,711	509	77	23
1987	2,246	1,738	509	77	23
1988	2,379	1,832	547	77	23
1989	2,341	1,811	530	77	23
1990	2,257	1,768	488	78	22
1991	2,278	1,788	490	78	22
1992	2,184	1,690	493	77	23
1993	2,161	1,676	485	78	22
1994	2,133	1,661	472	78	22
Projections					
1995	2,084	1,626	458	78	22
1996	2,086	1,627	459	78	22
1997	2,113	1,648	465	78	22
2000	2,234	1,743	491	78	22

Note: Data for 1950 are for 1st-time students; other years are for first-time freshmen. Prior to 1970, data exclude students in occupational programs not creditable to a baccalaureate.

Figures for 1995 and later are based on the 1994 share of undergraduate enrollments that first-time freshmen represented and on projections for undergraduate enrollments. Public/independent distributions are based on 1994 distributions.

Sources: 1 USOE, Opening Enrollment in Higher Education, 1960 Analytic Report (Washington: GPO, 1961), p. 11.

2 NCES, Digest of Education Statistics, 1996 (Washington: GPO, 1996), tbls.177, 183.

3 _____, Projections of Education Statistics to 2007 (Washington: GPO, 1997), tbl. 14.

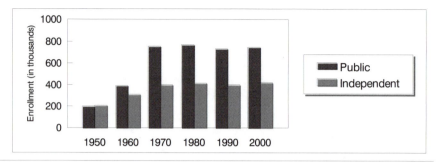

Year	Number (in thousands)			Percentage	
	Total	Public	Independent	Public	Independent
1950	410	204	206	50	50
1955	530	283	247	53	47
1960	709	396	313	56	44
1965	1,041	642	399	62	38
1970	1,151	754	397	66	34
1975	1,167	772	395	66	34
1980	1,183	765	418	65	35
1982	1,135	731	404	64	36
1984	1,117	714	403	64	36
1985	1,116	717	399	64	36
1986	1,112	720	392	65	35
1987	1,163	758	405	65	35
1988	1,209	783	426	65	35
1989	1,176	762	414	65	35
1990	1,127	727	400	65	35
1991	1,111	718	393	65	35
1992	1,105	697	408	63	37
1993	1,113	702	411	63	37
1994	1,115	709	406	64	36
Projections					
1995	1,088	694	394	64	36
1996	1,089	695	395	64	36
1997	1,103	704	400	64	36
2000	1,167	744	423	64	36

Note: Data for 1950 are for 1st-time students; other years are for first-time freshmen. Prior to 1970, data exclude students in occupational programs not creditable to a baccalaureate.

Figures for 1995 and later are based on the 1994 share of undergraduate enrollments that first-time freshmen represented and on projections for undergraduate enrollments. Public/independent and 4-year/2-year distributions are based on 1994 distributions.

Sources: 1 USOE, Opening Enrollment in Higher Education, 1960 Analytic Report (Washington: GPO, 1961), p. 11.

2 NCES, Digest of Education Statistics, 1996 (Washington: GPO, 1996), tbls.177, 183.

3 _____, Projections of Education Statistics to 2007 (Washington: GPO, 1997), tbl. 14.

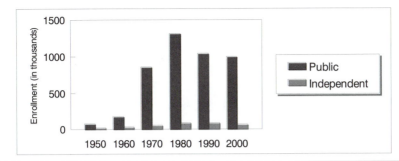

Year	Number (in thousands)			Percentage	
	Total	Public	Independent	Public	Independent
1950	107	82	25	77	23
1955	140	117	23	84	16
1960	214	182	32	85	15
1965	401	348	53	87	13
1970	912	854	58	94	6
1975	1,348	1,284	64	95	5
1980	1,405	1,314	91	94	6
1982	1,370	1,254	116	92	8
1984	1,240	1,130	110	91	9
1985	1,176	1,060	116	90	10
1986	1,108	991	117	89	11
1987	1,084	980	104	90	10
1988	1,170	1,049	121	90	10
1989	1,165	1,049	116	90	10
1990	1,129	1,041	88	92	8
1991	1,167	1,070	97	92	8
1992	1,078	993	85	92	8
1993	1,048	974	74	93	7
1994	1,018	952	66	94	6
Projections					
1995	996	932	64	94	6
1996	997	933	64	94	6
1997	1,010	945	65	94	6
2000	1,067	999	69	94	6

Note: Data for 1950 are for 1st-time students; other years are for first-time freshmen. Prior to 1970, data exclude students in occupational programs not creditable to a baccalaureate.

Figures for 1995 and later are based on the 1994 share of undergraduate enrollments that first-time freshmen represented and on projections for undergraduate enrollments. Public/independent and 4-year/2-year distributions are based on 1994 distributions.

Sources: 1 USOE, Opening Enrollment in Higher Education, 1960 Analytic Report (Washington: GPO, 1961), p. 11.

2 NCES, Digest of Education Statistics, 1996 (Washington: GPO, 1996), tbls.177, 183.

3 _____, Projections of Education Statistics to 2007 (Washington: GPO, 1997), tbl. 14.

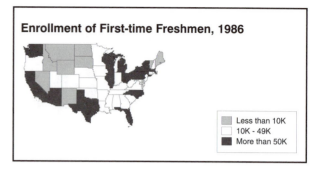

Enrollment of First-time Freshmen, 1986

Less than 10K
10K - 49K
More than 50K

Region and State	Number of First-time Freshmen (in thousands)			
	1986	1990	1994	1997 Estimate
50 States & D.C.	**2,219.2**	**2,256.6**	**2,133.2**	**2,113**
New England	**149.3**	**132.7**	**125.3**	**124**
Connecticut	30.2	25.6	21.3	21
Maine	9.2	9.6	8.1	8
Massachusetts	79.4	67.0	65.8	65
New Hampshire	11.0	10.8	11.4	11
Rhode Island	12.6	13.1	12.6	12
Vermont	6.9	6.6	6.1	6
Mideast	**364.9**	**358.5**	**345.7**	**342**
Delaware	7.5	7.7	6.9	7
D.C.	10.4	8.1	9.7	10
Maryland	31.7	30.7	31.6	31
New Jersey	45.2	45.0	43.1	43
New York	166.0	160.1	155.9	154
Pennsylvania	104.1	106.9	98.5	98
Southeast	**441.3**	**468.4**	**449.4**	**445**
Alabama	39.2	42.1	41.5	41
Arkansas	16.8	17.8	16.4	16
Florida	76.2	71.2	71.3	71
Georgia	38.1	50.2	59.0	58
Kentucky	27.2	30.7	29.0	29
Louisiana	29.2	29.9	31.0	31
Mississippi	25.4	29.4	25.9	26
North Carolina	67.4	63.4	51.3	51
South Carolina	28.7	33.1	28.6	28
Tennessee	32.8	35.7	34.2	34
Virginia	46.7	47.9	45.3	45
West Virginia	13.6	17.0	15.9	16
Great Lakes	**408.6**	**405.3**	**378.2**	**375**
Illinois	106.1	122.9	111.3	110
Indiana	47.4	54.1	48.1	48
Michigan	98.1	85.3	83.7	83
Ohio	104.6	93.5	88.6	88
Wisconsin	52.4	49.5	46.5	46

Continued on next page.

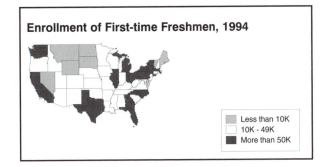

Enrollment of First-time Freshmen, 1994

Less than 10K
10K - 49K
More than 50K

Region and State	Number of First-time Freshmen (in thousands)			
	1986	1990	1994	1997 Estimate
Plains	**176.8**	**184.2**	**173.4**	**172**
Iowa	35.3	36.5	35.2	35
Kansas	26.6	26.8	24.6	24
Minnesota	46.2	45.4	43.8	43
Missouri	36.2	41.5	38.5	38
Nebraska	18.6	20.0	16.6	16
North Dakota	8.0	7.8	8.1	8
South Dakota	5.9	6.2	6.6	7
Southwest	**218.8**	**233**	**203.9**	**202**
Arizona	56.2	57.1	32.8	32
New Mexico	8.7	14.4	13.9	14
Oklahoma	29.3	30.2	29.6	29
Texas	124.6	131.3	127.6	126
Rocky Mountains	**69.4**	**78.9**	**77.6**	**77**
Colorado	27.4	35.3	31.0	31
Idaho	9.7	10.6	10.6	10
Montana	5.6	5.6	6.8	7
Utah	21.5	21.6	24.4	24
Wyoming	5.2	5.8	4.8	5
Far West	**386**	**391.4**	**369.6**	**366**
Alaska	1.4	2.6	1.8	2
California	276.1	277.3	258.7	256
Hawaii	8.7	8.8	10.3	10
Nevada	6.0	8.7	6.9	7
Oregon	25.1	27.0	23.3	23
Washington	68.7	67.0	68.6	68
U.S. Service Schools	**4.2**	**4.2**	**9.9**	**10**

Note: 1994 data are preliminary. The 1997 total is based on the 1994 share of undergraduate enrollment represented by first-time freshmen and on projections of undergraduate enrollment. The distribution of the total among the states is based on each state's share of the 1994 total enrollment.

Sources: 1 NCES, Digest of Education Statistics (Washington: GPO), 1990, tbl. 166; 1994, tbl. 178; 1996, tbl. 178.

2 ____, Projections of Education Statistics to 2007 (Washington: GPO, 1997), tbl. 14.

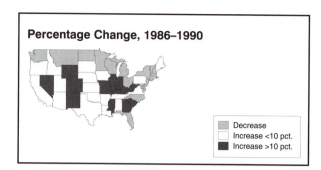

Percentage Change, 1986–1990

Decrease
Increase <10 pct.
Increase >10 pct.

Region and State	Percentage Change (4 years)	
	1986-1990	1990-1994
50 States & D.C.	**1.7**	**-5.5**
New England	**-11.1**	**-5.6**
Connecticut	-15.2	-16.8
Maine	4.3	-15.6
Massachusetts	-15.6	-1.8
New Hampshire	-1.8	5.6
Rhode Island	4.0	-3.8
Vermont	-4.3	-7.6
Mideast	**-1.8**	**-3.6**
Delaware	2.7	-10.4
D.C.	-22.1	19.8
Maryland	-3.2	2.9
New Jersey	-0.4	-4.2
New York	-3.6	-2.6
Pennsylvania	2.7	-7.9
Southeast	**6.1**	**-4.1**
Alabama	7.4	-1.4
Arkansas	6.0	-7.9
Florida	-6.6	0.1
Georgia	31.8	17.5
Kentucky	12.9	-5.5
Louisiana	2.4	3.7
Mississippi	15.7	-11.9
North Carolina	-5.9	-19.1
South Carolina	15.3	-13.6
Tennessee	8.8	-4.2
Virginia	2.6	-5.4
West Virginia	25.0	-6.5
Great Lakes	**-0.8**	**-6.7**
Illinois	15.8	-9.4
Indiana	14.1	-11.1
Michigan	-13.0	-1.9
Ohio	-10.6	-5.2
Wisconsin	-5.5	-6.1

Continued on next page.

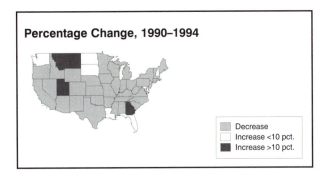

Percentage Change, 1990–1994

Decrease
Increase <10 pct.
Increase >10 pct.

Region and State	Percentage Change (4 years)	
	1986-1990	1990-1994
Plains	**4.2**	**-5.9**
Iowa	3.4	-3.6
Kansas	0.8	-8.2
Minnesota	-1.7	-3.5
Missouri	14.6	-7.2
Nebraska	7.5	-17.0
North Dakota	-2.5	3.8
South Dakota	5.1	6.5
Southwest	**6.5**	**-12.5**
Arizona	1.6	-42.6
New Mexico	65.5	-3.5
Oklahoma	3.1	-2.0
Texas	5.4	-2.8
Rocky Mountains	**13.7**	**-1.6**
Colorado	28.8	-12.2
Idaho	9.3	0.0
Montana	0.0	21.4
Utah	0.5	13.0
Wyoming	11.5	-17.2
Far West	**1.4**	**-5.6**
Alaska	85.7	-30.8
California	0.4	-6.7
Hawaii	1.1	17.0
Nevada	45.0	-20.7
Oregon	7.6	-13.7
Washington	-2.5	2.4
U.S. Service Schools	**0.0**	**135.7**

Source: Calculated from data in table on previous pages.

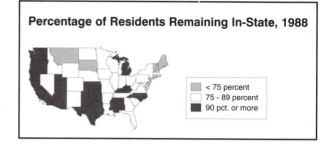

Percentage of Residents Remaining In-State, 1988

- < 75 percent
- 75 - 89 percent
- 90 pct. or more

| Region and State | 1988 First-time Residents of State | | | 1994 Freshman Residents of State | | |
| | | Remaining in State | | | Remaining in State | |
	Total	Number	Pct. of First-time Residents	Total	Number	Pct. of Fresh-man Residents
50 States & D.C.	**2,207.2**	**1,895.9**	**86**	**2,050.0**	**1,746.0**	**85**
New England						
Connecticut	36.5	22.6	62	25.7	14.7	57
Maine	9.4	6.5	70	9.3	5.9	63
Massachusetts	61.8	48.8	79	55.7	42.9	77
New Hampshire	9.6	5.6	58	9.3	5.6	60
Rhode Island	8.1	5.7	70	8.0	5.5	69
Vermont	4.7	3.0	63	4.6	2.6	56
Mideast						
Delaware	6.1	4.6	74	5.7	4.1	71
D.C.	3.5	1.7	50	3.9	2.3	60
Maryland	43.9	32.8	75	35.5	25.0	70
New Jersey	65.3	38.1	58	63.5	39.4	62
New York	142.8	114.1	80	157.0	131.0	83
Pennsylvania	92.3	76.1	82	91.6	76.8	84
Southeast						
Alabama	35.7	32.9	92	36.9	34.2	93
Arkansas	16.8	14.5	86	15.7	13.5	86
Florida	67.1	55.7	83	67.8	57.3	85
Georgia	46.8	38.8	83	56.8	49.9	88
Kentucky	33.6	30.4	90	27.2	24.1	89
Louisiana	27.9	24.3	87	29.1	25.4	87
Mississippi	26.8	24.7	92	24.5	22.3	91
North Carolina	55.0	51.4	94	42.7	39.3	92
South Carolina	27.4	24.3	89	26.6	23.5	88
Tennessee	33.0	28.0	85	31.5	26.7	85
Virginia	42.8	33.3	78	41.2	33.0	80
West Virginia	14.1	12.1	85	13.8	11.7	85
Great Lakes						
Illinois	132.9	113.0	85	120.0	102.1	85
Indiana	42.8	37.8	88	42.5	37.0	87
Michigan	92.2	83.9	91	84.4	76.8	91
Ohio	90.0	78.3	87	86.8	75.7	87
Wisconsin	51.7	45.6	88	45.3	39.1	86

Continued on next page.

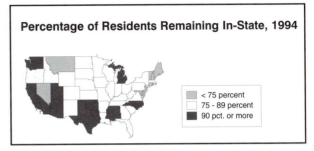

Percentage of Residents Remaining In-State, 1994

Legend:
- < 75 percent
- 75 - 89 percent
- 90 pct. or more

	1988			1994		
	First-time Residents of State			Freshman Residents of State		
		Remaining in State			Remaining in State	
Region and State	Total	Number	Pct. of First-time Residents	Total	Number	Pct. of Fresh-man Residents
Plains						
Iowa	35.1	30.8	88	31.4	27.7	88
Kansas	24.1	21.6	90	22.8	20.3	89
Minnesota	45.8	37.6	82	38.1	29.4	77
Missouri	35.6	30.2	85	35.7	30.0	84
Nebraska	17.7	15.1	85	16.5	13.9	84
North Dakota	7.6	6.4	84	7.0	5.5	79
South Dakota	6.1	4.4	72	6.0	4.5	75
Southwest						
Arizona	62.6	60.3	96	28.9	26.3	91
New Mexico	11.8	9.7	82	15.2	12.1	79
Oklahoma	28.2	25.3	90	28.8	26.0	90
Texas	155.5	147.1	95	124.8	114.9	92
Rocky Mountains						
Colorado	30.2	24.2	80	29.4	24.1	82
Idaho	7.4	5.8	78	9.8	7.7	79
Montana	6.5	4.7	72	7.2	5.2	72
Utah	13.4	12.0	90	19.4	18.1	93
Wyoming	5.1	4.1	81	4.6	3.6	77
Far West						
Alaska	3.0	1.3	43	3.0	1.5	50
California	268.8	256.0	95	254.4	235.9	93
Hawaii	8.9	6.9	77	10.3	8.3	81
Nevada	9.5	8.1	86	6.4	4.7	74
Oregon	34.7	31.8	92	22.0	18.2	83
Washington	69.1	63.9	92	65.5	60.3	92

Note: Data for 1988 describe undergraduates who enrolled at the reporting institutions for the first time and who reported living in a particular state when admitted to the reporting institution. Data for 1994 is restricted to first-time freshmen. Students shown as "attending in-state" are those who attended an institution in their state of residence. Excluded are students whose state of residence was not reported.

Source: NCES, Digest of Education Statistics (Washington: GPO), 1992, tbl. 190; 1996, tbl. 199.

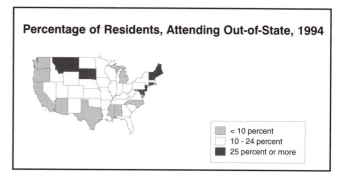

Percentage of Residents, Attending Out-of-State, 1994

< 10 percent
10 - 24 percent
25 percent or more

Region and State	1988 First-time Student Residents of State			1994 Freshman Residents of State		
		Attending Out-of-state			Attending Out-of-state	
	Total	Number	Pct. of First-time Residents	Total	Number	Pct. of Fresh-man Residents
50 States & D.C.	**2,207.2**	**311.2**	**14**	**2,050.0**	**304.0**	**15**
New England						
Connecticut	36.5	13.9	38	25.7	11.0	43
Maine	9.4	2.8	30	9.3	3.4	37
Massachusetts	61.8	13.0	21	55.7	12.8	23
New Hampshire	9.6	4.0	42	9.3	3.7	40
Rhode Island	8.1	2.4	30	8.0	2.4	30
Vermont	4.7	1.7	36	4.6	2.0	43
Mideast						
Delaware	6.1	1.6	26	5.7	1.7	30
D.C.	3.5	1.8	51	3.9	1.5	38
Maryland	43.9	11.1	25	35.5	10.5	30
New Jersey	65.3	27.2	42	63.5	24.2	38
New York	142.8	28.6	20	157.0	26.0	17
Pennsylvania	92.3	16.2	18	91.6	14.7	16
Southeast						
Alabama	35.7	2.8	8	36.9	2.6	7
Arkansas	16.8	2.3	14	15.7	2.3	15
Florida	67.1	11.4	17	67.8	10.5	15
Georgia	46.8	8.0	17	56.8	7.0	12
Kentucky	33.6	3.2	10	27.2	3.1	11
Louisiana	27.9	3.6	13	29.1	3.7	13
Mississippi	26.8	2.1	8	24.5	2.2	9
North Carolina	55.0	3.6	7	42.7	3.4	8
South Carolina	27.4	3.1	11	26.6	3.1	12
Tennessee	33.0	5.1	15	31.5	4.8	15
Virginia	42.8	9.5	22	41.2	8.2	20
West Virginia	14.1	2.1	15	13.8	2.1	15
Great Lakes						
Illinois	132.9	19.9	15	120.0	17.9	15
Indiana	42.8	5.0	12	42.5	5.5	13
Michigan	92.2	8.3	9	84.4	7.6	9
Ohio	90.0	11.7	13	86.8	11.1	13
Wisconsin	51.7	6.0	12	45.3	6.2	14

Continued on next page.

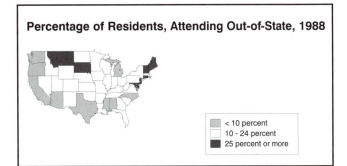

Percentage of Residents, Attending Out-of-State, 1988

< 10 percent
10 - 24 percent
25 percent or more

Region and State	1988 First-time Student Residents of State			1994 Freshman Residents of State		
		Attending Out-of -State			Attending Out-of -State	
	Total	Number	Pct. of First-time Residents	Total	Number	Pct. of Fresh-man Residents
Plains						
Iowa	35.1	4.2	12	31.4	3.7	12
Kansas	24.1	2.5	10	22.8	2.4	11
Minnesota	45.8	8.2	18	38.1	8.7	23
Missouri	35.6	5.4	15	35.7	5.7	16
Nebraska	17.7	2.6	15	16.5	2.6	16
North Dakota	7.6	1.2	16	7.0	1.5	21
South Dakota	6.1	1.7	28	6.0	1.5	25
Southwest						
Arizona	62.6	2.2	4	28.9	2.6	9
New Mexico	11.8	2.1	18	15.2	3.1	20
Oklahoma	28.2	2.9	10	28.8	2.8	10
Texas	155.5	8.4	5	124.8	9.8	8
Rocky Mountains						
Colorado	30.2	5.9	20	29.4	5.3	18
Idaho	7.4	1.6	22	9.8	2.0	20
Montana	6.5	1.8	28	7.2	2.0	28
Utah	13.4	1.4	10	19.4	1.3	7
Wyoming	5.1	1.0	20	4.6	1.0	22
Far West						
Alaska	3.0	1.7	57	3.0	1.5	50
California	268.8	12.8	5	254.4	18.6	7
Hawaii	8.9	2.0	22	10.3	2.0	19
Nevada	9.5	1.3	14	6.4	1.7	27
Oregon	34.7	2.9	8	22.0	3.8	17
Washington	69.1	5.2	8	65.5	5.2	8

Note: Data for 1988 describe undergraduates who enrolled at the reporting institutions for the first time and who reported living in a particular state when admitted to the reporting institution. Data for 1994 is restricted to first-time freshmen. Students shown as "attending out-of-state" are those who attended an institution NOT in their state of residence. Excluded are students whose state of residence was not reported.

Source: NCES, Digest of Education Statistics (Washington: GPO), 1992, tbl. 190; 1996, tbl. 199.

Percentage of Out-of-State 1st-time Undergrads, 1988

Legend:
- Less than 15 percent
- 15 - 29 percent
- 30 percent or more

Region and State	1988 Total First-time Undergrad. Students	1988 First-time Undergraduate Students from Out-of-state Number	1988 Pct. of First-time Enrollment	1994 Total First-time Freshmen	1994 First-time Freshman Students from Out-of-state Number	1994 Pct. of First-time Freshmen
50 States & D.C.	**2,337.4**	**441.4**	**19**	**2,111.3**	**365.3**	**17**
New England						
Connecticut	29.1	6.5	22	21.5	6.8	32
Maine	9.2	2.7	29	8.1	2.2	27
Massachusetts	72.2	23.4	32	65.8	22.9	35
New Hampshire	11.5	5.9	51	11.4	5.8	51
Rhode Island	12.9	7.2	56	12.6	7.1	56
Vermont	6.8	3.9	57	6.1	3.5	57
Mideast						
Delaware	8.0	3.4	43	6.9	2.8	41
D.C.	9.7	7.9	81	9.7	7.4	76
Maryland	39.6	6.8	17	32.7	7.8	24
New Jersey	44.3	6.2	14	43.1	3.7	9
New York	178.3	64.2	36	155.8	24.8	16
Pennsylvania	99.1	23.0	23	98.0	21.2	22
Southeast						
Alabama	41.8	9.0	22	41.5	7.3	18
Arkansas	17.1	2.6	15	16.2	2.7	17
Florida	71.5	15.8	22	70.2	12.9	18
Georgia	48.3	9.5	20	59.0	9.1	15
Kentucky	34.7	4.3	12	28.6	4.5	16
Louisiana	29.2	4.9	17	30.9	5.5	18
Mississippi	28.4	3.7	13	25.9	3.5	14
North Carolina	63.4	12.0	19	51.3	12.1	24
South Carolina	30.4	6.1	20	28.5	5.0	18
Tennessee	35.6	7.6	21	33.9	7.2	21
Virginia	49.0	15.7	32	45.3	12.3	27
West Virginia	17.0	5.0	29	15.8	4.1	26
Great Lakes						
Illinois	123.1	10.0	8	110.4	8.3	8
Indiana	50.4	12.6	25	48.1	11.0	23
Michigan	98.9	15.0	15	83.4	6.6	8
Ohio	91.0	12.6	14	88.5	12.7	14
Wisconsin	54.3	8.6	16	46.5	7.4	16

Continued on next page.

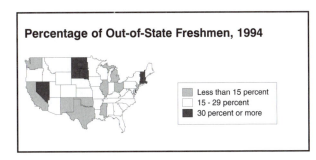

Percentage of Out-of-State Freshmen, 1994

Less than 15 percent
15 - 29 percent
30 percent or more

Region and State	1988			1994		
	Total First-time Undergrad. Students	First-time Undergraduate Students from Out-of-state		Total First-time Freshmen	First-time Freshman Students from Out-of-state	
		Number	Pct. of First-time Enrollment		Number	Pct. of First-time Freshmen
Plains						
Iowa	37.2	6.4	17	35.2	7.5	21
Kansas	26.3	4.7	18	24.6	4.3	17
Minnesota	46.7	9.1	19	38.0	8.6	23
Missouri	38.4	8.2	21	38.3	8.3	22
Nebraska	17.5	2.4	14	16.6	2.7	16
North Dakota	9.0	2.7	30	8.1	2.6	32
South Dakota	6.1	1.7	28	6.6	2.1	32
Southwest						
Arizona	69.6	9.3	13	32.8	6.4	20
New Mexico	11.5	1.8	16	13.9	1.8	13
Oklahoma	27.7	2.4	9	29.3	3.3	11
Texas	159.6	12.5	8	127.2	12.2	10
Rocky Mountains						
Colorado	30.9	6.7	22	32.1	8.0	25
Idaho	9.9	4.1	41	10.6	2.9	27
Montana	5.5	0.8	15	6.8	1.6	24
Utah	18.7	6.7	36	24.4	6.3	26
Wyoming	5.4	1.2	22	4.8	1.2	25
Far West						
Alaska	1.6	0.3	19	1.8	0.3	17
California	283.3	27.3	10	255.3	19.5	8
Hawaii	7.8	0.9	12	10.3	2.0	19
Nevada	9.2	1.0	11	6.9	2.2	32
Oregon	38.9	7.1	18	23.3	5.1	22
Washington	71.8	7.9	11	68.6	8.3	12

Note: Data for 1988 describe undergraduates who enrolled at the reporting institutions for the first time and who reported living in a particular state when admitted to the reporting institution. Data for 1994 is restricted to first-time freshmen. Students shown as being from "out-of-state" are those who attended an institution NOT in their state of residence. Excluded are students whose state of residence was not reported. Data for U.S. Service Schools are included in state totals.

Source: NCES, Digest of Education Statistics (Washington: GPO), 1992, tbl. 190; 1996, tbl. 199.

Full-time Equivalent (FTE) Enrollment, at All Institutions, Selected Years, 1970–2000

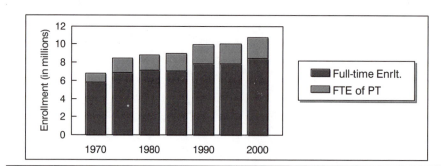

	Fall Enrollment, All Institutions (in thousands)				
Year	Full-time Equivalent Enrollment	Total Full-time Enrollment	Full-time Equivalent of Part-time (FTEPT)	Total Part-time Enrollment	Ratio of FTEPT to Total Part-time
1970	6,737.8	5,816.3	921.5	2,764.6	0.33
1975	8,479.7	6,841.3	1,638.4	4,343.5	0.38
1980	8,819.0	7,098.0	1,721.0	4,998.9	0.34
1982	9,091.6	7,220.6	1,871.0	5,205.2	0.36
1984	8,951.7	7,098.4	1,853.3	5,143.6	0.36
1985	8,943.4	7,075.2	1,868.2	5,171.8	0.36
1986	9,064.2	7,119.6	1,944.6	5,384.0	0.36
1987	9,229.7	7,231.1	1,998.6	5,535.6	0.36
1988	9,464.3	7,436.8	2,027.5	5,618.6	0.36
1989	9,780.9	7,661.0	2,119.9	5,877.6	0.36
1990	9,983.4	7,821.0	2,162.4	5,997.7	0.36
1991	10,360.6	8,115.3	2,245.3	6,243.6	0.36
1992	10,436.8	8,162.1	2,274.7	6,325.2	0.36
1993	10,351.4	8,127.6	2,223.8	6,177.2	0.36
1994	10,348.1	8,137.8	2,210.3	6,141.0	0.36
Projections					
1995	10,020.0	7,828.0	2,192.0	6,085.0	0.36
1996	10,002.0	7,798.0	2,204.0	6,119.0	0.36
1997	10,135.0	7,911.0	2,224.0	6,174.0	0.36
2000	10,750.0	8,469.0	2,281.0	6,331.0	0.36

Sources: 1 NCES, Digest of Education Statistics (Washington: GPO), 1990, tbl. 163; 1996, tbls. 175, 196.
   2 _____, Projections of Education Statistics to 2007 (Washington: GPO, 1997), tbls. 3, 23

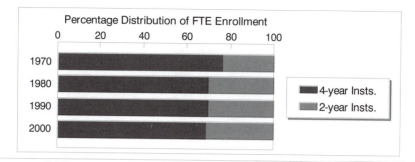

Percentage Distribution of FTE Enrollment

Fall Enrollment, All Institutions (in thousands)				
	FTE Enrollment All Insts.	FTE Enrollment 4-yr Insts.	FTE Enrollment 2-yr. Insts.	Percentage Distribution of FTE Enrollment
Year				4-yr Insts.	2-yr. Insts.
1970	6,737.8	5,145.4	1,592.4	76	24
1975	8,479.7	5,900.4	2,579.3	70	30
1980	8,819.0	6,161.4	2,657.6	70	30
1982	9,091.6	6,248.9	2,842.7	69	31
1984	8,951.7	6,292.7	2,659.0	70	30
1985	8,943.4	6,294.3	2,649.1	70	30
1986	9,064.2	6,360.3	2,703.8	70	30
1987	9,229.7	6,486.5	2,743.2	70	30
1988	9,464.3	6,664.1	2,800.1	70	30
1989	9,780.9	6,813.6	2,967.3	70	30
1990	9,983.4	6,968.0	3,015.4	70	30
1991	10,360.6	7,081.5	3,279.2	68	32
1992	10,436.8	7,129.4	3,307.4	68	32
1993	10,351.4	7,120.9	3,230.5	69	31
1994	10,348.1	7,137.3	3,210.7	69	31
Projections					
1995	10,020.0	6,895.0	3,125.0	69	31
1996	10,002.0	6,861.0	3,142.0	69	31
1997	10,135.0	6,945.0	3,190.0	69	31
2000	10,750.0	7,374.0	3,375.0	69	31

Sources: 1 NCES, Digest of Education Statistics 1996 (Washington: GPO, 1996), tbl. 196.
   2 _____, Projections of Education Statistics to 2007 (Washington: GPO, 1997), tbl. 23.

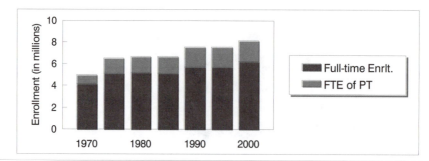

Year	Fall Enrollment, Public Institutions (in thousands)				
	Full-time Equivalent Enrollment	Total Full-time Enrollment	Full-time Equivalent of Part-time (FTEPT)	Total Part-time Enrollment	Ratio of FTEPT to Total Part-time
1970	4,953.1	4,215.6	737.5	2,212.4	0.33
1975	6,522.3	5,132.4	1,389.9	3,702.2	0.38
1980	6,642.3	5,187.7	1,454.6	4,269.8	0.34
1982	6,850.6	5,284.0	1,566.6	4,412.0	0.36
1984	6,684.7	5,147.6	1,537.1	4,329.8	0.36
1985	6,667.8	5,120.3	1,547.5	4,359.0	0.36
1986	6,778.0	5,162.8	1,615.2	4,551.1	0.35
1987	6,937.7	5,267.1	1,670.6	4,706.2	0.35
1988	7,096.9	5,410.3	1,686.6	4,751.0	0.35
1989	7,371.6	5,608.7	1,762.9	4,969.2	0.35
1990	7,558.0	5,750.6	1,807.4	5,094.1	0.35
1991	7,862.8	5,974.5	1,888.3	5,335.0	0.35
1992	7,911.7	6,010.9	1,900.8	5,373.7	0.35
1993	7,812.4	5,962.5	1,849.9	5,226.5	0.35
1994	7,784.4	5,950.8	1,833.6	5,183.0	0.35
			Projections		
1995	7,560.0	5,740.0	1,820.0	5,144.0	0.35
1996	7,555.0	5,725.0	1,830.0	5,170.0	0.35
1997	7,658.0	5,812.0	1,846.0	5,216.0	0.35
2000	8,124.0	6,230.0	1,894.0	5,353.0	0.35

Sources: 1 NCES, Digest of Education Statistics (Washington: GPO), 1990, tbl. 163;
1996, tbls. 175, 196.
2 _____, Projections of Education Statistics to 2007 (Washington: GPO, 1997), tbls. 10, 11, 24.

Full-time Equivalent (FTE) Enrollment, at Independent Institutions, Selected Years, 1970–2000

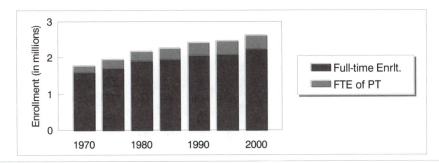

Year	Fall Enrollment, Independent Institutions (in thousands)				
	Full-time Equivalent Enrollment	Total Full-time Enrollment	Full-time Equivalent of Part-time (FTEPT)	Total Part-time Enrollment	Ratio of FTEPT to Total Part-time
1970	1,784.7	1,600.7	184.0	552.1	0.33
1975	1,957.4	1,709.0	248.4	641.5	0.39
1980	2,176.7	1,910.2	266.5	729.3	0.37
1982	2,241.1	1,936.5	304.6	793.2	0.38
1984	2,267.0	1,950.7	316.3	813.8	0.39
1985	2,275.7	1,955.0	320.7	812.8	0.39
1986	2,286.1	1,956.8	329.3	833.0	0.40
1987	2,292.0	1,964.1	327.9	829.4	0.40
1988	2,367.4	2,026.4	341.0	867.5	0.39
1989	2,409.3	2,052.2	357.1	908.2	0.39
1990	2,425.5	2,070.5	355.0	903.3	0.39
1991	2,497.8	2,140.7	357.1	908.6	0.39
1992	2,525.1	2,151.2	373.9	951.5	0.39
1993	2,539.0	2,165.0	374.0	950.7	0.39
1994	2,563.7	2,187.0	376.7	958.2	0.39
1995	2,460.0	2,088.0	372.0	942.0	0.39
1996	2,448.0	2,073.0	375.0	949.0	0.40
1997	2,477.0	2,099.0	378.0	958.0	0.39
2000	2,625.0	2,239.0	386.0	978.0	0.39

Sources: 1 NCES, Digest of Education Statistics (Washington: GPO), 1990, tbl. 163; 1996, tbls. 175, 196.

2 _____, Projections of Education Statistics to 2007 (Washington: GPO, 1997), tbls. 12, 13, 25.

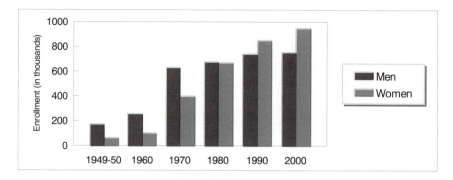

	Number of Students (in thousands)			Percentage	
Year	Total	Men	Women	Men	Women
1929-30	47.3	29.1	18.2	62	38
1939-40	105.7	67.4	38.3	64	36
1949-50	237.6	172.3	65.3	73	27
1960	356.0	253.0	103.0	71	29
1970	1,030.0	630.0	400.0	61	39
1980	1,343.0	675.0	670.0	50	50
1985	1,376.0	677.0	700.0	49	51
1986	1,435.0	693.0	742.0	48	52
1987	1,452.0	693.0	759.0	48	52
1988	1,472.0	697.0	774.0	47	53
1989	1,522.0	710.0	811.0	47	53
1990	1,586.0	737.0	849.0	46	54
1991	1,639.0	761.0	878.0	46	54
1992	1,669.0	772.0	896.0	46	54
1993	1,688.0	771.0	917.0	46	54
1994	1,721.0	776.0	945.0	45	55
Projections					
1995	1,667.0	760.0	906.0	46	54
1996	1,663.0	754.0	910.0	45	55
1997	1,672.0	753.0	919.0	45	55
2000	1,694.0	751.0	943.0	44	56

Note: Data for 1970 and later include unclassified postbaccalaureate students.

Sources: 1 USOE, Statistics of Higher Education (Washington: GPO), 1947-48, pp. 72-77;
1955-56, pp, 124, 135;
2 NCES, Digest of Education Statistics, 1996 (Washington: GPO, 1996), tbl. 184.
3 ____, Projections of Education Statistics (Washington: GPO), to 1979-80, p.34;
to 2007, tbl. 17.

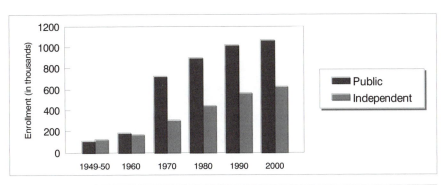

	Number of Students (in thousands)			Percentage	
Year	Total	Public	Independent	Public	Independent
1929-30	47.3	20.2	27.1	43	57
1939-40	105.7	44.6	61.2	42	58
1949-50	237.6	108.3	129.3	46	54
1960	356.0	187.0	169.0	53	47
1970	1,031.0	724.0	306.0	70	30
1980	1,343.0	900.0	442.0	67	33
1985	1,376.0	891.0	486.0	65	35
1986	1,435.0	941.0	494.0	66	34
1987	1,452.0	945.0	507.0	65	35
1988	1,472.0	949.0	522.0	64	35
1989	1,522.0	978.0	544.0	64	36
1990	1,586.0	1,023.0	563.0	65	35
1991	1,639.0	1,051.0	589.0	64	36
1992	1,669.0	1,058.0	611.0	63	37
1993	1,688.0	1,063.0	625.0	63	37
1994	1,721.0	1,075.0	647.0	62	38
Projections					
1995	1,667.0	1,052.0	614.0	63	37
1996	1,663.0	1,050.0	613.0	63	37
1997	1,672.0	1,056.0	616.0	63	37
2000	1,694.0	1,070.0	625.0	63	37

Note: Data for 1970 and later include unclassified postbaccalaureate students.

Sources: 1 USOE, Statistics of Higher Education (Washington: GPO), 1947-48, pp. 72-77; 1955-56, pp, 124, 135;

2 NCES, Digest of Education Statistics, 1996 (Washington: GPO, 1996), tbl. 184.

3 _____, Projections of Education Statistics (Washington: GPO), to 1979-80, p.34; to 2007, tbls. 18, 19.

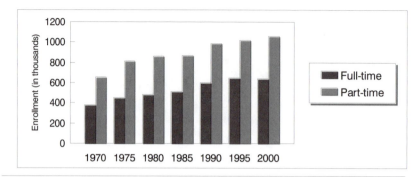

	Number of Students (in thousands)			Percentage	
Year	Total	Full-time	Part-time	Full-time	Part-time
1970	1,031.0	379.0	651.0	37	63
1975	1,263.0	453.0	810.0	36	64
1980	1,343.0	485.0	860.0	36	64
1985	1,376.0	509.0	867.0	37	63
1986	1,435.0	522.0	913.0	36	64
1987	1,452.0	527.0	925.0	36	64
1988	1,472.0	553.0	919.0	38	62
1989	1,522.0	572.0	949.0	38	62
1990	1,586.0	599.0	987.0	38	62
1991	1,639.0	642.0	997.0	39	61
1992	1,669.0	666.0	1,003.0	40	60
1993	1,688.0	688.0	1,000.0	41	59
1994	1,721.0	706.0	1,016.0	41	59
Projections					
1995	1,667.0	647.0	1,019.0	39	61
1996	1,663.0	631.0	1,033.0	38	62
1997	1,672.0	629.0	1,043.0	38	62
2000	1,694.0	637.0	1,057.0	38	62

Note: Data for 1970 and later include unclassified postbaccalaureate students.

Sources: 1 NCES, Digest of Education Statistics, 1996 (Washington: GPO, 1996), tbl. 184.
2 ____, Projections of Education Statistics to 2007 (Washington: GPO, 1997) tbl. 17.

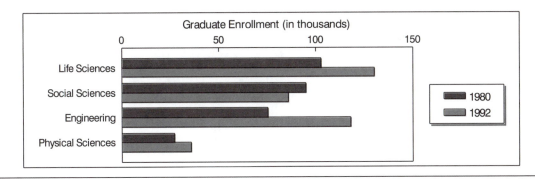

Field of Study	Graduate Enrollment (in thousands)				Percentage Distribution	
	1980	1985	1990	1992	1980	1992
All Science and Engineering Fields	**383.1**	**405.6**	**454.1**	**495.9**	**100**	**100**
Engineering, total	**75.1**	**96.2**	**107.7**	**118.0**	**19.6**	**23.8**
Aerospace	1.7	2.5	3.9	4.0	0.4	0.8
Chemical	6.0	7.2	6.7	7.4	1.6	1.5
Civil	13.5	14.9	15.6	19.4	3.5	3.9
Electrical	19.2	28.2	33.7	36.3	5.0	7.3
Mechanical	9.9	14.2	16.8	18.8	2.6	3.8
Other	24.8	29.2	31.0	32.1	6.5	6.5
Sciences, total	**308.0**	**309.4**	**346.3**	**377.9**	**80.4**	**76.2**
Computer sciences	13.6	29.6	34.3	36.9	3.5	7.4
Earth, atmospheric, ocean sciences	14.2	15.6	14.2	15.6	3.7	3.1
Life sciences	102.5	104.0	117.1	129.8	26.8	26.2
Agricultural	12.3	11.4	11.1	11.6	3.2	2.3
Biological	47.9	46.2	50.1	54.4	12.5	11.0
Health	42.4	46.4	55.9	63.8	11.1	12.9
Mathematical sciences	15.4	17.6	19.8	20.4	4.0	4.1
Physical sciences	27.0	31.0	34.1	35.5	7.0	7.2
Astronomy	0.6	0.7	0.8	0.9	0.2	0.2
Chemistry	16.2	18.3	19.1	19.9	4.2	4.0
Physics	9.9	11.7	13.9	14.3	2.6	2.9
Other	0.2	0.3	0.4	0.5	0.1	0.1
Psychology	40.6	41.2	48.7	53.8	10.6	10.8
Social sciences	94.8	70.5	78.0	85.8	24.7	17.3
Economics	13.1	12.4	12.3	13.3	3.4	2.7
Political science	31.2	27.0	30.6	33.8	8.1	6.8
Sociology and anthropology	15.5	13.3	15.5	17.1	4.0	3.4
Other	34.9	17.8	19.6	21.7	9.1	4.4

Note: Figures for "economics" exclude "agricultural economics."

Source: NSF, Academic Science/engineering Graduate Enrollment and Support Surveys as reported in:
NCES, Digest of Education Statistics (Washington: GPO), 1990, tbl. 198; 1996, tbl. 209.

Graduate Enrollment, by Region and State, Selected Years, 1960–1997

Graduate Enrollment, 1980

▨	Less than 5K
☐	5K - 24.9K
■	25K or more

Region and State	Graduate Enrollment (in thousands)					Estimate
	1960	1970	1980	1990	1994	1997
50 States & D.C.	**313.9**	**813.6**	**1,099.7**	**1,586.2**	**1,721.5**	**1,672.0**
New England	**28.3**	**68.0**	**87.1**	**129.2**	**138.3**	**134.3**
Connecticut	7.2	19.8	25.9	31.9	30.7	29.8
Maine	0.2	1.1	1.6	4.8	5.8	5.6
Massachusetts	18.9	40.1	48.3	71.0	79.4	77.1
New Hampshire	0.6	1.4	3.2	7.9	9.0	8.7
Rhode Island	1.2	4.7	5.8	9.5	9.3	9.0
Vermont	0.2	0.9	2.3	4.1	4.1	4.0
Mideast	**97.5**	**227.0**	**249.0**	**347.0**	**370.1**	**359.5**
Delaware	1.0	2.1	1.9	3.3	4.6	4.5
D.C.	7.6	16.6	20.6	22.5	25.2	24.5
Maryland	5.3	16.4	21.3	36.2	41.5	40.3
New Jersey	8.6	26.1	30.9	41.6	42.9	41.7
New York	54.4	115.4	118.8	167.4	173.4	168.4
Pennsylvania	20.6	50.4	55.5	76.0	82.5	80.1
Southeast	**31.4**	**106.4**	**187.7**	**280.4**	**326.5**	**317.1**
Alabama	2.5	7.6	14.3	20.2	23.3	22.6
Arkansas	1.2	2.8	6.4	6.4	7.4	7.2
Florida	3.9	14.7	26.4	52.6	62.6	60.8
Georgia	2.6	12.0	22.2	29.6	35.4	34.4
Kentucky	2.9	7.4	16.2	18.1	19.9	19.3
Louisiana	4.0	11.8	18.6	20.3	24.9	24.2
Mississippi	1.2	4.5	8.2	10.4	11.0	10.7
North Carolina	4.4	11.5	18.6	29.7	35.0	34.0
South Carolina	1.8	4.0	9.2	16.8	22.6	22.0
Tennessee	4.0	10.7	14.5	22.3	25.8	25.1
Virginia	2.0	15.1	22.4	45.2	47.1	45.7
West Virginia	0.9	4.3	10.7	8.8	11.5	11.2
Great Lakes	**64.4**	**160.5**	**208.6**	**270.7**	**293.4**	**285.0**
Illinois	16.8	44.0	62.4	88.7	96.7	93.9
Indiana	9.1	27.0	28.3	31.4	34.0	33.0
Michigan	18.9	36.6	46.9	58.6	66.3	64.4
Ohio	13.7	35.4	51.6	62.5	65.7	63.8
Wisconsin	5.9	17.5	19.4	29.5	30.7	29.8

For sources, see next page

Note: Detail may not sum to totals because of rounding. Comparability of the data is limited by changes in definitions of "graduate enrollment." Data for 1960 and 1970 come from the "advanced degree" enrollment surveys whose definitions were more stringent than later surveys. For example, the later surveys have included "unclassified postbaccalaureate students." Data exclude enrollment for "first-professional" degrees such as M.D., J.D., etc. Estimates for 1997 are based on national projections and the 1994 percentage distribution among the states.

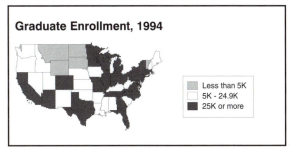

Graduate Enrollment, 1994

Less than 5K
5K - 24.9K
25K or more

Region and State	Graduate Enrollment (in thousands)					Estimate
	1960	1970	1980	1990	1994	1997
Plains	**22.2**	**57.6**	**80.7**	**117.3**	**123.9**	**120.3**
Iowa	4.1	9.4	14.2	19.5	16.5	16.0
Kansas	3.9	8.6	14.9	19.4	20.5	19.9
Minnesota	5.6	12.3	16.0	25.4	31.8	30.9
Missouri	5.8	18.9	24.0	35.0	36.1	35.1
Nebraska	1.7	5.0	8.1	12.2	12.3	11.9
North Dakota	0.6	1.7	1.6	2.2	2.7	2.6
South Dakota	0.5	1.7	1.9	3.6	4.0	3.9
Southwest	**20.2**	**61.9**	**107.9**	**154.5**	**170.2**	**165.3**
Arizona	3.1	10.5	17.0	26.8	32.1	31.2
New Mexico	2.0	4.6	6.3	10.1	12.6	12.2
Oklahoma	3.7	9.6	14.8	20.7	22.3	21.7
Texas	11.4	37.2	69.8	96.9	103.2	100.2
Rocky Mountains	**7.0**	**20.9**	**26.6**	**55.4**	**63.9**	**62.1**
Colorado	3.5	9.9	13.3	32.8	37.0	35.9
Idaho	0.4	1.4	2.7	6.7	8.1	7.9
Montana	0.5	1.7	1.9	3.5	3.4	3.3
Utah	2.3	6.9	7.6	9.5	12.7	12.3
Wyoming	0.3	1.0	1.1	2.9	2.7	2.6
Far West	**42.4**	**109.2**	**149.2**	**228.9**	**231.8**	**225.1**
Alaska	0.1	0.4	0.9	1.2	1.6	1.6
California	35.5	85.7	118.5	180.0	175.5	170.5
Hawaii	0.2	3.0	3.7	6.7	8.0	7.8
Nevada	0.1	1.6	1.6	5.3	6.8	6.6
Oregon	2.1	7.7	10.1	15.8	16.3	15.8
Washington	4.4	10.8	14.4	19.9	23.6	22.9
U.S. Service Schools	**0.5**	**2.1**	**2.7**	**2.8**	**3.7**	**3.6**

For notes, see previous page.

Sources: 1 NCES, Digest of Education Statistics (Washington: GPO), 1982, tbl. 74; 1994, tbl. 193; 1996, tbl. 193.
2 ____, Students Enrolled for Advanced Degrees (Washington: GPO), Fall 1960, p. 28; Fall 1970, Summary Data, p.11.
3 ____, Projections of Education Statistics to 2007 (Washington: GPO, 1997), tbl. 17.

III

Institutions and Finance, Faculty, Staff, and Students

Highlights on Institutions and Finance, Faculty, Staff, and Students

INSTITUTIONS

- As of fall 1995, there were 3,706 institutions of higher education in the 50 states and the District of Columbia. In addition to the institutions of higher education described here, there are thousands of other institutions of postsecondary education offering programs of instruction—in business skills, data processing, cosmetology, etc.—that require a high school diploma for entrance. Institutions described here are those listed in the U.S. Department of Education's official directory of institutions of higher education.
- Less than half (45 percent) of the colleges and universities are publicly controlled. That proportion has changed only slightly since 1970 when it stood at 43 percent.
- A little more than one-third (39 percent) of the nation's institutions of higher education are two-year institutions. The proportion of these colleges increased rapidly in the 1960s, but has changed little since 1980.
- About 700 institutions offer as their highest degree a bachelor's or first-professional degree. About 1,450 institutions offer graduate study; of these, 550 award the doctorate.

FINANCES

Current-fund Revenue

- Current-fund revenues totaled $179 billion in Fiscal Year (FY) 1993–94.
- Student tuition and fees provided a little more than one-quarter of all revenues (27 percent) for all institutions. However, independent institutions receive 42 percent of their current-fund revenue, and public institutions 18 percent, from this source.
- State funds provided one-third (36 percent) of the revenues for public institutions. For independent institutions, state funding provided only 2 percent of their total revenues.
- State funding, in terms of constant dollars, have dropped in the 1990s. In 1990, public institutions received $42.7 billion in constant 1993–94 dollars from the states; in 1993–94 they received $40.5 billion.
- Federal funds accounted for 11 percent of current-fund revenues at public institutions and 15 percent at independent institutions in 1993–94. For public institutions, this is a slight increase from 1990 when federal funds accounted for 10 percent. Independent institutions reported a slight drop, from 16 percent in 1990 to 15 percent in 1994. These figures, however, do not include Pell Grant funds, which for reporting purposes are considered grants to the individual student, not the institution. Thus the several billions of dollars that that program provides each year appears in the financial reports as tuition and fee auxiliary enterprise revenue, not as revenue from the federal government.

Current-fund Expenditures

- Current-fund expenditures for 1993–94 were $173 billion—slightly less than revenues. Public institutions spent $109 billion, and independent colleges, $64 billion. These expenditures were distributed among major categories as follows:

Instruction and academic support	37 percent
Research (nondepartmental)	11 percent
Public service programs (including hospitals)	14 percent
Student services (including student aid)	21 percent
Institutional support	17 percent

- Changes in these distributions have been relatively small since 1984–85 when the percentages were 39, 10, 12, 20, and 19, respectively.
- Constant dollar revenue and expenditures both increased by about 40 percent between 1984–85 and 1993–94. During the same period, full-time equivalent enrollment increased by 16 percent.

FACULTY AND STAFF

- As of fall 1997, institutions of higher education employed over 900,000 faculty members, one-third of whom were women; 60 percent were employed full-time.
- Tenure is held by 70 percent of the full-time male faculty and by half of the full-time female faculty.
- Average faculty salaries for the four major faculty ranks in academic year 1995–96 were:

Full professor	$65,440
Associate professor	48,310
Assistant professor	40,050
Instructor	30,830

- Fringe benefits for faculty vary by rank. The average figure for a full-time faculty member in 1995–96 amounted to about one-quarter of the individual's salary.
- Minorities represented a smaller proportion of full-time faculty than they did of the student body. Twelve percent of the nation's faculty in 1993 were members of minority racial/ethnic groups. Racial/ethnic minorities constitute about one-quarter of the student body.
- Minorities comprised 28 percent of the nonprofessional staff at colleges and universities in 1993. They made up 13 percent of the professional staff.

STUDENT DATA

- One-fifth of full-time, first-time entering students in fall 1996 were minority students.
- In 1996, 14 percent of the entering women and 6 percent of the entering men identified education (elementary, secondary, or college teaching) as their probable career occupations. In 1987, comparable figures for women and men were 13 percent and 4 percent, respectively.
- Average college costs in fall 1995 for four-year colleges were estimated at $6,823 for students at public institutions and $17,631 at independent institutions. These figures represent increases of 17 percent and 13 percent in constant dollar costs since 1990.

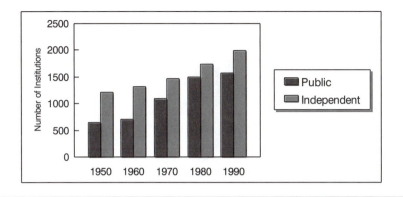

	Institutions of Higher Education				
	Number			Percentage Distribution	
Year	All Institutions	Public	Independent	Public	Independent
1950-51	1,852	636	1,216	34	66
1960-61	2,021	700	1,321	35	65
1970-71	2,556	1,089	1,467	43	57
1980-81	3,231	1,497	1,734	46	54
1982-83	3,280	1,493	1,787	46	54
1984-85	3,331	1,501	1,830	45	55
1985-86	3,340	1,498	1,842	45	55
1986-87	3,406	1,533	1,873	45	55
1987-88	3,587	1,591	1,996	44	56
1988-89	3,565	1,582	1,983	44	56
1989-90	3,535	1,563	1,972	44	56
1990-91	3,559	1,567	1,992	44	56
1991-92	3,601	1,598	2,003	44	56
1992-93	3,638	1,624	2,014	45	55
1993-94	3,632	1,625	2,007	45	55
1994-95	3,688	1,641	2,047	44	56
1995-96	3,706	1,655	2,051	45	55

Note: Data for 1980 and later include separate counts for branch campuses. Caution must be used in making year-to-year comparisons because institutions may change how they want their campuses categorized. One year a multi-campus institution may report its campuses separately, another year it may want the institution counted as a single entity.
Institutional counts in this table may vary from other tables because data come from different surveys with different categorization rules. See Guide to Sources chapter.

Source: NCES, Digest of Education Statistics, 1996 (Washington: GPO, 1996), tbl. 236.

Number of Institutions of Higher Education, by Type of Institutions, Selected Years, 1950–1995

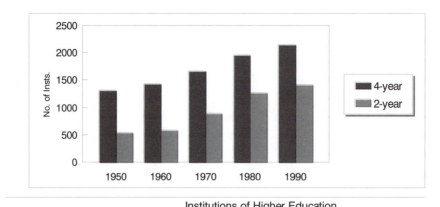

	Institutions of Higher Education				
	Number			Percentage Distribution	
Year	All Institutions	4-year	2-year	4-year	2-year
1950-51	1,852	1,312	540	71	29
1960-61	2,021	1,431	590	71	29
1970-71	2,556	1,665	891	65	35
1980-81	3,231	1,957	1,274	61	39
1982-83	3,280	1,984	1,296	60	40
1984-85	3,331	2,025	1,306	61	39
1985-86	3,340	2,029	1,311	61	39
1986-87	3,406	2,070	1,336	61	39
1987-88	3,587	2,135	1,452	60	40
1988-89	3,565	2,129	1,436	60	40
1989-90	3,535	2,127	1,408	60	40
1990-91	3,559	2,141	1,418	60	40
1991-92	3,601	2,157	1,444	60	40
1992-93	3,638	2,169	1,469	60	40
1993-94	3,632	2,190	1,442	60	40
1994-95	3,688	2,215	1,473	60	40
1995-96	3,706	2,244	1,462	61	39

Note: Data for 1980 and later include separate counts for branch campuses. Caution must be used in making year-to-year comparisons because institutions may change how they want their campuses categorized. One year a multi-campus institution may report its campuses separately, but another year it may want the institution counted as a single entity. Institutional counts in this table may vary from other tables because data come from different surveys with different categorization rules. See Guide to Sources chapter.

Source: NCES, Digest of Education Statistics, 1996 (Washington: GPO, 1996), tbl. 236.

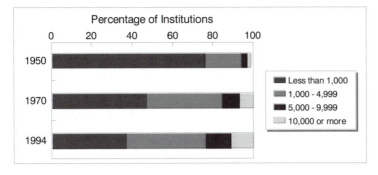

Year (Fall)	All Institutions	Percentage of Institutions with Enrollment of -			
		Less than 1,000	1,000 - 4,999	5,000 - 9,999	10,000 & Over
All Institutions					
1950	100	77	18	3	2
1960	100	63	28	5	4
1970	100	47	37	9	7
1980	100	36	40	12	12
1990	100	38	39	12	11
1992	100	37	39	12	12
1994	100	37	39	13	11
Public Institutions					
1990	100	10	46	22	22
1992	100	10	45	22	23
1994	100	10	45	23	22
Independent Institutions					
1990	100	60	34	4	2
1992	100	59	34	4	2
1994	100	58	35	4	2

Note: Detail may not sum to totals because of rounding. These data should be used with caution inasmuch as the growth and changing autonomy of branch campuses complicates this kind of analysis. A university reported as one institution in 1950 may have been reported as a main campus and three branch campuses in 1960. It therefore would be counted as four institutions in the latter year. Thus, some of the change results from differences in reporting rather than growth in the number of institutions. Data for recent years are counts of institutions that are included in the NCES IPEDS fall enrollment survey.

Sources: 1 USOE, Opening Fall Enrollment series, 1950 through 1970.
  2 CES computer tapes containing fall enrollment data from HEGIS, 1980.
  3 NCES, Digest of Education Statistics (Washington: GPO), 1992, tbl. 203; 1994, tbl 210; 1996, tbl. 210.

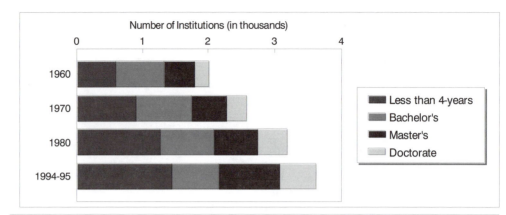

		Number of Institutions Offering as Highest Level -				
Year	All Institutions	Two, but less than Four, Years beyond the 12th Grade	Bachelor's and/or 1st-Professional Degree	Master's and beyond, but less than Doctorate	Doctor of Philosophy and Equivalent	Other
1950-51	1,859	527	800	360	155	17
1960-61	2,040	593	741	455	219	32
Fall 1970	2,573	897	850	528	298	na
Fall 1980	3,231	1,274	808	659	440	50
Fall 1982	3,280	1,296	810	658	452	64
Fall 1984	3,331	1,306	798	718	473	36
Fall 1986	3,434	1,291	731	737	462	213
1989-90	3,535	1,384	910	702	495	44
1991-92	3,601	1,420	889	714	545	33
1994-95	3,688	1,455	701	911	552	69

Note: Data prior to 1980 are for U.S. and outlying parts; for later years data are for 50 states and D.C.

Data prior to 1970 for master's degree institutions are those whose highest award was the master's or second professional degree.

Data for 1986 and later are not strictly comparable to earlier figures. The later data come from the Integrated Postsecondary Data System (IPEDS) which uses degree-level categories somewhat different from the earlier (HEGIS) surveys.

Data in the "Other" column include institutions that did not provide degree level information.

Sources: 1 NCES, Directory of Postsecondary Institutions (Washington: GPO), various years.

2 Computer tapes from NCES surveys of institutional characterisitcs.

3 NCES, 1995 Directory of Postsecondary Institutions; Vol 1, 4-year and 2-year Institutions (Washington: GPO, 1996), tbl. 9.

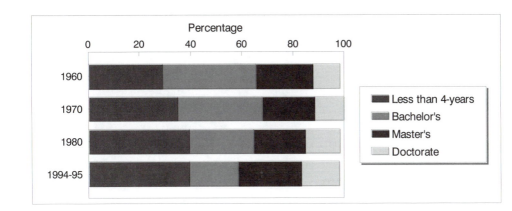

Year	All Institutions	Two, but less than Four, Years beyond the 12th Grade	Bachelor's and/or 1st-Professional Degree	Master's and beyond, but less than Doctorate	Doctor of Philosophy and Equivalent	Graduate Study (Master's & Doctorate)
		Percentage of Institutions Offering as Highest Level -				
1950-51	100	28	43	19	8	28
1960-61	100	29	36	22	11	33
Fall 1970	100	35	33	21	12	32
Fall 1980	100	39	25	20	14	34
Fall 1982	100	40	25	20	14	34
Fall 1984	100	39	24	22	14	36
Fall 1986	100	38	21	21	13	35
1989-90	100	39	26	20	14	34
1991-92	100	39	25	20	15	35
1994-95	100	39	19	25	15	40

Note: Data prior to 1980 are for U.S. and outlying parts; for later years data are for 50 states and D.C.

Data prior to 1970 for master's degree institutions are those whose highest award was the master's or second professional degree.

Data for 1986 and later are not strictly comparable to earlier figures. The later data come from the Integrated Post-secondary Data System (IPEDS) which uses degree-level categories somewhat different from the earlier (HEGIS) surveys.

Detail may not sum to 100 because percentage of "Other" institutions is not shown.

Source: Calculated from data shown on the opposite page.

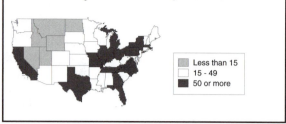

Number of 4-year institutions, 1995–96

Less than 15
15 - 49
50 or more

Region and State	1989-90			1995-96			Percentage Change, All Institutions
	All Institutions	4-year	2-year	All Institutions	4-year	2-year	
50 States & D.C.	**3,535**	**2,127**	**1,408**	**3,706**	**2,244**	**1,462**	**4.8**
New England	**258**	**178**	**80**	**257**	**185**	**72**	**-0.4**
Connecticut	48	28	20	42	26	16	-12.5
Maine	31	21	10	33	21	12	6.5
Massachusetts	117	85	32	118	90	28	0.9
New Hampshire	29	17	12	30	19	11	3.4
Rhode Island	11	10	1	12	10	2	9.1
Vermont	22	17	5	22	19	3	0.0
Mideast	**689**	**472**	**217**	**674**	**452**	**222**	**-2.2**
Delaware	10	7	3	9	6	3	-10.0
D.C.	17	17	0	19	19	0	11.8
Maryland	57	35	22	57	34	23	0.0
New Jersey	62	39	23	61	35	26	-1.6
New York	326	228	98	311	212	99	-4.6
Pennsylvania	217	146	71	217	146	71	0.0
Southeast	**836**	**443**	**393**	**870**	**486**	**384**	**4.1**
Alabama	87	36	51	82	36	46	-5.7
Arkansas	37	20	17	38	20	18	2.7
Florida	95	53	42	114	68	46	20.0
Georgia	95	51	44	120	56	64	26.3
Kentucky	59	32	27	61	37	24	3.4
Louisiana	34	24	10	36	27	9	5.9
Mississippi	47	21	26	46	21	25	-2.1
North Carolina	126	53	73	121	58	63	-4.0
South Carolina	64	32	32	59	34	25	-7.8
Tennessee	86	52	34	76	52	24	-11.6
Virginia	78	48	30	89	54	35	14.1
West Virginia	28	21	7	28	23	5	0.0
Great Lakes	**554**	**352**	**202**	**578**	**368**	**210**	**4.3**
Illinois	166	103	63	169	107	62	1.8
Indiana	78	55	23	78	54	24	0.0
Michigan	97	63	34	109	71	38	12.4
Ohio	152	90	62	156	92	64	2.6
Wisconsin	61	41	20	66	44	22	8.2

For sources, see next page

Note: Caution should be used in making year to year comparisons because institutions may change how they want their campuses categorized.

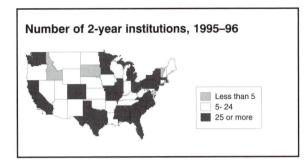

Number of 2-year institutions, 1995–96

Legend:
- Less than 5
- 5- 24
- 25 or more

Region and State	1989-90 All Institutions	4-year	2-year	1995-96 All Institutions	4-year	2-year	Percentage Change, All Institutions
Plains	**357**	**224**	**133**	**397**	**238**	**159**	**11.2**
Iowa	58	37	21	59	39	20	1.7
Kansas	54	30	24	54	31	23	0.0
Minnesota	81	44	37	107	48	59	32.1
Missouri	89	65	24	101	70	31	13.5
Nebraska	36	21	15	35	22	13	-2.8
North Dakota	20	10	10	20	10	10	0.0
South Dakota	19	17	2	21	18	3	10.5
Southwest	**284**	**150**	**134**	**304**	**161**	**143**	**7.0**
Arizona	37	17	20	45	23	22	21.6
New Mexico	26	10	16	35	15	20	34.6
Oklahoma	47	27	20	45	25	20	-4.3
Texas	174	96	78	179	98	81	2.9
Rocky Mountains	**107**	**53**	**54**	**123**	**63**	**60**	**15.0**
Colorado	54	30	24	59	34	25	9.3
Idaho	11	7	4	12	8	4	9.1
Montana	19	9	10	26	11	15	36.8
Utah	14	6	8	17	9	8	21.4
Wyoming	9	1	8	9	1	8	0.0
Far West	**441**	**247**	**194**	**493**	**282**	**211**	**11.8**
Alaska	8	7	1	9	6	3	12.5
California	310	171	139	348	199	149	12.3
Hawaii	14	8	6	17	10	7	21.4
Nevada	8	3	5	10	5	5	25.0
Oregon	46	32	14	45	30	15	-2.2
Washington	55	26	29	64	32	32	16.4
U.S. Service Schools	**9**	**8**	**1**	**10**	**9**	**1**	**11.1**

For notes, see previous page.

Source: NCES, Digest of Education Statistics (Washington: GPO), 1990, tbl. 218; 1996, tbl. 237.

Number of Institutions

Carnegie Classification	1970	1976	1987	1994
All institutions	2,837	3,072	3,389	3,595
Doctorate-granting universities	*173*	*184*	*213*	*236*
Research universities I	52	51	70	88
Research universities II	40	47	34	37
Doctoral universities I	53	56	51	51
Doctoral universities II	28	30	58	60
Master's colleges and universities	*456*	*594*	*595*	*529*
Master's colleges and universities I	323	381	424	435
Master's colleges and universities II	133	213	171	94
Baccalaureate colleges	*721*	*583*	*572*	*637*
Baccalaureate colleges I	146	123	142	166
Baccalaureate colleges II	575	460	430	471
Associate of arts colleges	1,063	1,146	1,367	1,471
Specialized institutions	424	559	642	693
Institutions for nontraditional study	ni	6	ni	ni
Tribal colleges	ni	ni	ni	29.00

ni: Institutional category not included in the study this year.
Note: Italics indicates subtotals.

The following classifications were first used in the 1994 report: "Master's degree-granting institution," "Baccalaureate colleges," and "Associate of arts colleges." They replace the following categories used in previous reports: "Comprehensive universities and colleges," "Liberal arts colleges," and "Two-year institutions."

Source: The Carnegie Foundation for the Advancement of Teaching (CFAT), Classification of Institutions of Higher Education (Berkeley: Univ. of California Press, 1994), tbls. 1 - 4. Used with permission.

Percentage Distribution of Institutions of Higher Education, by Carnegie Classification Code, Selected Years, 1970–1994

Carnegie Classification	1970	1976	1987	1994
All institutions	100	100	100	100
Doctorate-granting universities	6	6	6	7
Research universities I	2	2	2	2
Research universities II	1	2	1	1
Doctoral universities I	2	2	2	1
Doctoral universities II	1	1	2	2
Master's colleges and universities	16	19	18	15
Master's colleges and universities I	11	12	13	12
Master's colleges and universities II	5	7	5	3
Baccalaureate colleges	25	19	17	18
Baccalaureate colleges I	5	4	4	5
Baccalaureate colleges II	20	15	13	13
Associate of arts colleges	37	37	40	41
Specialized institutions	15	18	19	19
Institutions for nontraditional study	ni	<1	ni	ni
Tribal colleges	ni	ni	ni	1

Source: Calculated from data on the opposite page.

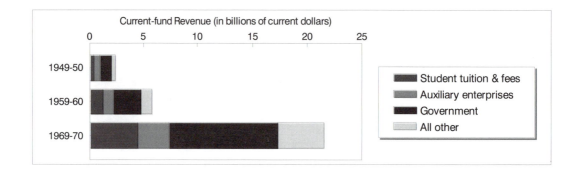

Current-fund Revenue (in billions of current dollars)

Legend:
- Student tuition & fees
- Auxiliary enterprises
- Government
- All other

Kind of Revenue	Amount (millions of current dollars)				
	1929-30	1939-40	1949-50	1959-60	1969-70
Total Current-fund Revenue	$554.5	$715.2	$2,374.6	$5,785.5	$21,515.2
Total educational & general revenue	*483.1*	*571.3*	*1,833.8*	*4,688.4*	*17,337.3*
Student tuition & fees	144.1	200.9	394.5	1,157.5	4,419.8
All government	*171.5*	*214.5*	*1,077.6*	*2,563.2*	*10,013.6*
Federal	20.7	38.9	524.3	1,037.0	3,450.9
State	150.8	151.2	491.6	1,374.5	5,787.9
Local	nr	24.4	61.7	151.7	774.8
Endowment earnings	68.6	71.3	96.3	206.6	447.3
Private gifts, grants & contracts	26.2	40.5	118.6	382.6	1,001.5
Other educational & general	72.7	44.2	146.6	378.5	1,455.1
Auxiliary enterprises	60.4	143.9	511.3	1,004.3	2,900.4
Student aid grants	nr	nr	16.3	92.9	658.0
Other sources	11.0	nr	13.2	nr	619.6
Sales & service of hospitals	nr	nr	nr	nr	nr

Continued on next page.

nr: Not reported.

Note: Italicized figures are subtotals. Data prior to 1959-60 include only the 48 contiguous states & D.C. Because of rounding, detail may not sum to totals. Data prior to 1979-80 are not strictly comparable to later data because of a major change in reporting categories and definitions. Student aid was eliminated as a revenue source; such revenue is included in either government revenue totals or private gifts and grants. However, Pell grant funds are excluded from federal revenue and included under student tuition and fees or auxiliary enterprises. Revenue for Federally Funded Research Centers are included in federal revenue. State revenue for 1929-30 includes revenue from local sources.

Estimates for 1996-97 are Fact Book estimates based on relationships betwen current-fund expenditures and current-fund revenues for the period 1990-94, projections for current-fund expenditures, and 1993-94 distribution among revenue sources.

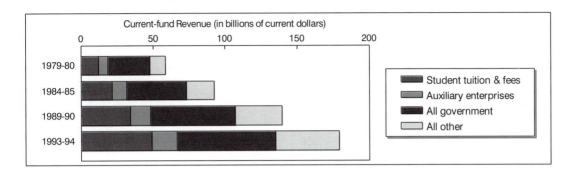

Current-fund Revenue (in billions of current dollars)

Legend:
- Student tuition & fees
- Auxiliary enterprises
- All government
- All other

Kind of Revenue	Amount (millions of current dollars)				
	1979-80	1984-85	1989-90	1993-94	1996-97 Estimate
	Millions of Current Dollars				
Total Current-fund Revenue	$58,520.0	$92,472.6	$139,635.6	$179,226.6	$207,300
Student tuition & fees	11,930.4	21,283.3	33,926.1	48,646.5	56,500
All government	*28,868.7*	*41,479.3*	*59,244.0*	*68,985.0*	*79,400*
Federal	8,902.8	11,509.1	17,254.9	22,076.4	25,600
State	18,378.3	27,583.0	38,349.2	41,910.3	48,000
Local	1,587.6	2,387.2	3,639.9	4,998.3	5,800
Endowment earnings	1,176.6	2,096.3	3,143.7	3,669.5	4,300
Private gifts, grants & contracts	2,808.1	4,896.3	7,781.4	10,203.1	11,900
Sales & services, total	*12,094.3*	*19,701.9*	*30,787.3*	*41,791.3*	*48,300*
Educational activities	1,239.4	2,126.9	3,632.1	5,294.0	6,100
Auxiliary enterprises	6,481.5	10,100.4	13,938.5	17,537.5	20,300
Hospitals	4,373.4	7,474.6	13,216.7	18,959.8	21,900
Other sources	1,642.0	3,015.5	4,753.1	5,931.2	6,900

Total revenue from students (Tuition & fees plus auxiliary enterprises)

	1979-80	1984-85	1989-90	1993-94	1996-97 Estimate
Amount	18,411.9	31,383.7	47,864.6	66,184.0	76,900

Sources: 1 NCES,"Financial Statistics of Institutions of Higher Education" surveys.

2 NCES, Digest of Education Statistics (Washington: GPO), 1990, tbl 291; 1996, tbl. 321.

3 _____, Projections of Education Statistics to 2007 (Washington: GPO, 1997), tbl. 37.

95 Percentage Distribution of Current-fund Revenues of All Institutions, by Kind of Revenue, Selected Years, 1979/80–1996/97

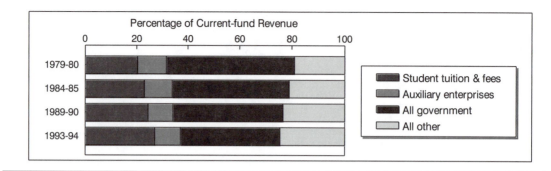

	Percentage of Current-fund Revenue			
Student tuition & fees				
Auxiliary enterprises				
All government				
All other				

Kind of Revenue	1979-80	1984-85	1989-90	1993-94	FB Estimate for 1996-97
	Percentage Distribution				
Total Current-fund Revenue	100.0	100.0	100.0	100.0	100.0
Student tuition & fees	20.4	23.0	24.3	27.1	27.3
All government	*49.3*	*44.9*	*42.4*	*38.5*	*38.3*
Federal	15.2	12.4	12.4	12.3	12.3
State	31.4	29.8	27.5	23.4	23.2
Local	2.7	2.6	2.6	2.8	2.8
Endowment earnings	2.0	2.3	2.3	2.0	2.1
Private gifts, grants & contracts	4.8	5.3	5.6	5.7	5.7
Sales & services, total	*20.7*	*21.3*	*22.0*	*23.3*	*23.3*
Educational activities	2.1	2.3	2.6	3.0	2.9
Auxiliary enterprises	11.1	10.9	10.0	9.8	9.8
Hospitals	7.5	8.1	9.5	10.6	10.6
Other sources	2.8	3.3	3.4	3.3	3.3

Total revenue from students (Tuition & fees plus auxiliary enterprises)

Percent of total current-fund revenue	31.5	33.9	34.3	36.9	37.0

Calculated from data in preceding table.

Current-fund Revenue of All Institutions of Higher Education, in Constant 1993–94 Dollars, Selected Years, 1979/80–1996/97

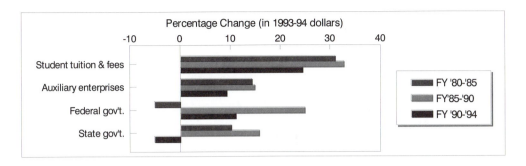

Kind of Revenue	1979-80	1984-85	1989-90	1993-94	FB Estimate for 1996-97
	Millions of Constant 1993-94 Dollars				
Total Current-fund Revenue	$110,252.9	$127,856.9	$160,812.6	$179,226.6	$190,200
Student tuition & fees	22,477.1	29,427.3	39,071.3	48,646.5	52,000
All government	*54,389.2*	*57,351.2*	*68,228.9*	*68,985.0*	*72,700*
Federal	16,773.1	15,913.0	19,871.8	22,076.4	23,500
State	34,625.1	38,137.5	44,165.2	41,910.3	44,000
Local	2,991.1	3,300.7	4,191.9	4,998.3	5,200
Endowment earnings	2,216.7	2,898.4	3,620.5	3,669.5	4,000
Private gifts, grants & contracts	5,290.5	6,769.8	8,961.5	10,203.1	10,800
Sales & services, total	*22,785.9*	*27,240.7*	*35,456.5*	*41,791.3*	*44,400*
Educational activities	2,335.1	2,940.7	4,182.9	5,294.0	5,600
Auxiliary enterprises	12,211.3	13,965.3	16,052.4	17,537.5	18,700
Hospitals	8,239.6	10,334.7	15,221.1	18,959.8	20,100
Other sources	3,093.6	4,169.4	5,473.9	5,931.2	6,300

	Percentage Change (in Constant 1993-94 Dollars)		
	1979-80 to 1984-85	1984-85 to 1989-90	1989-90 to 1993-94
Kind of Revenue	(5 years)	(5 years)	(4 years)
Total Current-fund Revenue	16.0	25.8	11.5
Student tuition & fees	30.9	32.8	24.5
All government	5.4	19.0	1.1
Federal	-5.1	24.9	11.1
State	10.1	15.8	-5.1
Local	10.4	27.0	19.2
Endowment earnings	30.8	24.9	1.4
Private gifts, grants & contracts	28.0	32.4	13.9
Sales & services, total	19.6	30.2	17.9
Educational activities	25.9	42.2	26.6
Auxiliary enterprises	14.4	14.9	9.3
Hospitals	25.4	47.3	24.6
Other sources	34.8	31.3	8.4
Total revenue from students (Tuition & fees plus auxiliary enterprises)	25.1	27.0	20.1

See note for table 94 for explanation of 1996-97 estimates.

Sources: 1 NCES, Digest of Education Statistics (Washington: GPO), 1990, tbl. 292; 1996, tbls. 37, 323.

2 _____, Projections of Education Statistics to 2007 (Washington: GPO, 1997), tbls. 37, B8.

Current-fund Revenue of Public Institutions of Higher Education in Current Dollars, Selected Fiscal Years, 1979/80–1996/97

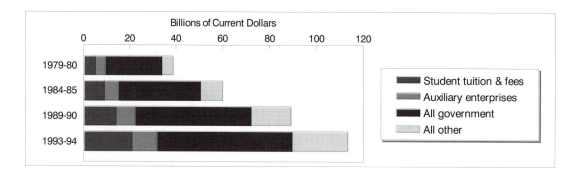

Kind of Revenue	1979-80	1984-85	1989-90	1993-94	FB Estimate for 1996-97
	Millions of Current Dollars				
Total Current-fund Revenue	$38,824.2	$59,794.2	$88,911.4	$112,968.1	$129,300
Student tuition & fees	4,860.2	8,647.6	13,820.2	20,825.4	23,800
All government	24,483.8	35,454.0	49,488.1	57,510.0	65,900
Federal	5,073.5	6,309.8	9,171.5	12,465.0	14,300
State	17,973.8	26,965.4	37,052.3	40,536.4	46,400
Local	1,436.5	2,178.8	3,264.3	4,508.6	5,200
Endowment earnings	191.0	342.8	461.7	639.3	700
Private gifts, grants & contracts	978.7	1,845.6	3,368.6	4,521.5	5,200
Sales & services, total	7,443.0	11,967.5	19,330.5	26,404.3	30,200
Educational activities	819.2	1,424.9	2,423.8	3,329.7	3,800
Auxiliary enterprises	4,088.5	6,296.3	8,473.3	10,814.8	12,400
Hospitals	2,535.3	4,246.3	8,433.4	12,259.8	14,000
Other sources	867.5	1,536.6	2,442.3	3,067.6	3,500
	Percentage Distribution				
Total Current Fund Revenue	100.0	100.0	100.0	100.0	100.0
Student tuition & fees	12.5	14.5	15.5	18.4	18.4
All government	63.1	59.3	55.7	50.9	50.9
Federal	13.1	10.6	10.3	11.0	11.1
State	46.3	45.1	41.7	35.9	35.9
Local	3.7	3.6	3.7	4.0	4.0
Endowment earnings	0.5	0.6	0.5	0.6	0.5
Private gifts, grants & contracts	2.5	3.1	3.8	4.0	4.0
Sales & services, total	19.2	20.0	21.7	23.4	23.4
Educational activities	2.1	2.4	2.7	2.9	2.9
Auxiliary enterprises	10.5	10.5	9.5	9.6	9.6
Hospitals	6.5	7.1	9.5	10.9	10.8
Other sources	2.2	2.6	2.7	2.7	2.7

Total revenue from students (Tuition & fees plus auxiliary enterprises)

	1979-80	1984-85	1989-90	1993-94	1996-97
Amount	8,948.7	14,943.9	22,293.5	31,640.2	36,200
Percent of total current-fund revenue	23.0	25.0	25.1	28.0	28.0

See note for table 94 for explanation of 1996-97 estimates.

Sources: 1 NCES, Digest of Education Statistics (Washington: GPO), 1990, tbl. 292; 1996, tbl. 322.

2 _____, Projections of Education Statistics to 2007 (Washington: GPO, 1997), tbl. 37.

Current-fund Revenue of Public Institutions of Higher Education, in Constant 1993–94 Dollars, Selected Fiscal Years, 1979/80–1996/97

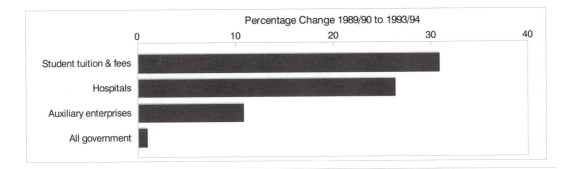

Percentage Change 1989/90 to 1993/94

Kind of Revenue	1979-80	1984-85	1989-90	1993-94	FB Estimate for 1996-97
			Millions of Constant 1993-94 Dollars		
Total Current-fund Revenue	$73,145.6	$82,674.2	$102,395.6	$112,968.1	$118,600
Student tuition & fees	9,156.7	11,956.6	15,916.2	20,825.4	21,900
All government	*46,128.0*	*49,020.3*	*56,993.4*	*57,510.0*	*60,300*
Federal	9,558.6	8,724.2	10,562.4	12,465.0	13,100
State	33,863.0	37,283.6	42,671.6	40,536.4	42,500
Local	2,706.4	3,012.5	3,759.4	4,508.6	4,700
Endowment earnings	359.8	474.0	531.7	639.3	700
Private gifts, grants & contracts	1,843.9	2,551.8	3,879.5	4,521.5	4,700
Sales & services, total	*14,022.8*	*16,546.8*	*22,262.1*	*26,404.3*	*27,800*
Educational activities	1,543.4	1,970.1	2,791.4	3,329.7	3,500
Auxiliary enterprises	7,702.8	8,705.6	9,758.4	10,814.8	11,400
Hospitals	4,776.6	5,871.1	9,712.4	12,259.8	12,900
Other sources	1,634.4	2,124.6	2,812.7	3,067.6	3,200

	Percentage Change (in Constant 1993-94 Dollars)		
	1979-80 to 1984-85 (5 years)	1984-85 to 1989-90 (5 years)	1989-90 to 1993-94 (4 years)
Total Current Fund Revenue	13.0	23.9	10.3
Student tuition & fees	30.6	33.1	30.8
All government	6.3	16.3	0.9
Federal	-8.7	21.1	18.0
State	10.1	14.5	-5.0
Local	11.3	24.8	19.9
Endowment earnings	31.7	12.2	20.2
Private gifts, grants & contracts	38.4	52.0	16.5
Sales & services, total	18.0	34.5	18.6
Educational activities	27.6	41.7	19.3
Auxiliary enterprises	13.0	12.1	10.8
Hospitals	22.9	65.4	26.2
Other sources	30.0	32.4	9.1
Total revenue from students (Tuition & fees plus auxiliary enterprises)	22.6	24.3	23.2

See note for table 94 for explanation of 1996-97 estimates.

Sources: NCES, Digest of Education Statistics (Washington: GPO), 1990, tbl. 292; 1996, tbls. 37, 322.
2 _____, Projections of Education Statistics to 2007 (Washington: GPO, 1997), tbls. 37, B8.

99

Current-fund Revenue of Independent Institutions of Higher Education, in Current Dollars, Selected Fiscal Years, 1979/80–1996/97

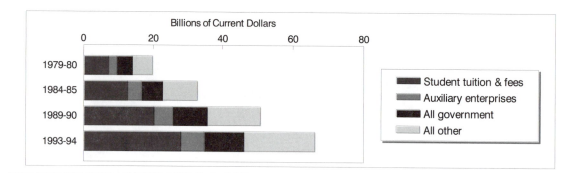

Billions of Current Dollars

Kind of Revenue	1979-80	1984-85	1989-90	1993-94	FB Estimate for 1996-97
			Millions of Current Dollars		
Total Current Fund Revenue	$19,695.8	$32,678.5	$50,724.0	$66,258.5	$78,000
Student tuition & fees	7,070.2	12,635.7	20,105.8	27,821.1	32,700
All government	4,385.0	6,025.4	9,755.9	11,474.9	13,500
Federal	3,829.4	5,199.3	8,083.4	9,611.3	11,300
State	404.5	617.6	1,296.9	1,373.9	1,600
Local	151.1	208.5	375.6	489.7	600
Endowment earnings	985.6	1,753.5	2,682.0	3,030.2	3,600
Private gifts, grants & contracts	1,829.4	3,050.7	4,412.8	5,681.6	6,700
Sales & services, total	4,651.3	7,734.4	11,456.8	15,387.0	18,100
Educational activities	420.3	702.0	1,208.3	1,964.3	2,300
Auxiliary enterprises	2,392.9	3,804.1	5,465.2	6,722.7	7,900
Hospitals	1,838.1	3,228.3	4,783.3	6,700.0	7,900
Other sources	774.4	1,478.9	2,310.7	2,863.5	3,400
			Percentage Distribution		
Total Current Fund Revenue	100.0	100.0	100.0	100.0	100.0
Student tuition & fees	35.9	38.7	39.6	42.0	41.9
All government	22.3	18.4	19.2	17.3	17.3
Federal	19.4	15.9	15.9	14.5	14.5
State	2.1	1.9	2.6	2.1	2.1
Local	0.8	0.6	0.7	0.7	0.8
Endowment earnings	5.0	5.4	5.3	4.6	4.6
Private gifts, grants & contracts	9.3	9.3	8.7	8.6	8.6
Sales & services, total	23.6	23.7	22.6	23.2	23.2
Educational activities	2.1	2.1	2.4	3.0	2.9
Auxiliary enterprises	12.1	11.6	10.8	10.1	10.1
Hospitals	9.3	9.9	9.4	10.1	10.1
Other sources	3.9	4.5	4.6	4.3	4.4

Total revenue from students (Tuition & fees plus auxiliary enterprises)

	1979-80	1984-85	1989-90	1993-94	1996-97
Amount	9,463.1	16,439.8	25,571.0	34,543.8	40,600
Percent of total current-fund revenue	48.0	50.3	50.4	52.1	52.1

See note for table 94 for explanation of 1996-97 estimates.

Sources: 1 NCES, Digest of Education Statistics (Washington: GPO), 1990, tbl. 293; 1996, tbl. 323.

2 _____, Projections of Education Statistics to 2007 (Washington: GPO, 1997), tbl. 37.

Current-fund Revenue of Independent Institutions of Higher Education, in Constant 1993–94 Dollars, Selected Years, 1979/80–1996/97

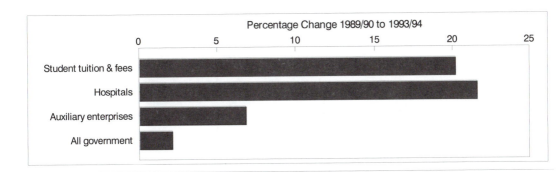

Percentage Change 1989/90 to 1993/94

Kind of Revenue	1979-80	1984-85	1989-90	1993-94	FB Estimate for 1996-97
		Millions of Constant 1993-94 Dollars			
Total Current-fund Revenue	$37,107.3	$45,182.8	$58,416.7	$66,258.5	$71,600
Student tuition & fees	13,320.4	17,470.7	23,155.0	27,821.1	30,100
All government	8,261.4	8,331.0	11,235.5	11,474.9	12,400
Federal	7,214.7	7,188.8	9,309.3	9,611.3	10,400
State	762.1	853.9	1,493.6	1,373.9	1,500
Local	284.7	288.3	432.6	489.7	500
Endowment earnings	1,856.9	2,424.5	3,088.7	3,030.2	3,300
Private gifts, grants & contracts	3,446.6	4,218.0	5,082.0	5,681.6	6,100
Sales & services, total	8,763.1	10,693.9	13,194.3	15,387.0	16,600
Educational activities	791.9	970.6	1,391.5	1,964.3	2,100
Auxiliary enterprises	4,508.3	5,259.7	6,294.0	6,722.7	7,300
Hospitals	3,463.0	4,463.6	5,508.7	6,700.0	7,200
Other sources	1,459.0	2,044.8	2,661.1	2,863.5	3,100

	Percentage Change (in Constant 1993-94 Dollars)		
	1979-80 to 1984-85 (5 years)	1984-85 to 1989-90 (5 years)	1989-90 to 1993-94 (4 years)
Total Current Fund Revenue	21.8	29.3	13.4
Student tuition & fees	31.2	32.5	20.2
All government	0.8	34.9	2.1
Federal	-0.4	29.5	3.2
State	12.1	74.9	-8.0
Local	1.3	50.0	13.2
Endowment earnings	30.6	27.4	-1.9
Private gifts, grants & contracts	22.4	20.5	11.8
Sales & services, total	22.0	23.4	16.6
Educational activities	22.6	43.4	41.2
Auxiliary enterprises	16.7	19.7	6.8
Hospitals	28.9	23.4	21.6
Other sources	40.2	30.1	7.6
Total revenue from students (Tuition & fees plus auxiliary enterprises)	27.5	29.6	17.3

See note for table 94 for explanation of 1996-97 estimates.

Sources: NCES, Digest of Education Statistics (Washington: GPO), 1990, tbl. 292; 1996, tbls. 37, 322.
2 _____, Projections of Education Statistics to 2007 (Washington: GPO, 1997), tbls. 37, B8.

Current-fund Expenditures of All Institutions of Higher Education, in Current Dollars, Selected Fiscal Years, 1929/30–1996/97

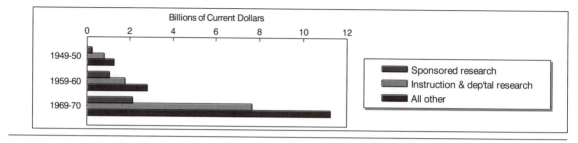

Billions of Current Dollars

Sponsored research
Instruction & dep'tal research
All other

Kind of Expenditure	1929-30	1939-40	1949-50	1959-60	1969-70
			Millions of Current Dollars		
Total Current-fund expenditures	$507.1	$674.7	$2,245.7	$5,601.4	$21,043.1
Educational & general expenditures	*377.9*	*522.0*	*1,706.4*	*4,513.2*	*15,788.7*
General administration & general expense	42.6	62.8	213.1	583.2	2,628.0
Instruction & departmental research	221.6	280.2	781.0	1,793.3	7,653.1
Extension & public service	25.0	35.3	86.7	205.6	521.1
Libraries	9.7	19.5	56.1	135.4	652.6
Plant operation and maintenance	60.9	69.6	225.1	469.9	1,541.7
Sponsored research	18.1	27.3	225.3	1,022.4	2,144.1
Related activities	nr	27.2	119.1	294.3	648.1
Other educational & general expenditures	nr	nr	nr	9.1	nr
Auxiliary enterprises	nr	124.2	476.4	916.1	2,769.3
Student aid expenditures	nr	nr	nr	172.1	984.6
Other current expenditures	129.2	28.5	62.8	nr	1,500.5

Figures in italics are subtotals. nr: Not reported.

Note: Data for 1969-70 are not directly comparable with earlier data because of a change in data gathering instruments. "Other current expenditures" catagory includes "major public service programs" that had been previously included in "sponsored research", "extension & public service", and "related activities".

Data for 1996-97 are Fact Book estimates based on projections for current-fund expenditures and the 1993-94 distribution among expenditure categories.

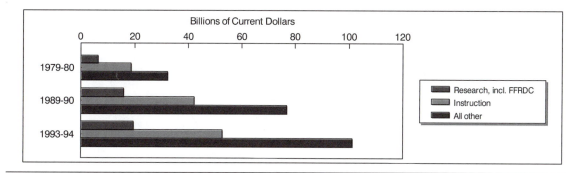

Billions of Current Dollars

Legend:
- Research, incl. FFRDC
- Instruction
- All other

Kind of Expenditure	1979-80	1984-85	1989-90	1993-94	FB Estimate for 1996-97
			Millions of Current Dollars		
Total Current-fund expenditures	$56,913.6	$89,951.3	$134,655.5	$173,350.6	$200,600
Educational and general expenditures	*44,542.8*	*70,061.3*	*105,585.1*	*136,024.3*	*157,100*
Instruction	18,496.7	28,777.2	42,146.0	52,775.6	61,000
Academic support minus libraries	2,252.6	3,712.5	6,183.4	7,769.6	9,000
Libraries	1,623.8	2,361.8	3,254.3	3,908.4	4,500
Student services	2,566.8	4,178.2	6,388.1	8,562.8	9,800
Institutional support	5,054.4	8,587.2	12,674.0	15,926.2	18,400
Plant operation and maintenance	4,700.1	7,345.5	9,458.3	11,368.5	13,100
Research	5,099.1	7,551.9	12,505.9	16,117.6	18,600
Public service	1,816.5	2,861.1	4,689.8	6,242.4	7,200
Student aid	2,200.5	3,670.4	6,655.6	11,238.0	13,000
Mandatory transfers	732.4	1,015.6	1,629.7	2,115.3	2,500
Auxiliary enterprises	6,485.6	10,012.3	13,204.0	16,429.4	19,000
Hospitals	4,757.4	8,010.2	12,679.3	17,509.6	20,400
Independent operations (FFRDCs)	1,127.7	1,867.6	3,187.3	3,387.4	4,200

Sources: 1 NCES, Digest of Education Statistics (Washington: GPO), 1983-84, tbl. 26; 1990, tbl. 301; 1996, tbl. 336.

2 _____, Projections of Education Statistics to 2007 (Washington: GPO, 1997), tbl. 37.

102

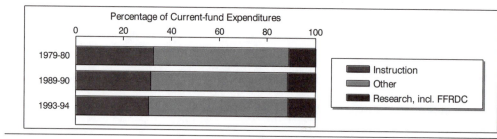

Percentage of Current-fund Expenditures

Kind of Expenditure	1979-80	1984-85	1989-90	1993-94	FB Estimate for 1996-97
			Percentage Distribution		
Total Current-fund expenditures	100.0	100.0	100.0	100.0	100.0
Educational and general expenditures	78.3	77.9	78.4	78.5	78.4
Instruction	32.5	32.0	31.3	30.4	30.4
Academic support minus libraries	4.0	4.1	4.6	4.5	4.5
Libraries	2.9	2.6	2.4	2.3	2.3
Student services	4.5	4.6	4.7	4.9	4.9
Institutional support	8.9	9.5	9.4	9.2	9.2
Plant operation and maintenance	8.3	8.2	7.0	6.6	6.6
Research	9.0	8.4	9.3	9.3	9.3
Public service	3.2	3.2	3.5	3.6	3.6
Student aid	3.9	4.1	4.9	6.5	6.5
Mandatory transfers	1.3	1.1	1.2	1.2	1.2
Auxiliary enterprises	11.4	11.1	9.8	9.5	9.5
Hospitals	8.4	8.9	9.4	10.1	10.1
Independent operations (FFRDCs)	2.0	2.1	2.4	2.0	2.0

Calculated from data in preceding table.

103

Current-fund Expenditures of All Institutions of Higher Education, in Constant 1993–94 Dollars, Selected Fiscal Years, 1979/80–1996/97

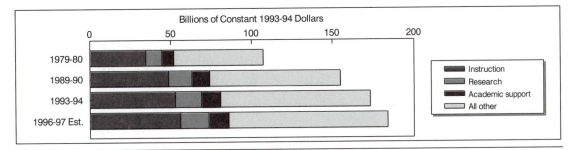

Kind of Expenditure	1979-80	1984-85	1989-90	1993-94	FB Estimate for 1996-97
	Millions of Constant 1993-94 Dollars				
Total Current-fund expenditures	$107,181.9	$124,299.4	$155,012.9	$173,350.6	$184,200
Educational and general expenditures	*83,884.7*	*96,814.4*	*121,547.6*	*136,024.3*	*144,300*
Instruction	34,833.7	39,765.8	48,517.7	52,775.6	56,100
Academic support minus libraries	4,242.2	5,130.1	7,118.2	7,769.6	8,200
Libraries	3,058.0	3,263.7	3,746.3	3,908.4	4,100
Student services	4,833.9	5,773.7	7,353.9	8,562.8	9,000
Institutional support	9,518.6	11,866.2	14,590.1	15,926.2	16,900
Plant operation and maintenance	8,851.4	10,150.4	10,888.2	11,368.5	12,100
Research	9,602.8	10,435.6	14,396.6	16,117.6	17,100
Public service	3,420.9	3,953.6	5,398.8	6,242.4	6,600
Student aid	4,144.1	5,072.0	7,661.8	11,238.0	11,900
Mandatory transfers	1,379.3	1,403.4	1,876.1	2,115.3	2,300
Auxiliary enterprises	12,213.9	13,835.5	15,200.2	16,429.4	17,500
Hospitals	8,959.3	11,068.9	14,596.2	17,509.6	18,600
Independent operations (FFRDCs)	2,123.7	2,580.7	3,669.2	3,387.4	3,800

	Percentage Change		
	1979/80 to 1984/85	1984/85 to 1989-90	1989-90 to 1993-94
Total Current-fund expenditures	16.0	24.7	11.8
Educational and general expenditures	15.4	25.5	11.9
Instruction	14.2	22.0	8.8
Academic support minus libraries	20.9	38.8	9.2
Libraries	6.7	14.8	4.3
Student services	19.4	27.4	16.4
Institutional support	24.7	23.0	9.2
Plant operation and maintenance	14.7	7.3	4.4
Research	8.7	38.0	12.0
Public service	15.6	36.6	15.6
Student aid	22.4	51.1	46.7
Mandatory transfers	1.7	33.7	12.8
Auxiliary enterprises	13.3	9.9	8.1
Hospitals	23.5	31.9	20.0
Independent operations (FFRDCs)	21.5	42.2	-7.7

See note for table 100 for explanation of 1996-97 estimates. Subtotals are in italics.

Sources: 1 NCES, Digest of Education Statistics (Washington: GPO), 1990, tbl. 300; 1996, tbl. 335.

2 _____, Projections of Education Statistics to 2007 (Washington: GPO, 1997), tbls. 37, B8.

104

Current-fund Expenditures of Public Institutions of Higher Education, in Current Dollars, Selected Fiscal Years, 1979/80–1996/97

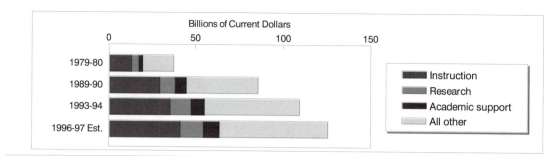

Kind of Expenditure	1979-80	1984-85	1989-90	1993-94	FB Estimate for 1996-97
			Millions of Current Dollars		
Total Current-fund expenditures	$37,768.0	$58,314.6	$85,770.5	$109,309.5	$125,300
Educational and general expenditures	*30,627.4*	*46,873.5*	*69,164.0*	*87,139.2*	*100,700*
Instruction	13,318.7	20,287.4	29,257.2	35,688.5	41,200
Academic support minus libraries	1,671.3	2,710.2	4,432.4	5,586.5	6,500
Libraries	1,114.4	1,557.5	2,102.7	2,449.1	2,800
Student services	1,754.8	2,684.3	4,021.3	5,315.4	6,100
Institutional support	3,135.5	5,191.7	7,490.1	9,328.2	10,800
Plant operation and maintenance	3,267.4	5,040.9	6,333.6	7,433.2	8,600
Research	3,408.6	5,119.2	8,542.2	11,180.4	12,900
Public service	1,512.8	2,316.3	3,688.7	4,741.7	5,500
Student aid	970.4	1,374.8	2,386.5	4,222.9	4,900
Mandatory transfers	473.5	591.3	909.2	1,193.4	1,400
Auxiliary enterprises	4,131.9	6,431.6	8,282.3	10,637.8	11,800
Hospitals	2,947.9	4,914.6	8,114.0	11,317.7	12,600
Independent operations (FFRDCs)	60.7	94.9	210.3	214.9	200
			Percentage Distribution		
Total Current-fund expenditures	100.0	100.0	100.0	100.0	100.0
Educational and general expenditures	*81.1*	*80.4*	*80.6*	*79.7*	*80.4*
Instruction	35.3	34.8	34.1	32.6	32.9
Academic support minus libraries	4.4	4.6	5.2	5.1	5.2
Libraries	3.0	2.7	2.5	2.2	2.3
Student services	4.6	4.6	4.7	4.9	4.9
Institutional support	8.3	8.9	8.7	8.5	8.6
Plant operation and maintenance	8.7	8.6	7.4	6.8	6.9
Research	9.0	8.8	10.0	10.2	10.3
Public service	4.0	4.0	4.3	4.3	4.4
Student aid	2.6	2.4	2.8	3.9	3.9
Mandatory transfers	1.3	1.0	1.1	1.1	1.1
Auxiliary enterprises	10.9	11.0	9.7	9.7	9.4
Hospitals	7.8	8.4	9.5	10.4	10.0
Independent operations (FFRDCs)	0.2	0.2	0.2	0.2	0.2

See note for table 100 for explanation of 1996-97 estimates. Subtotals are in italics.

Sources: 1 NCES, Digest of Education Statistics (Washington: GPO), 1990, tbl. 300; 1996, tbl. 335.

2 _____, Projections of Education Statistics to 2007 (Washington: GPO, 1997), tbl. 37.

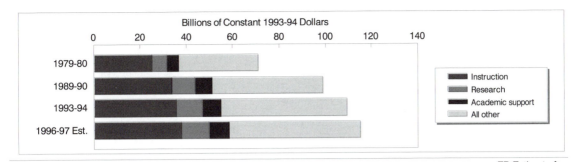

Billions of Constant 1993-94 Dollars

Kind of Expenditure	1979-80	1984-85	1989-90	1993-94	FB Estimate for 1996-97
		Millions of Constant 1993-94 Dollars			
Total Current-fund expenditures	$71,126.2	$80,628.4	$98,778.3	$109,309.5	$115,000
Educational and general expenditures	57,678.7	64,809.4	79,653.3	87,139.2	*92,500*
Instruction	25,082.3	28,050.3	33,694.3	35,688.5	37,900
Academic support minus libraries	3,147.5	3,747.2	5,104.6	5,586.5	5,900
Libraries	2,098.7	2,153.5	2,421.6	2,449.1	2,600
Student services	3,304.7	3,711.4	4,631.2	5,315.4	5,600
Institutional support	5,904.9	7,178.3	8,626.0	9,328.2	9,900
Plant operation and maintenance	6,153.3	6,969.8	7,294.1	7,433.2	7,900
Research	6,419.2	7,078.0	9,837.7	11,180.4	11,900
Public service	2,849.0	3,202.6	4,248.1	4,741.7	5,000
Student aid	1,827.5	1,900.9	2,748.4	4,222.9	4,500
Mandatory transfers	891.7	817.6	1,047.1	1,193.4	1,300
Auxiliary enterprises	7,781.4	8,892.6	9,538.4	10,637.8	10,800
Hospitals	5,551.6	6,795.2	9,344.6	11,317.7	11,500
Independent operations (FFRDCs)	114.3	131.2	242.2	214.9	200

	Percentage Change		
Kind of Expenditure	1979/80 to 1984/85	1984/85 to 1989-90	1989-90 to 1993-94
Total Current-fund expenditures	13.4	22.5	10.7
Educational and general expenditures	12.4	22.9	9.4
Instruction	11.8	20.1	5.9
Academic support minus libraries	19.1	36.2	9.4
Libraries	2.6	12.5	1.1
Student services	12.3	24.8	14.8
Institutional support	21.6	20.2	8.1
Plant operation and maintenance	13.3	4.7	1.9
Research	10.3	39.0	13.6
Public service	12.4	32.6	11.6
Student aid	4.0	44.6	53.6
Mandatory transfers	-8.3	28.1	14.0
Auxiliary enterprises	14.3	7.3	11.5
Hospitals	22.4	37.5	21.1
Independent operations (FFRDCs)	14.8	84.6	-11.3

See note for table 100 for explanation of 1996-97 estimates. Subtotals are in italics.

The Consumer Price Index was used to convert current dollars to constant 1993-94 dollars.

Sources: 1 NCES, Digest of Education Statistics (Washington: GPO), 1990, tbl. 300; 1996, tbl. 335.

2 _____, Projections of Education Statistics to 2007 (Washington: GPO, 1997), tbls. 37, B8.

106

Current-fund Expenditures of Independent Institutions of Higher Education, in Current Dollars, Selected Fiscal Years, 1979/80–1996/97

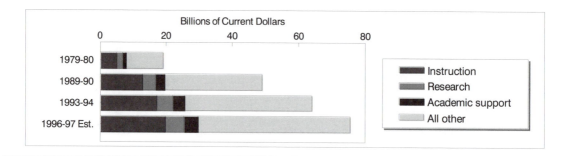

Billions of Current Dollars

Kind of Expenditure	1979-80	1984-85	1989-90	1993-94	FB Estimate for 1996-97
			Millions of Current Dollars		
Total Current-fund expenditures	$19,145.6	$31,636.7	$48,885.0	$64,041.1	$75,400
Educational and general expenditures	*13,915.4*	*23,187.8*	*36,421.1*	*48,885.1*	*56,400*
Instruction	5,178.0	8,489.8	12,888.8	17,087.1	19,800
Academic support minus libraries	581.3	1,002.3	1,751.0	2,183.1	2,500
Libraries	509.4	804.3	1,151.6	1,459.3	1,700
Student services	812.0	1,493.9	2,366.8	3,247.4	3,700
Institutional support	1,918.9	3,395.5	5,183.9	6,598.0	7,600
Plant operation and maintenance	1,432.7	2,304.6	3,124.7	3,935.3	4,500
Research	1,690.5	2,432.7	3,963.7	4,937.2	5,700
Public service	303.7	544.8	1,001.1	1,500.7	1,700
Student aid	1,230.1	2,295.6	4,269.1	7,015.1	8,100
Mandatory transfers	258.9	424.3	720.5	921.9	1,100
Auxiliary enterprises	2,353.7	3,580.7	4,921.7	5,791.6	7,200
Hospitals	1,809.5	3,095.6	4,565.3	6,191.9	7,800
Independent operations (FFRDCs)	1,067.0	1,772.7	2,977.0	3,172.5	4,000
			Percentage Distribution		
Total Current-fund expenditures	100.0	100.0	100.0	100.0	100.0
Educational and general expenditures	*72.7*	*73.3*	*74.5*	*76.3*	*74.8*
Instruction	27.0	26.8	26.4	26.7	26.1
Academic support minus libraries	3.0	3.2	3.6	3.4	3.3
Libraries	2.7	2.5	2.4	2.3	2.2
Student services	4.2	4.7	4.8	5.1	5.0
Institutional support	10.0	10.7	10.6	10.3	10.1
Plant operation and maintenance	7.5	7.3	6.4	6.1	6.0
Research	8.8	7.7	8.1	7.7	7.6
Public service	1.6	1.7	2.0	2.3	2.3
Student aid	6.4	7.3	8.7	11.0	10.7
Mandatory transfers	1.4	1.3	1.5	1.4	1.4
Auxiliary enterprises	12.3	11.3	10.1	9.0	9.6
Hospitals	9.5	9.8	9.3	9.7	10.3
Independent operations (FFRDCs)	5.6	5.6	6.1	5.0	5.3

See note for table 100 for explanation of 1996-97 estimates. Subtotals are in italics.

Sources: 1 NCES, Digest of Education Statistics (Washington: GPO), 1990, tbl. 301; 1996, tbl. 336.

2 _____, Projections of Education Statistics to 2007 (Washington: GPO, 1997), tbl. 37.

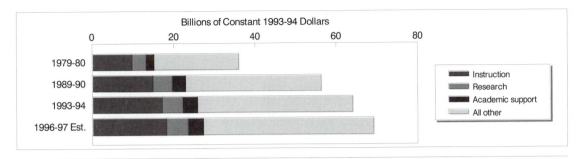

Billions of Constant 1993-94 Dollars

Legend:
- Instruction
- Research
- Academic support
- All other

Years: 1979-80, 1989-90, 1993-94, 1996-97 Est.

Kind of Expenditure	1979-80	1984-85	1989-90	1993-94	FB Estimate for 1996-97
	Millions of Constant 1993-94 Dollars				
Total Current-fund expenditures	$36,055.7	$43,742.4	$56,298.8	$64,041.1	$69,200
Educational and general expenditures	*26,216.9*	*32,042.1*	*41,927.3*	*48,885.1*	*51,800*
Instruction	9,755.5	11,731.7	14,837.3	17,087.1	18,200
Academic support minus libraries	1,095.2	1,385.0	2,015.7	2,183.1	2,300
Libraries	959.7	1,111.4	1,325.7	1,459.3	1,500
Student services	1,529.8	2,064.3	2,724.6	3,247.4	3,400
Institutional support	3,615.2	4,692.1	5,967.6	6,598.0	7,000
Plant operation and maintenance	2,699.2	3,184.6	3,597.1	3,935.3	4,200
Research	3,184.9	3,361.6	4,562.9	4,937.2	5,200
Public service	572.2	752.8	1,152.4	1,500.7	1,600
Student aid	2,317.5	3,172.2	4,914.5	7,015.1	7,400
Mandatory transfers	487.8	586.3	829.4	921.9	1,000
Auxiliary enterprises	4,434.4	4,948.0	5,665.8	5,791.6	6,700
Hospitals	3,409.1	4,277.7	5,255.5	6,191.9	7,100
Independent operations (FFRDCs)	2,010.3	2,449.6	3,427.1	3,172.5	3,600

	Percentage Change		
	1979/80 to 1984/85	1984/85 to 1989-90	1989-90 to 1993-94
Total Current-fund expenditures	21.3	28.7	13.8
Educational and general expenditures	22.2	30.9	16.6
Instruction	20.3	26.5	15.2
Academic support minus libraries	26.5	45.5	8.3
Libraries	15.8	19.3	10.1
Student services	34.9	32.0	19.2
Institutional support	29.8	27.2	10.6
Plant operation and maintenance	18.0	13.0	9.4
Research	5.5	35.7	8.2
Public service	31.6	53.1	30.2
Student aid	36.9	54.9	42.7
Mandatory transfers	20.2	41.5	11.1
Auxiliary enterprises	11.6	14.5	2.2
Hospitals	25.5	22.9	17.8
Independent operations (FFRDCs)	21.9	39.9	-7.4

See note for table 100 for explanation of 1996-97 estimates. Subtotals are in italics.

Sources: 1 NCES, Digest of Education Statistics (Washington: GPO), 1990, tbl. 300; 1996, tbl. 335.

2 _____, Projections of Education Statistics to 2007 (Washington: GPO, 1997), tbls. 37, B8.

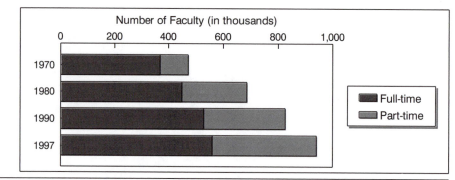

Year	Employment Status (in thousands)			Type of Institution	
	Total	Full-time	Part-time	4-year	2-year
1970	474	369	104	382	92
1975	628	440	188	467	161
1980	686	450	236	494	192
1981	705	461	244	493	212
1982	710	462	248	493	217
1983	725	471	254	504	220
1984	717	462	255	504	213
1985	715	459	256	504	211
1986	722	459	263	506	216
1987	793	523	270	548	246
1988	808	523	285	566	243
1989	824	524	300	584	241
1990	826	530	296	588	238
1991	826	536	291	591	235
1992	905	528	377	629	276
1993	915	546	370	626	290
1994	915	546	370	626	290
1995	909	542	367	622	288
1996	924	551	374	632	293
1997	940	561	380	643	298

Note: Italicized figures are estimates based on enrollment. Data prior to 1988 are not directly comparable with more recent figures because of revised survey methods. Data for 1992 come from a survey of individual faculty members; most of the other data are from institutional surveys.

Senior instructional staff includes full, associate, and assistant professors, instructors, and adjunct professors; it excludes graduate/teaching assistants.

Sources: 1 NCES, Digest of Educational Statistics, 1996 (Washington: GPO, 1996), tbls. 216, 220, 222.

2 _____, Projections of Education Statistics to 2006 (Washington: GPO, 1996), tbls. 24, 25.

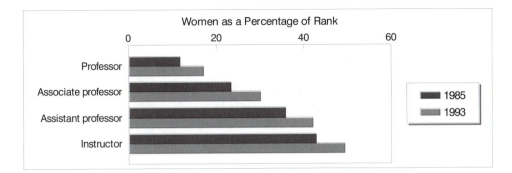

Rank	Number (in thousands)			Percentage	
	Total	Men	Women	Men	Women
Fall 1985					
All ranks	464.1	336.2	128.0	72.4	27.6
Professor	129.3	114.3	15.0	88.4	11.6
Associate professor	111.1	85.2	25.9	76.7	23.3
Assistant professor	111.3	71.5	39.8	64.2	35.8
Instructor	75.4	43.3	32.2	57.4	42.7
Lecturer	9.8	5.1	4.7	52.0	48.0
Other	27.2	16.8	10.4	61.8	38.2
Fall 1991					
All ranks	520.3	355.1	165.2	68.2	31.8
Professor	144.3	123.2	21.2	85.4	14.7
Associate professor	116.6	84.3	32.3	72.3	27.7
Assistant professor	126.3	76.1	50.2	60.3	39.7
Instructor	78.1	41.1	37.0	52.6	47.4
Lecturer	11.3	5.4	5.9	47.8	52.2
Other	43.7	25.0	18.6	57.3	42.7
Fall 1993					
All ranks	545.7	363.4	182.3	66.6	33.4
Professor	157.3	130.6	26.7	83.0	17.0
Associate professor	120.7	84.5	36.2	70.0	30.0
Assistant professor	129.2	74.8	54.3	57.9	42.0
Instructor	67.7	34.3	33.4	50.7	49.3
Lecturer	13.7	6.7	7.0	48.9	51.1
Other	57.2	32.5	24.7	56.8	43.2

Note: Totals may not agree with those in other tables because of varying methodologies used in different surveys.

Source: NCES, Digest of Education Statistics (Washington: GPO), 1990, tbl. 207; 1995, tbl. 218; 1996, tbl. 221.

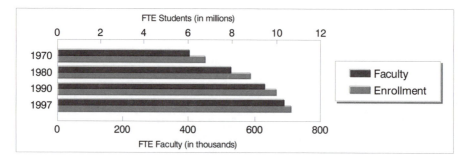

Year	Instructional Staff (in thousands)				Full-time Equivalent Enrollment (in thousands)	Ratio of FTE Staff to FTE Enrollment
	Total	Full-time	Part-time	Full-time Equivalent (FTE)		
1970	474	369	104	402	6,737	1:16.8
1975	628	440	188	501	8,480	1:16.9
1980	686	450	236	529	8,819	1:16.7
1981	705	461	244	542	9,014	1:16.6
1982	710	462	248	545	9,092	1:16.7
1983	724	471	254	556	9,166	1:16.5
1984	717	462	255	547	8,952	1:16.4
1985	715	459	256	*549*	8,943	1:16.3
1986	722	459	263	*555*	9,064	1:16.3
1987	793	523	270	613	9,230	1:15.0
1988	*808*	*523*	*285*	*619*	9,467	1:15.3
1989	824	524	300	624	9,781	1:15.7
1990	*826*	*530*	*296*	*629*	9,984	1:15.9
1991	826	536	291	633	10,361	1:16.4
1992	905	528	377	*677*	10,436	1:15.4
1993	915	546	370	*669*	10,352	1:15.5
1994	*915*	*546*	*370*	*669*	10,179	1:15.2
1995	*909*	*542*	*367*	*665*	10,286	1:15.5
1996	*924*	*551*	*374*	*676*	10,457	1:15.5
1997	*940*	*561*	*380*	*687*	10,638	1:15.5

NOTE: Italicized figures are estimates. Those showing faculty counts for 1994 and later are based on enrollment. Those for faculty full-time equivalents (FTE) are based on relations between totals and FTE figures for adjacent years. Data prior to 1988 are not directly comparable to more recent figures because of revised survey methods. Data for 1992 come from a survey of individual faculty members; most of the other data are from institutional surveys.

Sources: 1 NCES, Digest of Educational Statistics (Washington: GPO), 1990, tbl. 203; 1993, tbl. 215; 1996, tbls. 216, 220, 222.
2 _____, Projections of Education Statistics (Washington: GPO), 1977 edition, tables 8, 22, 23; to 2006, tbl 23.

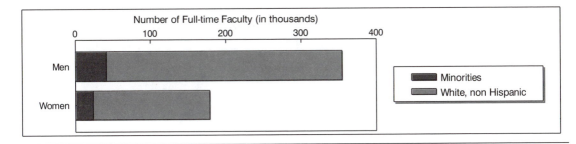

Rank	Total	White, non-Hispanic	Total Minority	Black, non-Hispanic	Hispanic	Asian, or Pacific Islander	American Indian or Alaskan Native	Non-resident alien	Race/ethnicity Unknown
				All Full-time Faculty					
All ranks	545.7	468.8	64.8	25.7	12.1	25.3	2.0	10.8	1.1
Professor	157.3	141.8	14.3	4.5	2.4	7.0	0.4	0.9	0.1
Associate professor	120.7	106.0	13.4	5.3	2.3	5.5	0.3	1.1	0.1
Assistant professor	129.2	105.1	19.1	7.7	3.4	7.6	0.4	4.6	0.3
Instructor	67.7	56.9	9.6	4.7	2.2	2.1	0.6	0.9	0.3
Lecturer	13.7	11.3	1.9	0.9	0.4	0.6	0.1	0.5	0.0
Other	57.2	47.6	6.5	2.5	1.3	2.5	0.2	2.7	0.2
				Men					
All ranks	363.5	313.3	41.1	13.4	7.5	18.9	1.2	8.4	0.8
Professor	130.7	118.3	11.3	3.0	1.8	6.2	0.3	0.8	0.1
Associate professor	84.5	74.2	9.3	3.1	1.6	4.4	0.2	0.9	0.1
Assistant professor	74.8	59.7	11.3	3.8	2.0	5.3	0.2	3.6	0.2
Instructor	34.3	28.8	4.8	2.1	1.2	1.1	0.4	0.6	0.2
Lecturer	6.7	5.5	0.9	0.4	0.2	0.3	<0.1	0.3	<0.1
Other	32.5	26.8	3.5	1.0	0.7	1.7	0.1	2.0	0.1
				Women					
All ranks	182.3	155.5	23.7	12.3	4.6	6.3	0.8	2.5	0.3
Professor	26.7	23.5	3.0	1.5	0.6	0.8	0.1	0.1	<0.1
Associate professor	36.2	31.8	4.1	2.2	0.7	1.1	0.1	0.2	<0.1
Assistant professor	54.3	45.4	7.8	3.9	1.4	2.3	0.2	1.0	0.1
Instructor	33.4	28.1	4.8	2.6	1.0	1.0	0.2	0.3	0.1
Lecturer	7.0	5.8	1.0	0.5	0.2	0.3	<.1	0.2	<0.1
Other	24.7	20.8	3.0	1.5	0.6	0.8	0.1	0.7	0.1

Note: Totals may not agree with data in other tables because of varying methodologies used in different surveys.

Source: NCES, E.D. Tabs, Fall Staff in Postsecondary Institutions, 1993, NCES 96-323 (Washington: NCES, 1996), tbl. B-7a.

Number of Faculty, Academic Year, 1995–96

Less than 2,500
2,500 - 9.999
10,000 or more

Region and State	All Ranks	Professor	Associate Professor	Assistant Professor	Instructor	Lecturer	No Academic Rank
50 States & D.C.	**384,960**	**118,944**	**93,437**	**89,836**	**21,353**	**7,986**	**53,404**
New England	**28,311**	**11,710**	**7,844**	**6,419**	**933**	**655**	**750**
Connecticut	5,447	2,227	1,468	1,375	210	126	41
Maine	1,851	453	591	422	58	23	304
Massachusetts	15,016	6,686	4,004	3,204	460	389	273
New Hampshire	1,976	770	662	482	47	7	8
Rhode Island	2,552	1,117	704	605	89	37	0
Vermont	1,469	457	415	331	69	73	124
Mideast	**71,802**	**25,882**	**20,778**	**18,638**	**3,597**	**1,739**	**1,168**
Delaware	1,261	324	382	281	88	8	178
D.C.	3,274	1,269	1,026	813	150	16	0
Maryland	6,700	2,390	1,879	1,689	364	271	107
New Jersey	8,506	3,004	2,377	2,364	502	169	90
New York	31,462	12,035	8,973	7,430	1,345	1,050	629
Pennsylvania	20,599	6,860	6,141	6,061	1,148	225	164
Southeast	**83,785**	**22,861**	**21,976**	**21,810**	**7,152**	**1,205**	**8,781**
Alabama	6,322	1,241	1,390	1,536	505	47	1,603
Arkansas	3,262	789	742	815	438	29	449
Florida	12,318	3,751	2,981	2,537	1,000	109	1,940
Georgia	8,729	2,133	2,517	3,121	812	71	75
Kentucky	5,549	1,609	1,729	1,668	378	112	53
Louisiana	6,575	1,721	1,670	2,000	1,020	45	119
Mississippi	4,365	726	675	849	360	32	1,723
North Carolina	10,172	2,825	2,617	2,428	307	499	1,496
South Carolina	5,881	1,472	1,309	1,177	601	91	1,231
Tennessee	7,908	2,532	2,270	2,205	802	44	55
Virginia	10,081	3,224	3,288	2,708	737	104	20
West Virginia	2,623	838	788	766	192	22	17
Great Lakes	**65,695**	**19,526**	**16,422**	**15,047**	**2,545**	**1,374**	**10,781**
Illinois	18,220	4,928	3,743	3,671	680	308	4,890
Indiana	9,411	2,861	2,553	2,704	411	252	630
Michigan	12,458	4,120	3,045	2,488	298	438	2,069
Ohio	15,626	4,937	4,926	4,366	1,030	117	250
Wisconsin	9,980	2,680	2,155	1,818	126	259	2,942

Continued on next page.

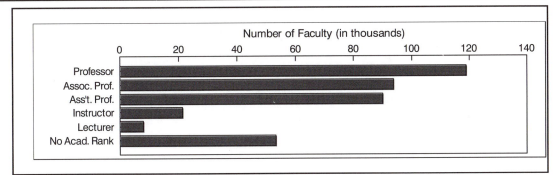

Region and State	All Ranks	Professor	Associate Professor	Assistant Professor	Instructor	Lecturer	No Academic Rank
Plains	**32,254**	**8,664**	**7,758**	**7,934**	**1,868**	**264**	**5,765**
Iowa	5,439	1,587	1,359	1,355	322	13	803
Kansas	4,863	1,164	1,118	1,085	253	42	1,201
Minnesota	8,440	2,378	1,795	1,549	252	4	2,462
Missouri	7,612	2,216	1,993	2,169	557	81	596
Nebraska	3,116	781	750	846	157	48	534
North Dakota	1,492	229	447	475	159	76	106
South Dakota	1,292	309	296	455	168	*	63
Southwest	**35,205**	**9,441**	**7,483**	**7,927**	**2,232**	**1,391**	**6,731**
Arizona	5,231	1,326	1,076	801	114	157	1,757
New Mexico	2,459	653	619	663	187	144	193
Oklahoma	4,622	1,248	965	1,366	487	27	529
Texas	22,893	6,214	4,823	5,097	1,444	1,063	4,252
Rocky Mountains	**13,964**	**4,320**	**3,352**	**3,267**	**840**	**230**	**1,955**
Colorado	5,631	1,972	1,397	1,247	287	78	650
Idaho	1,893	480	381	390	118	0	524
Montana	1,569	455	359	399	96	3	257
Utah	3,834	1,189	1,046	1,035	276	92	196
Wyoming	1,037	224	169	196	63	57	328
Far West	**50,636**	**16,515**	**8,207**	**7,159**	**1,201**	**1,046**	**16,508**
Alaska	798	204	245	243	71	0	35
California	34,705	12,366	5,059	4,278	413	698	11,891
Hawaii	1,678	559	383	440	296	0	0
Nevada	1,336	406	312	249	86	98	185
Oregon	4,689	1,113	911	814	227	28	1,596
Washington	7,430	1,867	1,297	1,135	108	222	2,801

Note: Includes only faculty on 9- and 10-month contracts which represent 86 percent of all faculty in institutions of higher education.

 * Number of faculty reported in this category was too small to yield reliable results.

Source: NCES, E.D. TABS: Salaries of Full-time Instructional Faculty on 9- and 10 Month and 11- and 12-Month Contracts, 1995-96, NCES 97-416 (Washington: NCES, 1997), tbl., 11.

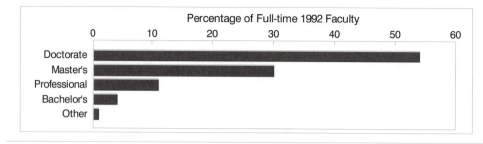

Percentage of Full-time 1992 Faculty

Percentage of Instructional Faculty				
			1987	1992	
Characteristic	1975	1984	Full-time Only	Full-time Only	Full- & part-time
Highest Degree Held					
All degrees	100	100	100	100	100
Doctorate	54	55	55	54	38
Master's	29	28	28	30	39
Professional	11	7	13	11	11
Bachelor's	5	4	2	4	9
Other	1	6	2	1	3
Employment Status					
Full-time	92	92	100	100	58
Part-time	8	8	-	-	42

Note: Data for 1975 and 1984 come from the Carnegie studies. Data for 1987 and 1992 come from NCES' National Study of Postsecondary Faculty (NSOPF). The differing coverage and sampling methods used by the studies limit their comparability.

Sources: 1 Carnegie Surveys, 1975. The Carnegie Foundation for the Advancement of Teaching. Used by permission.
2 Carnegie Survey of Faculty. Copyright 1985. The Carnegie Foundation for the Advancement of Teaching. Used by permission.
3 NCES, Digest of Education Statistics (Washington: GPO), 1994, tbl.221; 1996, tbl. 222.

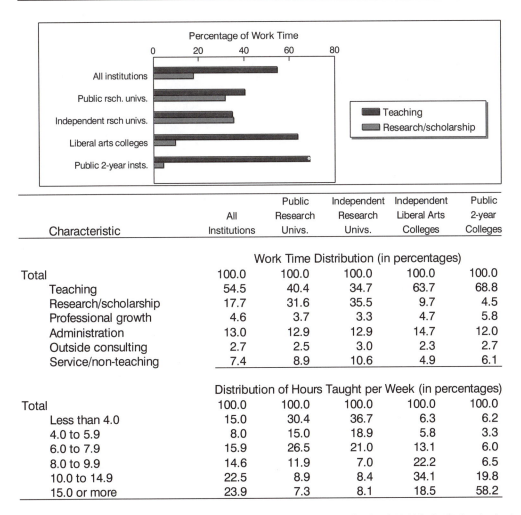

Characteristic	All Institutions	Public Research Univs.	Independent Research Univs.	Independent Liberal Arts Colleges	Public 2-year Colleges
	Work Time Distribution (in percentages)				
Total	100.0	100.0	100.0	100.0	100.0
Teaching	54.5	40.4	34.7	63.7	68.8
Research/scholarship	17.7	31.6	35.5	9.7	4.5
Professional growth	4.6	3.7	3.3	4.7	5.8
Administration	13.0	12.9	12.9	14.7	12.0
Outside consulting	2.7	2.5	3.0	2.3	2.7
Service/non-teaching	7.4	8.9	10.6	4.9	6.1
	Distribution of Hours Taught per Week (in percentages)				
Total	100.0	100.0	100.0	100.0	100.0
Less than 4.0	15.0	30.4	36.7	6.3	6.2
4.0 to 5.9	8.0	15.0	18.9	5.8	3.3
6.0 to 7.9	15.9	26.5	21.0	13.1	6.0
8.0 to 9.9	14.6	11.9	7.0	22.2	6.5
10.0 to 14.9	22.5	8.9	8.4	34.1	19.8
15.0 or more	23.9	7.3	8.1	18.5	58.2

Note: Percentages in "All Institutions" column describe full-time instructional faculty (528,000); institutional subcategories not shown separately here but included in the all institutions figure are doctoral, comprehensive, and "other" institutions. Faculty at the excluded categories accounted for approximately two-fifths of the Fall 1992 full-time instructional faculty. Data come from the 1992 National Study of Postsecondary Faculty (NSOPF), 1993, as summarized in the Source.

Source: NCES, Digest of Education Statistics, 1996 (Washington: GPO, 1996), tbl. 223.

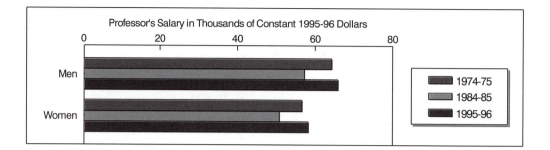

Year	Professor		Associate Professor		Assistant Professor		Instructor	
	Men	Women	Men	Women	Men	Women	Men	Women
	Current Dollars							
1974-75	21,532	19,012	16,282	15,481	13,458	12,858	13,350	11,740
1979-80	28,672	25,910	21,651	20,642	17,720	16,974	14,323	13,750
1984-85	40,269	35,824	30,392	28,517	25,330	23,575	21,159	19,362
1989-90	53,650	47,663	40,131	37,469	33,781	31,090	25,933	24,320
1991-92	58,494	51,621	43,814	40,766	36,969	34,063	33,359	28,873
1993-94	61,857	54,746	46,229	43,178	38,794	36,169	29,815	28,136
1994-95	64,046	56,555	47,705	44,626	39,923	37,352	30,528	29,072
1995-96	65,949	58,318	49,037	45,803	40,858	38,345	30,940	29,940
	Constant 1995-96 Dollars							
1974-75	64,222	56,706	48,563	46,174	40,140	38,351	39,818	35,016
1979-80	57,085	51,586	43,107	41,098	35,280	33,795	28,517	27,376
1984-85	57,183	50,871	43,158	40,495	35,970	33,477	30,047	27,495
1989-90	65,267	57,984	48,821	45,582	41,096	37,822	31,548	29,586
1991-92	65,389	57,706	48,979	45,572	41,327	38,078	37,291	32,277
1993-94	35,361	57,847	48,848	45,624	40,992	38,218	31,504	29,730
1994-95	65,789	58,093	49,003	45,840	41,009	38,368	31,359	29,863
1995-96	65,949	58,318	49,037	45,803	40,858	38,345	30,940	29,940

Note: Data describe average salaries of full-time instructional faculty on 9- and 10-month contracts.
   For conversion to constant dollars, the Consumer Price Index, adjusted to the academic year, was used.

Sources: 1 NCES, Digest of Education Statistics, 1996 (Washington: GPO, 1996), tbls. 37, 229.
   2 _____, E.D.Tabs: Salaries of Full-time Instructional Faculty on 9- and 10-Month and 11- and 12-Month
   Contracts, 1995-96 (Washington: NCES, 1997), tbls. 2, 3.

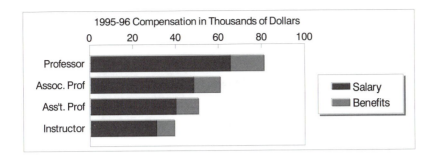

Year	Average Salary	Average Fringe Benefits	Average Compensation	Fringe Benefits as a Percentage of Compensation
		All Ranks		
1965-66	$9,816	$816	$10,632	7.7
1976-77	17,930	2,740	20,670	13.3
1986-87	35,470	7,780	43,250	18.0
1989-90	41,650	9,750	51,400	19.0
1995-96	50,980	12,770	63,750	20.0
		Professor		
1965-66	13,505	1,199	14,704	8.2
1976-77	23,930	3,610	27,540	13.1
1986-87	45,530	9,770	55,300	17.7
1989-90	53,540	12,070	65,610	18.4
1995-96	65,440	15,680	81,120	19.3
		Associate Professor		
1965-66	10,186	847	11,033	7.7
1976-77	18,100	2,790	20,890	13.4
1986-87	33,820	7,640	41,460	18.4
1989-90	39,790	9,630	49,420	19.5
1995-96	48,310	12,490	60,800	20.5
		Assistant Professor		
1965-66	8,429	685	9,114	7.5
1976-77	14,820	2,290	17,110	13.4
1986-87	27,920	6,170	34,090	18.1
1989-90	32,970	7,930	40,900	19.4
1995-96	40,050	10,390	50,440	20.6
		Instructor		
1965-66	6,737	487	7,224	6.7
1976-77	11,920	1,770	13,690	12.9
1986-87	21,330	4,710	26,040	18.1
1989-90	24,900	6,150	31,050	19.8
1995-96	30,830	8,370	39,200	21.4

Note: Figures in this table may differ from those shown elsewhere because of different coverage in the several surveys. Only institutions with academic ranks were included.

Sources: 1 "The Economic Status of the Profession", AAUP Bulletin, American Association of University Professors (AAUP), June 1966, p. 152; August 1977, p. 152.
2 AAUP, "The Annual Report on the Economic Status of the Profession," Academe, March-April issues, 1987 - 1996. Used with permission.

Percentage of Full-time Instructional Faculty with Tenure, by Rank, Sex, and Control of Institution, Selected Years, 1980/81–1994/95

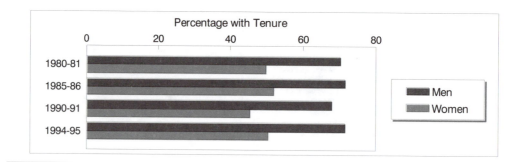

	Percentage with Tenure						
		By Rank				By Sex	
Year	All Ranks	Professor	Associate Professor	Assistant Professor	Instructor	Men	Women
			All Institutions				
1980-81	64.8	95.8	82.9	27.9	9.2	70.0	49.7
1985-86	66.0	95.8	82.2	25.1	10.7	71.3	51.7
1990-91	61.2	95.6	80.8	18.6	6.8	67.8	45.3
1993-94	64.2	96.0	81.8	17.0	7.0	71.0	49.9
1994-95	64.3	96.0	82.2	16.8	7.4	71.3	50.3
			Public 4-year Institutions				
1980-81	65.7	96.6	85.3	27.6	8.7	71.1	47.5
1985-86	66.9	96.6	84.9	24.4	7.3	72.5	49.3
1990-91	64.0	96.5	83.5	18.0	5.3	70.8	45.9
1993-94	65.1	97.4	85.7	16.3	5.2	72.5	47.1
1994-95	65.3	97.4	86.3	15.9	5.0	73.0	47.4
			Public 2-year Institutions				
1980-81	75.2	95.9	89.5	59.5	20.3	79.3	67.5
1985-86	75.7	95.2	89.0	57.4	28.0	79.5	69.2
1990-91	57.3	93.7	85.6	51.4	16.7	61.0	52.2
1993-94	73.2	93.0	84.4	47.8	16.2	78.4	66.6
1994-95	73.4	93.4	84.3	49.1	18.1	78.2	67.3
			Independent 4-year Institutions				
1980-81	56.0	93.8	75.2	17.4	2.8	62.2	37.2
1985-86	57.7	93.9	73.9	15.9	2.5	64.0	40.3
1990-91	56.8	93.9	73.8	11.6	1.4	63.7	39.8
1993-94	56.9	94.0	73.8	10.6	1.6	64.4	40.7
1994-95	57.2	93.7	73.8	10.5	1.7	64.6	41.4

Note: Calculated from data provided by institutions reporting tenure status.

Source: NCES, Digest of Education Statistics (Washington: GPO); 1990, tbl. 215; 1996, tbl. 235.

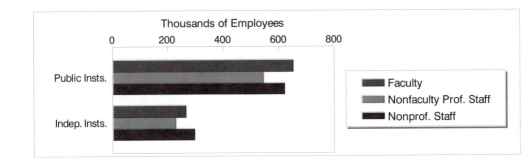

Control of Institution and Primary Occupation	Number of Employees (in thousands)		
	Total	Full-time	Part-time
All Institutions	**2,602.6**	**1,783.5**	**819.1**
Professional staff	*1,687.3*	*1,039.1*	*648.2*
Executive/administrative/management	143.6	137.8	5.8
Faculty (instruction/research)	915.5	545.7	369.8
Instruction/research assistants	202.8	na	202.8
Professional (support/service)	425.4	355.6	69.8
Nonprofessional staff	*915.3*	*744.4*	*170.9*
Technical & paraprofessionals	183.9	142.8	41.1
Clerical and secretarial	438.1	352.0	86.1
Skilled crafts	64.0	60.9	3.1
Service/maintenance	229.3	188.7	40.6
Public Institutions	**1,812.5**	**1,206.4**	**606.1**
Professional staff	*1,193.3*	*701.4*	*491.9*
Executive/administrative/management	81.2	78.0	3.2
Faculty (instruction/research)	650.4	382.7	267.7
Instruction/research assistants	173.7	na	173.7
Professional (support/service)	288.0	240.7	47.3
Nonprofessional staff	*619.2*	*505.0*	*114.2*
Technical & paraprofessionals	131.7	99.6	32.1
Clerical and secretarial	290.2	233.6	56.6
Skilled crafts	46.7	44.5	2.2
Service/maintenance	150.7	127.3	23.4
Independent Institutions	**790.1**	**577.1**	**213.0**
Professional staff	*494.0*	*337.7*	*156.3*
Executive/administrative/management	62.4	59.8	2.6
Faculty (instruction/research)	265.1	163.0	102.1
Instruction/research assistants	29.1	na	29.1
Professional (support/service)	137.4	114.9	22.5
Nonprofessional staff	*296.1*	*239.4*	*56.7*
Technical & paraprofessionals	52.2	43.2	9.0
Clerical and secretarial	147.9	118.4	29.5
Skilled crafts	17.3	16.4	0.9
Service/maintenance	78.6	61.4	17.2

Note: Faculty counts here may differ from data in other tables because of differences in survey methodologies.

na: Not applicable.

Source: NCES, E. D. TABS: Fall Staff in Postsecondary Institutions, 1993, NCES 96-32 (Washington: GPO, 1996), tbl. B-1a.

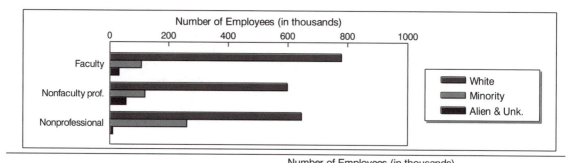

Number of Employees (in thousands)

Control of Institution and Primary Occupation	Total	White, non-Hispanic	Total Minority	Black, non-Hispanic	Other Minority	Nonres. Alien & Unknown
All Institutions	**2,602.6**	**2,022.0**	**484.0**	**274.6**	**209.4**	**96.6**
Professional staff	*1,687.3*	*1,375.9*	*224.8*	*103.3*	*121.4*	*86.6*
Executive/admin./management	143.6	123.7	19.4	12.6	6.8	0.5
Faculty (instruction/research)	915.5	779.0	106.2	45.2	61.0	30.3
Instruction/research assistants	202.8	131.2	28.2	7.5	20.7	43.4
Professional (support/service)	425.4	341.9	70.8	38.0	32.8	12.5
Nonprofessional staff	*915.3*	*646.1*	*259.2*	*171.2*	*88.0*	*10.0*
Technical & paraprofessionals	183.9	135.0	45.5	27.7	17.8	3.6
Clerical and secretarial	438.1	327.5	107.0	67.5	39.5	3.5
Skilled crafts	64.0	52.0	11.6	7.0	4.6	0.4
Service/maintenance	229.3	131.6	95.2	69.1	26.1	2.5
Public Institutions	**1,812.5**	**1,408.8**	**331.9**	**183.9**	**148.0**	**71.9**
Professional staff	*1,193.3*	*966.1*	*161.2*	*72.7*	*88.5*	*66.0*
Executive/administrative/manager	81.2	69.6	11.4	7.3	4.1	0.2
Faculty (instruction/research)	650.4	551.2	78.3	33.9	44.4	21.0
Instruction/research assistants	173.7	113.6	23.7	6.0	17.7	36.4
Professional (support/service)	288.0	231.7	47.7	25.5	22.2	8.4
Nonprofessional staff	*619.2*	*442.6*	*170.8*	*111.2*	*59.5*	*5.8*
Technical & paraprofessionals	131.7	99.2	30.4	18.6	11.8	2.0
Clerical and secretarial	290.2	218.0	70.0	42.8	27.2	2.1
Skilled crafts	46.7	37.9	8.4	5.0	3.4	0.3
Service/maintenance	150.7	87.5	61.8	44.8	17.0	1.4
Independent Institutions	**790.1**	**613.2**	**152.1**	**90.7**	**61.4**	**24.8**
Professional staff	*494.0*	*409.8*	*63.6*	*30.7*	*32.9*	*20.6*
Executive/administrative/manager	62.4	54.1	8.0	5.3	2.7	0.3
Faculty (instruction/research)	265.1	227.8	27.9	11.3	16.6	9.3
Instruction/research assistants	29.1	17.6	4.5	1.5	3.0	7.0
Professional (support/service)	137.4	110.2	23.1	12.5	10.6	4.1
Nonprofessional staff	*296.1*	*203.4*	*88.5*	*60.0*	*28.5*	*4.2*
Technical & paraprofessionals	52.2	35.8	14.9	9.1	5.8	1.6
Clerical and secretarial	147.9	109.5	37.0	24.7	12.3	1.4
Skilled crafts	17.3	14.1	3.2	2.0	1.2	0.1
Service/maintenance	78.6	44.1	33.4	24.3	9.1	1.1

Note: Faculty counts here may differ from data in other tables because of differences in survey methodologies.

Source: NCES, E. D. TABS: Fall Staff in Postsecondary Institutions, 1993, NCES 96-32 (Washington: GPO, 1996), tbl. B-1a.

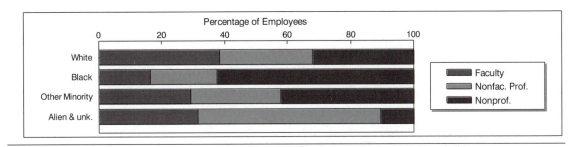

Control of Institution and Primary Occupation	Total	White, non-Hispanic	Total Minority	Black, non, Hispanic	Other Minority	Nonres. Alien & Unknown
All Institutions	**100.0**	**100.0**	**100.0**	**100.0**	**100.0**	**100.0**
Professional staff	*64.8*	*68.0*	*46.4*	*37.6*	*58.0*	*89.6*
Executive/admin./management	5.5	6.1	4.0	4.6	3.2	0.5
Faculty (instruction/research)	35.2	38.5	21.9	16.5	29.1	31.4
Instruction/research assistants	7.8	6.5	5.8	2.7	9.9	44.9
Professional (support/service)	16.3	16.9	14.6	13.8	15.7	12.9
Nonprofessional staff	*35.2*	*32.0*	*53.6*	*62.3*	*42.0*	*10.4*
Technical & paraprofessionals	7.1	6.7	9.4	10.1	8.5	3.7
Clerical and secretarial	16.8	16.2	22.1	24.6	18.9	3.6
Skilled crafts	2.5	2.6	2.4	2.5	2.2	0.4
Service/maintenance	8.8	6.5	19.7	25.2	12.5	2.6
Public Institutions	**69.6**	**69.7**	**68.6**	**67.0**	**70.7**	**74.4**
Professional staff	*45.9*	*47.8*	*33.3*	*26.5*	*42.3*	*68.3*
Executive/admin./management	3.1	3.4	2.4	2.7	2.0	0.2
Faculty (instruction/research)	25.0	27.3	16.2	12.3	21.2	21.7
Instruction/research assistants	6.7	5.6	4.9	2.2	8.5	37.7
Professional (support/service)	11.1	11.5	9.9	9.3	10.6	8.7
Nonprofessional staff	*23.8*	*21.9*	*35.3*	*40.5*	*28.4*	*6.0*
Technical & paraprofessionals	5.1	4.9	6.3	6.8	5.6	2.1
Clerical and secretarial	11.2	10.8	14.5	15.6	13.0	2.2
Skilled crafts	1.8	1.9	1.7	1.8	1.6	0.3
Service/maintenance	5.8	4.3	12.8	16.3	8.1	1.4
Independent Institutions	**30.4**	**30.3**	**31.4**	**33.0**	**29.3**	**25.7**
Professional staff	*19.0*	*20.3*	*13.1*	*11.2*	*15.7*	*21.3*
Executive/admin./management	2.4	2.7	1.7	1.9	1.3	0.3
Faculty (instruction/research)	10.2	11.3	5.8	4.1	7.9	9.6
Instruction/research assistants	1.1	0.9	0.9	0.5	1.4	7.2
Professional (support/service)	5.3	5.5	4.8	4.6	5.1	4.2
Nonprofessional staff	*11.4*	*10.1*	*18.3*	*21.8*	*13.6*	*4.3*
Technical & paraprofessionals	2.0	1.8	3.1	3.3	2.8	1.7
Clerical and secretarial	5.7	5.4	7.6	9.0	5.9	1.4
Skilled crafts	0.7	0.7	0.7	0.7	0.6	0.1
Service/maintenance	3.0	2.2	6.9	8.8	4.3	1.1

Note: Detail may not sum to totals because of rounding. Italics indicate subtotals.

Source: Calculated from table 119.

Percentage Distribution of Employees of Higher Education, by Primary Occupation and Race/Ethnicity, Fall 1993

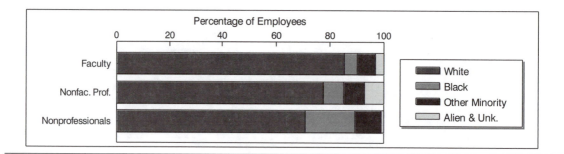

Control of Institution and Primary Occupation	Percentage Distribution of Employees (total horizontally)					
	Total	White, non-Hispanic	Total Minority	Black, non-Hispanic	Other Minority	Nonres. Alien & Unknown
All Institutions	**100.0**	**77.7**	**18.6**	**10.6**	**8.0**	**3.7**
Professional staff	*100.0*	*81.5*	*13.3*	*6.1*	*7.2*	*5.1*
Executive/admin./management	100.0	86.1	13.5	8.8	4.7	0.3
Faculty (instruction/research)	100.0	85.1	11.6	4.9	6.7	3.3
Instruction/research assistants	100.0	64.7	13.9	3.7	10.2	21.4
Professional (support/service)	100.0	80.4	16.6	8.9	7.7	2.9
Nonprofessional staff	*100.0*	*70.6*	*28.3*	*18.7*	*9.6*	*1.1*
Technical & paraprofessionals	100.0	73.4	24.7	15.1	9.7	2.0
Clerical and secretarial	100.0	74.8	24.4	15.4	9.0	0.8
Skilled crafts	100.0	81.3	18.1	10.9	7.2	0.6
Service/maintenance	100.0	57.4	41.5	30.1	11.4	1.1
Public Institutions	**100.0**	**77.7**	**18.3**	**10.1**	**8.2**	**4.0**
Professional staff	*100.0*	*81.0*	*13.5*	*6.1*	*7.4*	*5.5*
Executive/admin./management	100.0	85.7	14.0	9.0	5.0	0.2
Faculty (instruction/research)	100.0	84.7	12.0	5.2	6.8	3.2
Instruction/research assistants	100.0	65.4	13.6	3.5	10.2	21.0
Professional (support/service)	100.0	80.5	16.6	8.9	7.7	2.9
Nonprofessional staff	*100.0*	*71.5*	*27.6*	*18.0*	*9.6*	*0.9*
Technical & paraprofessionals	100.0	75.3	23.1	14.1	9.0	1.5
Clerical and secretarial	100.0	75.1	24.1	14.7	9.4	0.7
Skilled crafts	100.0	81.2	18.0	10.7	7.3	0.6
Service/maintenance	100.0	58.1	41.0	29.7	11.3	0.9
Independent Institutions	**100.0**	**77.6**	**19.3**	**11.5**	**7.8**	**3.1**
Professional staff	*100.0*	*83.0*	*12.9*	*6.2*	*6.7*	*4.2*
Executive/admin./management	100.0	86.7	12.8	8.5	4.3	0.5
Faculty (instruction/research)	100.0	85.9	10.5	4.3	6.3	3.5
Instruction/research assistants	100.0	60.5	15.5	5.2	10.3	24.1
Professional (support/service)	100.0	80.2	16.8	9.1	7.7	3.0
Nonprofessional staff	*100.0*	*68.7*	*29.9*	*20.3*	*9.6*	*1.4*
Technical & paraprofessionals	100.0	68.6	28.5	17.4	11.1	3.1
Clerical and secretarial	100.0	74.0	25.0	16.7	8.3	0.9
Skilled crafts	100.0	81.5	18.5	11.6	6.9	0.6
Service/maintenance	100.0	56.1	42.5	30.9	11.6	1.4

Note: Detail may not sum to totals because of rounding.

Source: Calculated from table 119.

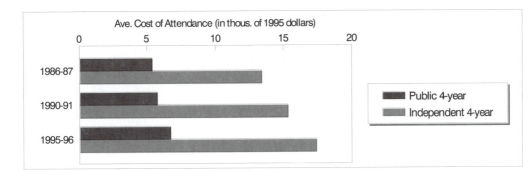

| Year | Cost of Attendance | | Tuition and Fees | | Disposable | |
	Public Four-year Institution	Independent Four-year Institution	Public Four-year Institution	Independent Four-year Institution	Personal Income (Per Capita)	Median Family Income
			Current Dollars			
1986-87	$3,921	$9,775	$1,285	$6,581	$13,000	$29,458
1987-88	4,199	10,455	1,485	7,048	13,528	30,970
1988-89	4,455	11,660	1,578	8,004	14,457	32,191
1989-90	4,715	12,557	1,696	8,663	15,291	34,213
1990-91	5,074	13,476	1,908	9,340	16,173	35,353
1991-92	5,452	14,188	2,107	9,812	16,730	35,939
1992-93	5,834	15,028	2,334	10,449	17,606	36,812
1993-94	6,212	15,795	2,535	11,007	18,151	36,959
1994-95	6,527	16,698	2,705	11,719	18,852	38,752
1995-96	6,823	17,631	2,860	12,432	19,729	40,611
			Constant 1995 Dollars			
1986-87	5,372	13,392	1,761	9,016	18,082	40,973
1987-88	5,525	13,756	1,954	9,273	18,145	41,541
1988-89	5,605	14,670	1,985	10,071	18,632	41,487
1989-90	5,658	15,068	2,035	10,395	18,799	42,062
1990-91	5,771	15,326	2,170	10,622	18,852	41,209
1991-92	6,009	15,637	2,322	10,814	18,712	40,196
1992-93	6,235	16,062	2,495	11,168	19,112	39,961
1993-94	6,470	16,452	2,640	11,465	19,137	38,966
1994-95	6,610	16,910	2,739	11,868	19,371	39,819
1995-96	6,731	17,392	2,821	12,264	19,729	40,611

Note: Cost of attendance describes undergraduate costs only and is weighted by enrollment.

Cost of attendance includes tuition, fees and on-campus room and board costs.

Income data are for the calendar year in which the academic year begins.

Sources: 1 The Washington Office of the College Board (WOCB), Trends in Student Aid, 1986-1996 (Washington: WOCB, 1996), tbl. 3. Used with permission.

2 Council of Economic Advisers, Economic Report of the President (Washington: GPO, 1997), tbl. B-31.

Aid Awarded to Postsecondary Students, in Current Dollars, Selected Academic Years, 1964–1996

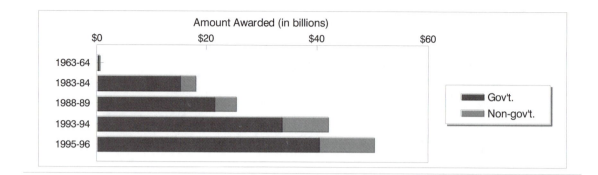

Amount Awarded (in billions)

Source and Type of Aid	Amount Awarded (in millions of current dollars)				
	1963-64	1983-84	1988-89	1993-94	Preliminary 1995-96
Federally supported programs					
Generally Available Aid					
Pell Grants	-	$2,792	$4,471	$5,652	$5,407
SEOG	-	361	422	564	579
SSIG	-	60	72	71	64
College Work-study	-	683	625	771	612
Perkins Loans	$114	682	874	919	957
Income Contingent Loans	-	-	5	-	-
Ford Direct Loans	-	-	-	-	8,542
(Subsidized Stafford)	-	-	-	-	5,112
(Unsubsidized Stafford)	-	-	-	-	2,544
(PLUS)	-	-	-	-	796
Family Education Loans	-	7,576	11,985	21,177	18,932
(Subsidized Stafford)	-	-	9,319	14,155	11,039
(Unsubsidized Stafford)	-	-	0	2,024	6,253
(SLS)	-	-	2,015	3,469	-
(PLUS)	-	-	651	1,529	1,640
Subtotal	*114*	*12,155*	*18,455*	*29,154*	*35,004*
Specially Directed Aid					
Veterans	67	1,148	724	1,192	1,372
Military	-	301	341	405	452
Other grants	9	285	102	167	171
Other loans	-	263	332	456	366
Subtotal	*76*	*1,996*	*1,498*	*2,221*	*2,361*
All Federal Aid	*190*	*14,151*	*19,952*	*31,375*	*37,365*
State grant programs	56	1,106	1,581	2,375	3,021
Institutional and other grants	300	2,881	3,978	8,233	9,962
Total aid	$546	$18,138	$25,511	$41,983	$50,349

Note: Over the 30-year period covered in this table, Federal student aid programs have changed greatly, thus limiting precise comparability. These data show general trends rather than exact comparisons. Institutional awards include awards from the institution's own funds and awards made from funds from government and private programs that allow the institution to select the recipient. Data for 1993-94 and later are estimates. Italics indicate subtotals. Dashes indicate no awards.

Source: The Washington Office of the College Board (WOCB), Trends in Student Aid (Washington: WOCB), Update: 1980-1988, p. 6; Update: 1986-1996, tbl 1. Used with permission.

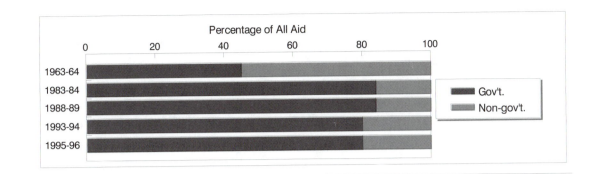

Source and Type of Aid	Amount Awarded (in millions of constant 1995 dollars)				
	1963-64	1983-84	1988-89	1993-94	Preliminary 1995-96
Federally supported programs					
Generally Available Aid					
Pell Grants	-	$4,180	$5,625	$5,886	$5,334
SEOG	-	540	532	588	571
SSIG	-	90	91	74	64
College Work-study	-	1,022	787	804	604
Perkins Loans	$564	1,021	1,099	957	944
Income Contingent Loans	-	-	6	-	-
Ford Direct Loans	-	-	-	-	*8,559*
(Subsidized Stafford)	-	-	-	-	5,042
(Unsubsidized Stafford)	-	-	-	-	2,509
(PLUS)	-	-	-	-	785
Family Education Loans	-	*11,342*	*15,079*	*22,057*	*18,676*
(Subsidized Stafford)	-	-	11,725	14,743	10,890
(Unsubsidized Stafford)	-	-	-	2,108	6,168
(SLS)	-	-	2,535	3,613	-
(PLUS)	-	-	819	1,592	1,618
Subtotal	*564*	*18,197*	*23,219*	*30,366*	*34,530*
Specially Directed Aid					
Veterans	332	1,719	911	1,242	1,354
Military	-	451	429	422	446
Other grants	45	427	128	174	168
Other loans	-	394	332	475	366
Subtotal	*376*	*2,988*	*1,885*	*2,313*	*2,329*
All Federal Aid	*940*	*21,185*	*25,104*	*32,679*	*36,859*
State grant programs	277	1,656	1,989	2,474	2,980
Institutional and other grants	1,484	4,313	5,005	8,576	9,828
Total aid	$2,702	$27,154	$32,098	$43,729	$49,667

Note: Over the 30-year period covered in this table, Federal student aid programs have changed greatly, thus limiting precise comparability. These data show general trends rather than exact comparisons. Institutional awards include awards from the institution's own funds and awards made from funds from government and private programs that allow the institution to select the recipient. Data for 1993- 94 and later are estimates. Italics indicate subtotals. CPI was used to convert current to constant dollars.

Source: The Washington Office of the College Board (WOCB), Trends in Student Aid (Washington: WOCB), Update: 1980-1988, p. 6; Update: 1986-1996, tbl 1. Used with permission.

125

Percentage of Undergraduates Receiving Student Aid, by Enrollment Status, Type and Control of Institution, and Source of Aid, 1992

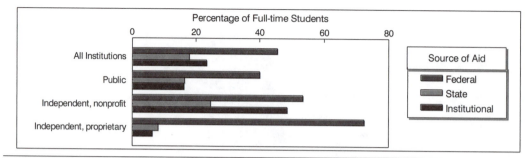

Type & Control of Institution	Percentage of Students Enrolled at Any Time in AY 1992-93						Number of Undergrads (in thousands)
	Any aid	Federal	State	Institutional	Other	No aid	
Full-time Students							
All Institutions	**57.9**	**45.6**	**17.9**	**23.4**	**9.7**	**42.1**	**6,000**
Public	51.9	40.0	16.5	16.2	8.8	48.1	4,110
4-year doctoral	53.7	39.3	14.9	20.8	9.7	46.3	1,772
Other 4-year	56.4	46.1	21.6	16.1	8.1	43.6	1,087
2-year	45.9	36.0	14.6	10.1	8.2	54.1	1,196
Less than 2-year	35.0	31.6	10.9	0.4	7.7	65.0	55
Independent, nonprofit	69.5	53.4	24.6	48.5	13.2	30.5	1,469
4-year doctoral	62.7	44.5	17.9	48.2	13.4	37.3	681
Other 4-year	75.5	60.8	31.0	51.2	13.3	24.5	719
2-year or less	73.9	63.9	23.2	23.8	10.4	26.1	70
Independent, proprietary	76.1	72.4	8.1	6.1	6.9	23.9	421
2-year and above	80.6	77.4	14.1	7.5	10.6	19.4	182
Less than 2-year	72.7	68.6	3.5	5.0	4.1	27.3	238
Part-time Students							
All Institutions	**32.9**	**25.0**	**6.7**	**6.6**	**6.6**	**67.1**	**12,293**
Public	27.1	19.8	6.2	4.9	6.1	72.9	9,911
4-year doctoral	36.5	27.5	7.6	9.5	6.9	63.5	1,504
Other 4-year	35.6	28.4	10.0	6.7	6.2	64.4	1,330
2-year	23.6	16.5	5.3	3.7	5.9	76.4	6,850
Less than 2-year	19.2	15.1	1.5	1.0	5.3	80.8	227
Independent, nonprofit	49.4	35.1	11.6	20.2	11.0	50.6	1,431
4-year doctoral	44.4	28.3	8.8	23.7	8.9	55.6	391
Other 4-year	52.2	38.1	13.4	19.8	13.3	47.8	818
2-year or less	47.6	35.8	10.0	15.3	6.4	52.4	223
Independent, proprietary	69.0	64.4	4.7	3.8	5.0	31.0	951
2-year and above	60.4	54.9	6.4	2.9	6.8	39.6	383
Less than 2-year	74.8	70.8	3.5	4.3	3.8	25.2	568

Note: The number of undergraduates will not agree with other enrollment figures because these figures came from a sample survey that included students who enrolled at any time during the academic year. Full-time students are those who attended full-time for the entire year. Because students may receive aid from various sources, the "any aid" figure will be less than a sum of the source columns. "Other" includes those who reported aid but did not report its source.

Source: NCES, Digest of Education Statistics, 1996 (Washington: GPO, 1996), tbl. 313.

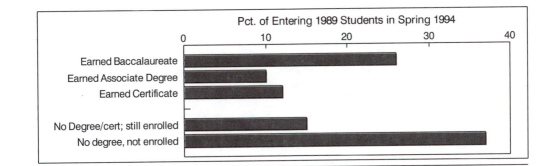

Characteristic	Attained -			Received No Degree/cert., but-	
	Bacca-laureate	Assoc. Degree	Certi-ficate	Are Still Enrolled	Are Not Enrolled
All Entering 1989-90 Students	26	10	12	15	37
Sex and Race/ethnicity					
Men					
White, non-Hispanic	26	9	10	16	39
Black, non-Hispanic	13	11	15	13	47
Hispanic	14	9	12	22	44
Asian/Pacific Islander	38	5	19	20	19
Women					
White, non-Hispanic	28	11	13	12	35
Black, non-Hispanic	19	6	16	14	45
Hispanic	21	12	19	17	32
Asian/Pacific Islander	32	10	6	21	31
Degree Aspiration/ Type of Institution Entered					
Baccalaureate/4-year institution	57	3	2	16	22
Baccalaureate/2-year institution	10	14	7	29	40
Associate degree/2-year inst.	8	23	11	13	45
Certificate/Public 2-year inst.	0	5	34	6	54
Certificate/For-profit 2-year inst.	1	2	61	4	32
Other combinations	9	9	23	8	52

Source: NCES, Beginning Postsecondary Students Study, as published in American Council on Education (ACE), ACE Fact Sheet on Higher Education, "Degree and Enrollment Status of 1989-90 Beginning Postsecondary Students," August 1997.

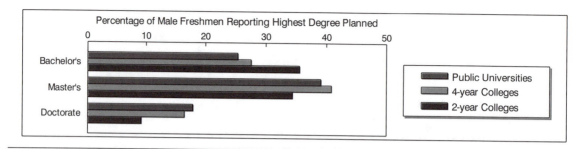

Percentage of Male Freshmen Reporting Highest Degree Planned

Legend: Public Universities, 4-year Colleges, 2-year Colleges

Student Characteristic	Percentage of Students					
	All Institutions		Public Universities		Independent Universities	
	Men	Women	Men	Women	Men	Women
Highest Degree Planned						
None	1.0	0.8	0.5	0.5	0.4	0.4
Vocational certificate	0.7	0.9	0.2	0.1	0.1	0.0
Associate Degree	3.0	4.1	0.6	0.6	0.1	0.1
Bachelor's	28.3	24.6	25.3	20.0	13.3	10.9
Master's	38.3	39.3	39.1	39.9	37.3	37.3
Ph.D. or Ed.D.	15.1	15.0	17.8	18.3	22.6	22.6
M.D., D. O., D.D.S., or D.V.M.	7.5	9.7	11.0	14.9	15.7	18.4
LL.B. or J.D.	3.5	3.7	4.0	4.2	8.8	8.9
B.D. or M.Div.	0.5	0.2	0.4	0.2	0.4	0.2
Other	2.1	1.7	1.2	1.2	1.3	1.2
Racial Background						
White/Caucasian	80.5	80.2	83.9	80.9	74.7	71.7
Black/Negro/African-American	8.7	10.5	5.6	9.5	7.8	11.8
American Indian	2.3	2.3	2.0	2.5	1.5	1.6
Asian American/Asian	5.0	3.8	7.1	6.0	11.8	11.1
Mexican-American/Chicano	2.9	3.1	1.4	1.5	3.1	3.1
Puerto Rican/other Latino	2.8	2.3	2.1	2.4	3.5	4.0
Other	2.5	2.4	2.4	2.6	3.5	3.8
Concern about Financing Education						
No concern	38.4	25.3	37.0	25.7	37.4	27.8
Some concern	47.3	53.7	50.6	54.9	48.6	52.0
Major concern	14.3	21.0	12.4	19.4	14.0	20.2
Average Grade in High School						
A-, A, A+	27.0	35.2	37.2	46.0	55.9	61.7
B-, B, B+	54.1	53.9	54.6	49.5	40.1	36.4
C, C+	18.4	10.7	8.0	4.5	3.9	1.9
D	0.6	0.2	0.1	0.0	0.1	0.0

Continued on next page.

na: Not available

Note: Weighted national norms for first-time full-time freshmen based on a sample of over 150,000 freshmen each year.
  Percentages in the racial background item will total more than 100 because multiple choice was permitted.

For Source see next page.

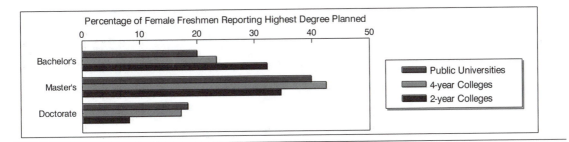

Percentage of Female Freshmen Reporting Highest Degree Planned

Legend: Public Universities, 4-year Colleges, 2-year Colleges

	Percentage of Students					
	Four-year Colleges		Two-year Colleges		Black Colleges	
Student Characteristic	Men	Women	Men	Women	Men	Women
Highest Degree Planned						
None	0.8	0.6	1.8	1.3	0.8	1.0
Vocational certificate	0.3	0.1	1.8	2.7	0.4	0.3
Associate Degree	0.7	0.6	8.9	12.3	0.6	0.7
Bachelor's	27.5	23.4	35.5	32.2	22.4	15.2
Master's	40.8	42.5	34.4	34.6	39.8	35.0
Ph.D. or Ed.D.	16.5	17.2	9.1	8.1	20.4	24.1
M.D., D. O., D.D.S., or D.V.M.	7.3	9.9	3.0	4.1	5.7	13.8
LL.B. or J.D.	3.7	3.8	1.7	2.1	5.4	7.3
B.D. or M.Div.	0.6	0.3	0.6	0.2	1.2	0.8
Other	1.9	1.6	3.2	2.4	3.3	1.7
Racial Background						
White/Caucasian	79.1	78.3	81.5	84.1	3.7	3.9
Black/Negro/African-American	11.8	13.2	6.6	7.1	94.9	95.8
American Indian	2.4	2.7	2.4	1.9	1.9	2.8
Asian American/Asian	4.0	3.4	3.2	1.7	0.8	0.3
Mexican-American/Chicano	2.8	2.9	4.2	4.2	0.1	0.2
Puerto Rican/other Latino	2.2	2.1	3.9	1.9	1.2	1.1
Other	2.5	2.5	2.3	1.9	1.4	2.2
Concern about Financing Education						
No concern	38.1	24.2	40.0	26.0	35.0	24.7
Some concern	48.3	55.3	43.4	51.1	46.5	50.0
Major concern	13.7	20.5	16.5	22.9	18.5	25.3
Average Grade in High School						
A-, A, A+	28.1	41.0	11.4	17.0	9.7	16.7
B-, B, B+	56.5	52.9	53.2	61.2	55.4	63.9
C, C+	15.0	7.1	33.6	21.4	34.3	19.2
D	0.2	0.1	1.8	0.4	0.5	0.2

Source: Linda Sax, Alexander Astin, William S. Korn, Kathryn M. Mahoney, The American Freshman, National Norms for Fall 1996
(Los Angeles: Higher Education Institute, UCLA, 1996), pp. 31 - 43; 49 - 61.

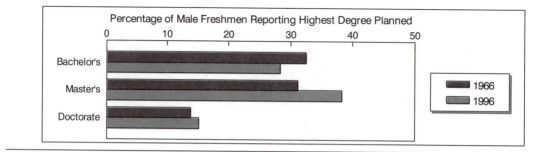

Percentage of Male Freshmen Reporting Highest Degree Planned

	Percentage of Freshmen at All Institutions					
	Men			Women		
Student Characteristic	1966	1987	1996	1966	1987	1996
Highest Degree Planned						
None	6.1	2.0	1.0	4.8	2.0	0.8
Vocational certificate	na	1.6	0.7	na	1.4	0.9
Associate Degree	4.1	4.4	3.0	7.3	6.2	4.1
Bachelor's	32.5	35.9	28.3	46.1	34.7	24.6
Master's	31.2	34.1	38.3	32.3	34.5	39.3
Ph.D. or Ed.D.	13.7	10.7	15.1	5.2	10.0	15.0
M.D., D. O., D.D.S., or D.V.M.	7.4	5.1	7.5	1.9	5.4	9.7
LL.B. or J.D.	2.5	4.2	3.5	0.3	4.2	3.7
B.D. or M.Div.	0.5	0.4	0.5	0.1	0.2	0.2
Other	2.1	1.5	2.1	1.8	1.4	1.7
Racial Background						
White/Caucasian	90.9	87.6	80.5	90.5	84.5	80.2
Black/Negro/African-American	4.5	7.2	8.7	5.6	10.0	10.5
American Indian	0.5	0.9	2.3	0.6	0.9	2.3
Asian American/Asian	0.8	2.6	5.0	0.7	2.1	3.8
Mexican-American/Chicano	na	0.9	2.9	na	1.1	3.1
Puerto Rican/other Latino	na	0.9	2.8	na	1.5	2.3
Other	3.3	1.6	2.5	2.7	1.7	2.4
Concern about Financing Education						
No concern	34.9	42.7	38.4	35.3	32.3	25.3
Some concern	57.0	45.9	47.3	55.5	51.8	53.7
Major concern	8.1	11.3	14.3	9.2	15.9	21.0
Average Grade in High School						
A-, A, A+	11.3	18.6	27.0	20.2	23.8	35.2
B-, B, B+	49.5	56.8	54.1	59.6	60.4	53.9
C, C+	37.9	23.9	18.4	19.9	15.6	10.7
D	1.3	0.6	0.6	0.3	0.2	0.2

Continued on next page.

na: Not available

Note: Weighted national norms for first-time full-time freshmen based on a sample of over 150,000 freshmen each year.

For Source see next page.

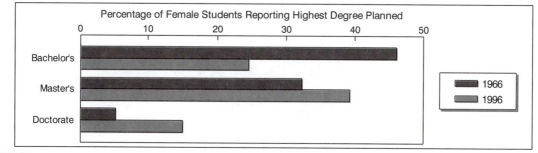

Percentage of Female Students Reporting Highest Degree Planned

Student Characteristic	Percentage of Freshmen at All Institutions					
	Men			Women		
	1966	1987	1996	1966	1987	1996
Objectives Considered to Be Essential or Very Important						
Help others in difficulty	59.2	50.0	53.4	79.5	66.5	69.8
Be an authority in my field	70.3	78.1	66.2	60.8	76.4	62.3
Be very well off financially	54.1	79.5	76.4	31.6	72.1	72.2
Raise a family	na	55.9	72.3	na	59.5	72.1
Obtain recognition from colleagues	48.0	59.5	53.1	36.3	57.3	52.0
Probable Career Occupation						
Artist (including performer)	4.6	3.0	3.4	8.9	3.3	2.7
Businessperson	18.5	28.0	12.9	3.3	24.2	7.4
Clergy or religious worker	1.2	0.4	0.7	0.8	0.1	0.1
Doctor (M.D. or D.D.S.)	7.4	4.2	5.8	1.7	3.8	6.9
Educator (college teacher)	2.1	0.4	0.6	1.5	0.3	0.5
Educator (secondary ed.)	10.5	2.7	3.9	18.4	3.5	3.9
Educator (elementary ed.)	0.8	0.7	1.6	15.7	8.8	9.3
Engineer	16.3	15.2	12.8	0.2	2.6	2.4
Farmer or forester	3.2	1.9	2.4	0.2	0.4	0.8
Health professional (non-M.D.)	3.1	2.7	5.4	6.6	9.2	11.8
Lawyer	6.7	4.5	3.1	0.7	4.5	3.5
Nurse	0.1	0.2	0.5	5.3	4.0	5.5
Research scientist	4.9	1.8	1.8	1.9	1.2	1.8
Other occupation	15.8	24.2	33.3	31.0	21.7	29.8
Undecided	5.0	9.9	11.8	3.6	12.6	13.6

Sources: 1 Alexander Astin, Robert J. Panos,and John A. Creager, National Norms for Entering College Freshmen (Washington: American Council on Education), Fall 1966, pp. 5-9, 12-16.

2 Alexander Astin, Kenneth C. Green, William S. Korn, and Marilyn Schalit, The American Freshman: National Norms for Fall 1987 (Los Angeles: Cooperative Institutional Research Program, UCLA), 1987, pp. 21-23, 37-39.

3 Linda Sax, Alexander Astin, William S. Korn, Kathryn M. Mahoney,The American Freshman, National Norms for Fall 1996 (Los Angeles: Higher Education Institute, UCLA, 1996), pp. 31-45; 49-63.

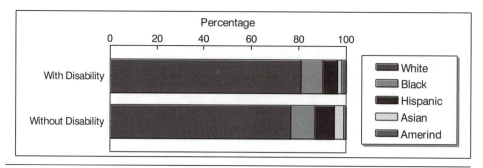

| Characteristic | Undergraduates | | |
	All	with Disabilities	without Disabilities
Both Sexes	100.0	100.0	100.0
Male	44.5	53.0	44.0
Female	55.5	47.0	56.0
Race/ethnicity	100.0	100.0	100.0
White, NonHispanic	76.8	80.8	76.6
Black, NonHispanic	10.3	9.3	10.3
Hispanic	8.0	6.3	8.1
Asian-American	4.0	1.7	4.1
American Indian	1.0	1.8	0.9
Attendance status	100.0	100.0	100.0
Full-time	52.6	46.3	52.9
Part-time	47.4	53.7	47.1
Age	100.0	100.0	100.0
15 to 23	55.1	37.8	56.1
24 to 29	17.1	15.2	17.2
30 or older	27.7	47.0	26.7
Dependency status	100.0	100.0	100.0
Dependent	47.9	32.9	48.7
Independent	32.9	37.0	32.7
Independent with dependents	19.2	30.1	18.6

Note: Students with disabilities are those with one or more of the following conditions:
hearing disability, visual handicap, hard of hearing, deafness, speech disability, orthopedic handicap, or health impairment.

Detail may not sum to totals because of rounding and/or survey item nonresponse. Data came from the 1992-93 National Postsecondary Student Aid Study.

Source: NCES, Digest of Education Statistics, 1996 (Washington: GPO, 1996), tbl. 206.

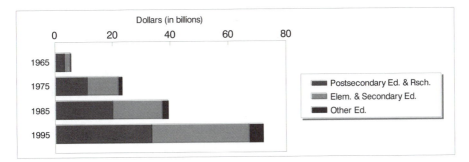

	Federal On-budget Support (in millions of current dollars)			
Fiscal Year	Total	Elementary & Secondary Education	Post-secondary Education	Other Education	Research at Educational Institutions
1965	$5,331.1	$1,942.6	$1,197.5	$374.7	$1,816.3
1970	12,526.5	5,830.4	3,447.7	964.7	2,283.6
1975	23,288.1	10,617.2	7,644.0	1,608.5	3,418.4
1980	34,493.5	16,027.7	11,115.9	1,548.7	5,801.2
1982	34,304.7	14,839.2	10,872.8	1,995.1	6,597.4
1984	36,104.5	15,292.4	10,163.2	2,710.4	7,938.6
1985	39,027.9	16,901.3	11,174.4	2,107.6	8,844.6
1986	39,745.0	17,049.9	11,065.6	2,620.0	9,009.4
1988	43,216.0	18,564.9	10,419.1	2,981.6	11,250.5
1990	51,624.3	21,984.4	13,650.9	3,383.0	12,606.0
1991	57,595.7	25,418.0	14,703.6	3,698.6	13,775.4
1992	60,479.8	27,926.9	14,384.1	3,992.0	14,176.9
1993	67,740.6	30,834.3	17,844.0	4,107.2	14,955.1
1994	68,811.5	32,304.4	16,734.4	4,483.7	15,289.1
1995	71,718.8	33,623.8	17,623.9	4,721.7	15,749.4
1996	70,857.0	35,202.8	14,802.3	4,941.4	15,910.6

Note: "Other education" includes funds for libraries, museums, cultural activities, and miscellaneous research.

Source: NCES, Federal Support for Education, Fiscal Years 1980 to 1996, NCES 97-384 (Washington: GPO, 1996), tbl. A.

IV

Earned Degrees

Highlights on Earned Degrees

ASSOCIATE DEGREES

- In academic year (AY) 1993–94, over half a million associate degrees were awarded in the 50 states and the District of Columbia.
- The number of associate degrees has increased by 20 percent since 1983–84, while the full-time enrollment (FTE) in two-year institutions increased by 14 percent in the same time period.
- Women were awarded nearly three-fifths (59 percent) of the associate degrees in 1993–94. That share has remained constant for the past several years.
- Public institutions awarded 84 percent of the associate degrees in 1993–94. The public share has ranged between 80 and 85 percent since 1980.

BACHELOR'S DEGREES

- Over one million bachelor's degrees were awarded in 1993–94. Although projections show a slight downturn in 1996–97, the figure remains in the 1.1 to 1.2 million range.
- The number of awards to women outstripped those to men by 100,000 in 1993–94, with 54 percent going to women. That difference is expected to continue to widen in the immediate future.
- Public institutions awarded more than twice as many bachelor's degrees—nearly 800,000—as independent institutions.
- Minorities earned 17 percent of the bachelor's degrees awarded in 1993–94. In 1984–85, the comparable figure was 12 percent.

FIRST-PROFESSIONAL DEGREES

- Slightly more than 75,000 first-professional degrees were awarded in 1993–94. The number of these degrees has stayed within a rather narrow range (70,000–75,000) since 1979–80. That figure is projected to rise to 77,000 for 1996–97.
- Three-fifths of these degrees were awarded to men. However, that proportion has been declining for the past 25 years. In 1969–70, men received 95 percent of first-professional degrees.
- The share of first-professional degrees awarded by independent institutions has held at around 60 percent for the past 25 years.
- Minorities were awarded 18 percent of the first-professional degrees in 1993–94. In 1984–85, they earned half that proportion (9 percent).

MASTER'S DEGREES

- The number of master's degrees awarded in 1993–94 reached 387,000. This is one-third greater than 10 years earlier (1983–84).
- Women now receive a greater proportion of these degrees (55 percent) than do men (45 percent). A decade ago, the split was about half male, half female.
- Independent institutions awarded about two-fifths of these degrees and have done so for the past decade.
- Minorities earned one-eighth (13 percent) of the master's degrees awarded in 1993–94. This compares with 10 percent of the degrees in 1984–85.
- More master's degrees were awarded in the field of education (99,000) than in any other major academic area.

DOCTORAL DEGREES

- The number of earned doctoral degrees awarded in 1993–94 was 43.2 thousand, topping the 40,000-degree mark for the third year in a row. The number is projected to reach 44.2 thousand in 1996–97.

- Men continued to receive a majority of these degrees—a proportion that has remained stable for the last 20 years.
- Minorities received 10 percent of the earned doctorates in 1993–94. In 1984–85, they received 9 percent.

- Just over one-quarter (27 percent) of the doctorates in 1993–94 were awarded to non-resident aliens. In 1984–85, the comparable figure was 16 percent.

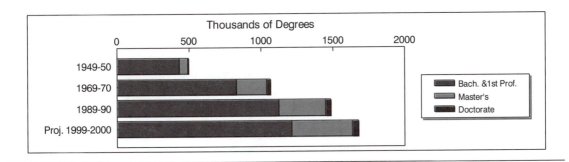

	Degrees Conferred						
	Number (in thousands)					Percentage Distribution	
	All		First-pro-			Bachelor's		
Year	Degrees	Bachelor's	fessional	Master's	Doctorate	& 1st Prof.	Master's	Doctorate
1949-50	496.7	432.1	na	58.2	6.4	87	12	1.3
1959-60	476.6	392.4	na	74.4	9.8	82	16	2.1
1964-65	659.8	493.8	28.3	121.2	16.5	79	18	2.5
1969-70	1,065.4	792.3	34.9	208.3	29.9	78	20	2.8
1974-75	1,305.4	922.9	55.9	292.5	34.1	75	22	2.6
1979-80	1,330.2	929.4	70.1	298.1	32.6	75	22	2.5
1981-82	1,353.2	953.0	72.0	295.5	32.7	76	22	2.4
1983-84	1,366.3	974.3	74.5	284.3	33.2	77	21	2.4
1984-85	1,373.7	979.4	75.1	286.3	32.9	77	21	2.4
1985-86	1,384.0	987.8	73.9	288.6	33.7	77	21	2.4
1987-88	1,399.7	994.8	70.7	299.3	34.9	76	21	2.5
1989-90	1,485.0	1,051.3	71.0	324.3	38.4	76	22	2.6
1990-91	1,542.9	1,094.5	71.9	337.2	39.3	76	22	2.5
1991-92	1,604.2	1,136.6	74.1	352.8	40.7	75	22	2.5
1992-93	1,652.3	1,165.2	75.4	369.6	42.1	75	22	2.5
1993-94	1,675.0	1,169.3	75.4	387.1	43.2	74	23	2.6
Projections								
1994-95	1,701.1	1,181.0	76.8	400.0	43.3	74	24	2.5
1995-96	1,714.3	1,186.0	78.7	406.0	43.6	74	24	2.5
1996-97	1,714.1	1,183.0	76.9	410.0	44.2	74	24	2.6
1999-2000	1,678.4	1,138.0	73.1	422.0	45.3	72	25	2.7

Note: Prior to 1964-65, first professional degrees are included with bachelor's degrees. Data are for 50 states and D.C. Percentages may not sum to 100 because of rounding.

Sources: See Guide to Sources.

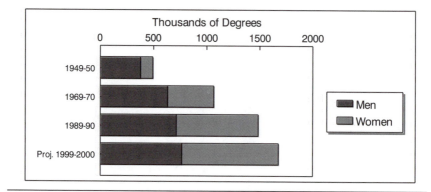

Year	Number of Degrees (All Levels) Conferred (in thousands)				
	Total	Men	Women	Public	Independent
1949-50	496.7	375.8	120.8	246.3	252.1
1959-60	476.6	313.8	162.9	262.8	216.4
1964-65	659.8	405.5	254.2	377.9	272.1
1969-70	1,065.4	635.7	429.7	692.5	379.7
1974-75	1,305.4	742.2	563.3	881.0	434.3
1979-80	1,330.2	699.9	630.2	860.1	470.1
1981-82	1,353.2	693.3	659.9	869.3	484.0
1983-84	1,366.3	699.4	666.9	867.4	498.9
1984-85	1,373.7	698.1	675.6	873.7	500.0
1985-86	1,384.0	700.5	683.4	879.5	504.4
1987-88	1,399.7	690.5	709.4	884.0	515.8
1989-90	1,485.0	713.8	771.2	939.5	545.4
1990-91	1,542.9	729.1	813.8	972.5	570.6
1991-92	1,604.2	753.3	850.9	1,019.1	585.1
1992-93	1,652.3	773.5	878.9	1,055.9	596.3
1993-94	1,675.0	779.8	895.2	1,068.8	606.0
Projections					
1994-95	1,701.1	792.6	908.5	1,080.2	620.9
1995-96	1,714.3	795.3	919.0	1,088.6	625.7
1996-97	1,714.1	795.0	919.1	1,088.5	625.6
1999-2000	1,678.4	768.2	909.2	1,065.8	612.6

Note: Prior to 1964-65, first professional degrees are included with bachelor's degrees. Data for men and women for all years are for 50 states and D.C. Data for the public and independent sectors prior to 1979-80 include "outlying parts" of the U.S., i.e., Puerto Rico, Canal Zone, etc. Projections for public/independent data for 1994-95 and later are based on the 1990-94 average distributions.

Sources: See Guide to Sources.

Bachelor's Degrees, by Sex of Student and Control of Institution, Selected Years, 1948–2000

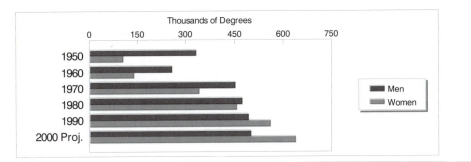

Year	Total	Men	Women	Public	Independent
			Number of Bachelor's Degrees (in thousands)		
1947-48	272.3	176.1	96.2	136.2	136.1
1949-50	433.7	329.8	103.9	217.4	216.3
1954-55	287.4	183.6	103.8	147.4	140.0
1959-60	394.9	255.5	139.4	214.7	180.2
1964-65	493.0	279.8	213.2	289.0	204.0
1969-70	792.3	451.1	341.2	519.6	272.8
1974-75	922.9	504.8	418.1	634.8	288.1
1979-80	929.4	473.6	455.8	624.1	305.3
1981-82	953.0	473.4	479.6	636.5	316.5
1983-84	974.3	482.3	492.0	646.0	328.3
1984-85	979.4	482.5	496.9	652.2	327.2
1985-86	987.8	485.9	501.9	658.6	329.2
1987-88	994.8	477.2	517.6	658.5	336.3
1989-90	1,051.3	491.7	559.6	700.0	351.3
1990-91	1,094.5	504.0	590.5	724.1	370.5
1991-92	1,136.5	520.8	615.7	759.5	377.1
1992-93	1,165.2	532.9	632.3	785.1	380.1
1993-94	1,169.3	532.4	636.9	789.1	380.1
			Projections		
1994-95	1,181.0	533.0	648.0	790.0	391.0
1995-96	1,186.0	531.0	655.0	793.0	393.0
1996-97	1,183.0	528.0	655.0	791.0	392.0
1999-2000	1,138.0	500.0	637.0	761.0	377.0

Note: Data prior to 1969-70 are for aggregate U.S. For later years, data are for 50 states and D.C. Figures through 1959-60 include first-professional degrees. Projections for public/independent data are based on average distributions for the 1990-94 period.

Sources: See Guide to Sources.

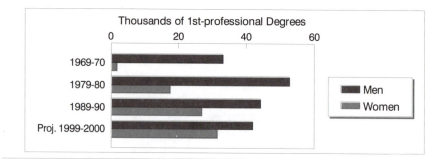

Year	Number of First-professional Degrees (in thousands)				
	Total	Men	Women	Public	Independent
1960-61	25.3	24.6	0.7	8.9	16.4
1964-65	28.3	27.3	1.0	11.2	17.1
1969-70	34.9	33.1	1.8	14.5	20.4
1974-75	55.9	49.0	7.0	23.6	32.3
1979-80	70.1	52.7	17.4	27.9	42.2
1981-82	72.0	52.2	19.8	29.6	42.4
1983-84	74.5	51.4	23.1	29.6	44.9
1984-85	75.1	50.5	24.6	30.2	44.9
1985-86	73.9	49.3	24.6	29.6	44.3
1987-88	70.7	45.5	25.3	29.2	41.6
1989-90	71.0	44.0	27.0	28.8	42.2
1990-91	71.9	43.8	28.1	29.6	42.4
1991-92	74.1	45.1	29.1	29.4	44.8
1992-93	75.4	45.2	30.2	29.6	45.8
1993-94	75.4	44.7	30.7	29.8	45.6
Projections					
1994-95	76.8	45.0	31.8	30.7	46.1
1995-96	78.7	45.6	33.1	31.5	47.2
1996-97	76.9	46.2	30.7	30.8	46.1
1999-2000	73.1	41.7	31.4	29.3	43.8

Note: Data are for 50 states and D.C.

Data show first-professional degrees that require at least two years of college work for admission and a total of six or more years of work for the degree. Projections for public/independent data are based on average distributions for the 1990-94 period.

Sources: See Guide to Sources.

135

Master's Degrees, by Sex of Student and Control of Institution, Selected Years, 1948–2000

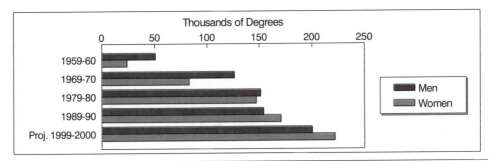

Year	Number of Master's Degrees (in thousands)				
	Total	Men	Women	Public	Independent
1947-48	42.4	28.9	13.5	17.7	24.7
1949-50	58.2	41.2	17.0	26.2	32.0
1954-55	58.2	38.7	19.5	32.3	25.9
1959-60	74.5	50.9	23.6	43.0	31.5
1964-65	112.2	76.2	36.0	68.2	44.0
1969-70	208.3	125.6	82.7	134.5	73.7
1974-75	292.5	161.6	130.9	193.8	98.6
1979-80	298.1	150.7	147.3	187.5	110.6
1981-82	295.5	145.5	150.0	182.3	113.3
1983-84	284.3	143.6	140.7	170.7	113.6
1984-85	286.3	143.4	142.9	170.0	116.3
1985-86	288.6	143.5	145.1	169.9	118.7
1987-88	299.3	145.2	154.2	173.8	125.5
1989-90	324.3	153.7	170.6	186.1	138.2
1990-91	337.2	156.5	180.7	193.1	144.1
1991-92	352.8	161.8	191.0	203.4	149.4
1992-93	369.6	169.3	200.3	213.8	155.7
1993-94	387.1	176.1	211.0	221.4	165.6
Projections					
1994-95	400.0	188.0	212.0	230.0	170.0
1995-96	406.0	192.0	214.0	233.0	173.0
1996-97	410.0	194.0	216.0	236.0	174.0
1999-2000	422.0	200.0	222.0	243.0	179.0

Note: Data prior to 1969-70 are for aggregate U.S. For later years, data are for 50 states and D.C.
Figures through 1964-65 generally exclude those master's degrees that are considered
first-professional degrees such as master of library science and social work. Data for later years
include all master's degrees. Public/independent data for projections are based on the 1990 - 1994
average distributions.

Sources: See Guide to Sources.

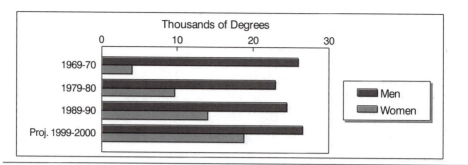

Year	Number of Doctoral Degrees (in thousands)				
	Total	Men	Women	Public	Independent
1947-48	4.0	3.5	0.5	1.6	2.4
1949-50	6.4	5.8	0.6	2.7	3.7
1954-55	8.8	8.0	0.8	4.5	4.3
1959-60	9.8	8.8	1.0	5.1	4.7
1964-65	16.5	14.7	1.8	9.5	7.0
1969-70	29.9	25.9	4.0	19.2	10.7
1974-75	34.1	26.8	7.3	22.2	11.9
1979-80	32.6	22.9	9.7	20.6	12.0
1981-82	32.7	22.2	10.5	20.9	11.8
1983-84	33.2	22.1	11.1	21.1	12.1
1984-85	32.9	21.7	11.2	21.3	11.6
1985-86	33.7	21.8	11.8	21.5	12.2
1987-88	34.9	22.6	12.3	22.5	12.4
1989-90	38.4	24.4	14.0	24.7	13.7
1990-91	39.3	24.8	14.5	25.7	13.6
1991-92	40.7	25.6	15.1	26.9	13.8
1992-93	42.1	26.1	16.1	27.4	14.7
1993-94	43.2	26.6	16.6	28.5	14.7
Projections					
1994-95	43.3	26.6	16.7	28.3	15.0
1995-96	43.6	26.7	16.9	28.5	15.1
1996-97	44.2	26.8	17.4	28.9	15.3
1999-2000	45.3	26.5	18.8	29.6	15.7

Note: Data prior to 1969-70 are for aggregate U.S. For later years, data are for 50 states
and D.C. In addition to the Ph.D., figures include data for Ed.D., S.T.D. Excluded are honorary
doctorates and first-professional degrees, such as M.D., D.D.S., D.V.M., and J.D.
Public/independent data for projections are based on the 1990 - 1994 average distributions.

Sources: See Guide to Sources.

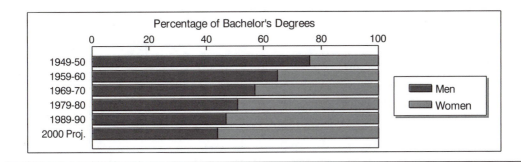

Percentage of Bachelor's Degrees

Percentage of Degrees								
	Bachelor's		1st-Professional		Master's		Doctorate	
Year	Men	Women	Men	Women	Men	Women	Men	Women
1947-48	65	35	na	na	68	32	88	13
1949-50	76	24	na	na	71	29	91	9
1954-55	64	36	na	na	66	34	91	9
1959-60	65	35	na	na	68	32	90	10
1964-65	57	43	96	4	68	32	89	11
1969-70	57	43	95	5	60	40	87	13
1974-75	55	45	88	13	55	45	79	21
1979-80	51	49	75	25	51	49	70	30
1981-82	50	50	73	28	49	51	68	32
1983-84	50	50	69	31	51	49	67	33
1984-85	49	51	67	33	50	50	66	34
1985-86	49	51	67	33	50	50	65	35
1987-88	48	52	64	36	49	52	65	35
1989-90	47	53	62	38	47	53	64	36
1990-91	46	54	61	39	46	54	63	37
1991-92	46	54	61	39	46	54	63	37
1992-93	46	54	60	40	46	54	62	38
1993-94	46	54	59	41	45	55	62	38
Projections								
1994-95	45	55	59	41	47	53	61	39
1995-96	45	55	58	42	47	53	61	39
1996-97	45	56	60	40	47	53	61	39
1999-2000	44	56	57	43	47	53	58	42

na: Not available.

Source: Calculated from preceding tables, 133 - 136.

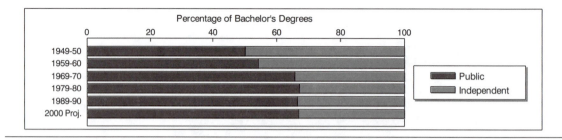

Percentage of Bachelor's Degrees

Percentage of Degrees								
	Bachelor's		1st-Professional		Master's		Doctorate	
Year	Public	Independent	Public	Independent	Public	Independent	Public	Independent
1947-48	50	50	na	na	42	58	40	60
1949-50	50	50	na	na	45	55	42	58
1954-55	51	49	na	na	55	45	51	49
1959-60	54	46	na	na	58	42	52	48
1964-65	59	41	39	61	61	39	58	42
1969-70	66	34	42	58	65	35	64	36
1974-75	69	31	42	58	66	34	65	35
1979-80	67	33	40	60	63	37	63	37
1981-82	67	33	41	59	62	38	64	36
1983-84	66	34	40	60	60	40	64	36
1984-85	67	33	40	60	59	41	65	35
1985-86	67	33	40	60	59	41	64	36
1987-88	66	34	41	59	58	42	64	36
1989-90	67	33	41	59	57	43	64	36
1990-91	66	34	41	59	57	43	65	35
1991-92	67	33	40	60	58	42	66	34
1992-93	67	33	39	61	58	42	65	35
1993-94	67	33	40	60	57	43	66	34
Projections								
1994-95	67	33	40	60	58	43	65	35
1995-96	67	33	40	60	57	43	65	35
1996-97	67	33	40	60	58	42	65	35
1999-2000	67	33	40	60	58	42	65	35

na: Not available.
Data for 1994-95 and beyond are based on average distributions for the 1990-94 period.

Source: Calculated from preceding tables, 133 - 136.

Percentage of Earned Doctorates Awarded to Women, by Selected Field of Study, Selected Years, 1950–1994

Percentage of Doctorates Awarded

Field of Study	Percentage of Doctorates Awarded to Women					
	1949-50	1959-60	1969-70	1974-75	1984-85	1993-94
All Fields	9	10	13	21	34	38
Humanities						
English	21	21	31	41	55	58
French	28	38	46	65	68	70
German	20	33	30	44	59	53
Philosophy	17	18	12	15	18	28
Spanish	24	35	39	47	65	71
Education	16	19	20	31	52	61
Social Sciences						
Anthropology	21	17	27	35	49	53
Economics	4	4	5	8	16	24
History	11	9	13	22	35	37
Political Science	8	8	11	16	26	29
Psychology	15	15	22	31	49	62
Sociology	18	16	19	30	52	51
Biological Sciences						
Bacteriology/ microbiology	19	14	21	26	37	43
Biochemistry	15	13	15	22	30	41
Biology, general	15	11	20	28	34	41
Botany	8	7	9	13	27	34
Zoology	18	14	10	24	30	36
Physical Sciences						
Chemistry	4	5	8	11	20	28
Mathematics	6	6	8	11	16	22
Physics	1	2	3	5	9	12

Source: USOE/US Department of Education, NCES, "Degrees & Other Formal Awards Conferred" surveys.

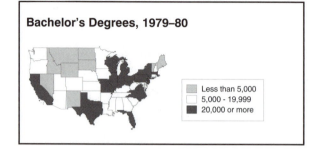

Bachelor's Degrees, 1979–80

Less than 5,000
5,000 - 19,999
20,000 or more

Region and State	Bachelor's Degrees (in thousands)			
	1969-70	1979-80	1989-90	1993-94
50 States & D.C.	**792.3**	**929.4**	**1,051.3**	**1,169.3**
New England	**56.4**	**73.0**	**82.6**	**83.6**
Connecticut	10.9	13.0	14.2	13.9
Maine	4.1	4.8	4.9	6.0
Massachusetts	29.5	38.3	43.5	42.4
New Hampshire	4.2	5.8	6.7	7.5
Rhode Island	4.8	7.1	8.8	9.1
Vermont	2.9	4.0	4.5	4.7
Mideast	**152.3**	**190.0**	**202.5**	**214.7**
Delaware	1.5	3.3	3.5	4.2
D.C.	5.9	6.5	7.5	7.2
Maryland	12.1	15.7	18.5	20.7
New Jersey	18.0	24.4	22.9	25.2
New York	67.5	85.1	89.6	93.1
Pennsylvania	47.3	55.0	60.5	64.3
Southeast	**152.3**	**186.2**	**211.1**	**251.2**
Alabama	12.9	16.3	17.1	21.2
Arkansas	7.3	7.0	7.5	8.5
Florida	19.8	28.6	35.6	44.1
Georgia	13.9	16.6	21.4	26.3
Kentucky	12.0	11.5	12.2	14.6
Louisiana	13.6	14.8	15.9	17.8
Mississippi	8.8	8.8	8.8	10.5
North Carolina	18.6	23.7	27.3	32.7
South Carolina	7.8	11.9	13.2	15.3
Tennessee	15.9	17.9	17.6	20.0
Virginia	13.7	21.7	27.1	31.2
West Virginia	8.0	7.4	7.4	9.0
Great Lakes	**158.6**	**168.5**	**193.2**	**206.5**
Illinois	38.4	44.2	49.8	52.3
Indiana	22.2	24.2	27.7	30.8
Michigan	35.3	37.6	42.4	44.9
Ohio	41.8	40.7	47.0	51.0
Wisconsin	20.9	21.8	26.3	27.5

Continued on next page.

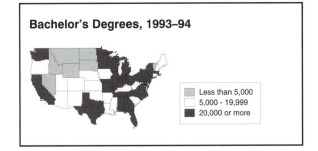

Bachelor's Degrees, 1993–94

Less than 5,000
5,000 - 19,999
20,000 or more

Region and State	Bachelor's Degrees (in thousands)			
	1969-70	1979-80	1989-90	1993-94
Plains	**80.7**	**80.8**	**92.6**	**103.5**
Iowa	14.3	13.5	16.1	17.8
Kansas	12.2	11.7	12.4	14.6
Minnesota	18.0	18.6	22.9	24.7
Missouri	18.3	21.8	24.7	27.5
Nebraska	9.4	7.6	8.7	10.1
North Dakota	3.9	3.7	4.2	4.6
South Dakota	4.6	3.9	3.6	4.2
Southwest	**64.2**	**81.2**	**93.9**	**107.2**
Arizona	7.9	10.2	14.3	16.1
New Mexico	4.1	4.7	5.0	6.1
Oklahoma	12.0	12.7	13.6	15.7
Texas	40.2	53.6	61.0	69.3
Rocky Mountains	**28.5**	**31.5**	**36.0**	**43.6**
Colorado	11.9	14.1	16.4	19.0
Idaho	2.7	2.9	3.2	4.2
Montana	3.7	3.9	3.9	4.4
Utah	8.8	9.3	10.9	14.2
Wyoming	1.4	1.3	1.6	1.8
Far West	**96.2**	**114.7**	**136.1**	**155.4**
Alaska	0.3	0.4	1.0	1.4
California	67.8	83.1	98.2	111.8
Hawaii	2.6	3.2	3.7	4.3
Nevada	1.0	1.4	2.2	3.3
Oregon	9.9	10.4	12.6	13.3
Washington	14.6	16.2	18.4	21.3
U.S. Service Schools	**2.8**	**3.2**	**3.3**	**3.4**

Note: Each year's data are for twelve months ending June 30.

Sources: 1 NCES, Digest of Education Statistics (Washington: GPO), 1983-84, tbl. 99;
    1993, tbl. 236; 1996, tbl. 240.
    2 _____, Earned Degrees Conferred, 1969-70, Summary Data (Washington: GPO, 1972), tbl. 3.

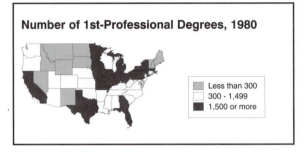

Number of 1st-Professional Degrees, 1980

Legend:
- Less than 300
- 300 - 1,499
- 1,500 or more

Region and State	First-professional Degrees			
	1969-70	1979-80	1989-90	1993-94
50 States & D.C.	**34,918**	**70,131**	**70,988**	**75,418**
New England	**2,388**	**4,949**	**5,105**	**5,075**
Connecticut	440	946	956	769
Maine	45	110	162	173
Massachusetts	1,845	3,480	3,653	3,771
New Hampshire	0	175	165	182
Rhode Island	0	61	82	87
Vermont	58	177	87	93
Mideast	**8,639**	**14,725**	**16,223**	**16,749**
Delaware	0	0	329	461
D.C.	1,453	2,375	2,498	2,420
Maryland	782	907	971	972
New Jersey	672	1,497	1,763	1,709
New York	3,517	6,255	7,200	7,442
Pennsylvania	2,215	3,691	3,462	3,745
Southeast	**6,225**	**12,666**	**13,699**	**14,726**
Alabama	413	893	832	908
Arkansas	191	371	324	441
Florida	632	1,799	2,138	2,382
Georgia	759	1,603	1,835	2,015
Kentucky	731	1,330	1,127	1,118
Louisiana	784	1,396	1,459	1,582
Mississippi	188	375	477	478
North Carolina	665	1,468	1,597	1,673
South Carolina	233	405	587	627
Tennessee	814	1,323	1,289	1,296
Virginia	657	1,352	1,732	1,839
West Virginia	158	351	302	367
Great Lakes	**6,859**	**13,233**	**12,293**	**12,738**
Illinois	2,254	4,532	4,412	4,321
Indiana	906	1,513	1,420	1,454
Michigan	1,408	2,705	2,418	2,746
Ohio	1,769	3,549	3,076	3,251
Wisconsin	522	934	967	966

Continued on next page.

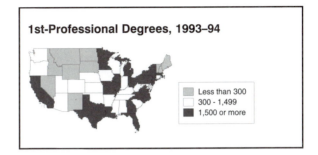

| Region | First-professional Degrees | | | |
and State	1969-70	1979-80	1989-90	1993-94
Plains	**3,573**	**7,163**	**6,706**	**6,944**
Iowa	526	1,675	1,427	1,442
Kansas	379	643	566	619
Minnesota	785	1,501	1,561	1,536
Missouri	1,391	2,333	2,283	2,206
Nebraska	407	776	658	811
North Dakota	37	111	109	189
South Dakota	48	124	102	141
Southwest	**2,667**	**5,333**	**5,619**	**6,268**
Arizona	132	348	408	462
New Mexico	58	165	179	192
Oklahoma	404	960	923	846
Texas	2,073	3,860	4,109	4,768
Rocky Mountains	**671**	**1,385**	**1,436**	**1,460**
Colorado	427	800	794	809
Idaho	26	80	124	148
Montana	34	74	71	70
Utah	153	371	380	367
Wyoming	31	60	67	66
Far West	**3,896**	**10,649**	**9,756**	**11,303**
Alaska	0	0	0	0
California	3,153	8,518	7,814	9,228
Hawaii	0	128	113	172
Nevada	0	36	49	39
Oregon	397	1,033	928	946
Washington	346	934	852	918
U.S. Service Schools	**0**	**28**	**151**	**155**

Note: Each year's data are for twelve months ending June 30.

Sources: 1 NCES, Digest of Education Statistics (Washington: GPO), 1983-84, tbl. 99;
1993, tbl. 236; 1996, tbl 240.

2 _____, Earned Degrees Conferred, 1969-70, Summary Data (Washington: GPO, 1972), tbl. 3.

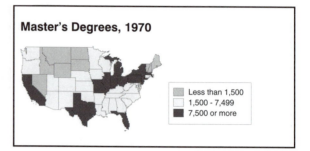

Master's Degrees, 1970

Less than 1,500
1,500 - 7,499
7,500 or more

Region and State	Master's Degrees (in thousands)			
	1969-70	1979-80	1989-90	1993-94
50 States & D.C.	**208.3**	**298.1**	**324.3**	**387.1**
New England	**17.6**	**24.5**	**29.5**	**33.6**
Connecticut	4.0	5.6	6.3	6.6
Maine	0.6	0.6	0.7	0.9
Massachusetts	10.8	14.7	17.8	20.7
New Hampshire	0.6	0.9	1.9	2.2
Rhode Island	1.1	1.5	1.8	2.0
Vermont	0.6	1.2	1.0	1.2
Mideast	**50.4**	**65.0**	**71.7**	**85.6**
Delaware	0.4	0.5	0.8	1.0
D.C.	4.1	5.5	5.1	6.3
Maryland	3.0	5.1	6.4	8.2
New Jersey	5.0	8.0	7.2	8.3
New York	26.8	32.8	37.4	42.9
Pennsylvania	11.1	13.1	14.8	18.9
Southeast	**29.0**	**55.5**	**57.0**	**71.5**
Alabama	2.3	5.5	4.5	5.8
Arkansas	1.2	1.8	1.7	2.0
Florida	4.3	8.3	10.8	14.1
Georgia	3.3	6.8	6.4	8.3
Kentucky	2.6	5.2	3.7	4.0
Louisiana	3.1	4.2	4.0	5.2
Mississippi	1.4	2.8	2.4	2.6
North Carolina	3.2	5.3	6.0	7.3
South Carolina	0.8	3.3	3.8	4.5
Tennessee	3.1	4.8	4.8	5.7
Virginia	2.6	5.3	7.2	10.0
West Virginia	1.2	2.2	1.7	2.0
Great Lakes	**45.9**	**58.0**	**58.8**	**67.5**
Illinois	12.7	16.3	19.3	23.7
Indiana	8.1	8.3	7.4	7.0
Michigan	12.0	15.1	13.3	15.5
Ohio	8.8	13.0	13.0	15.0
Wisconsin	4.2	5.3	5.8	6.3

Continued on next page.

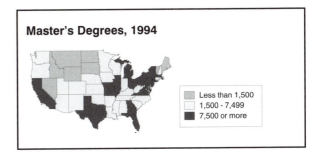

Master's Degrees, 1994

Less than 1,500
1,500 - 7,499
7,500 or more

Region and State	Master's Degrees (in thousands)			
	1969-70	1979-80	1989-90	1993-94
Plains	**15.9**	**19.3**	**22.4**	**27.8**
Iowa	2.2	2.6	3.0	3.5
Kansas	2.9	3.1	3.3	4.6
Minnesota	2.6	3.2	4.4	5.7
Missouri	5.3	7.6	8.6	10.1
Nebraska	1.2	1.7	1.7	2.2
North Dakota	0.7	0.5	0.6	0.7
South Dakota	0.9	0.6	0.8	1.0
Southwest	**15.5**	**25.9**	**29.0**	**35.5**
Arizona	2.8	3.9	5.2	6.4
New Mexico	1.3	1.7	1.8	2.3
Oklahoma	2.9	3.5	3.9	5.0
Texas	8.5	16.8	18.1	21.8
Rocky Mountains	**6.5**	**8.9**	**9.5**	**12.0**
Colorado	3.3	5.0	5.1	6.9
Idaho	0.4	0.7	0.8	1.0
Montana	0.6	0.6	0.7	0.8
Utah	1.8	2.3	2.5	2.8
Wyoming	0.3	0.3	0.4	0.5
Far West	**26.8**	**40.2**	**44.9**	**52.3**
Alaska	0.2	0.2	0.3	0.4
California	19.5	31.1	34.5	38.7
Hawaii	1.0	1.0	1.0	1.4
Nevada	0.2	0.4	0.5	0.9
Oregon	2.9	3.2	3.3	3.6
Washington	3.0	4.3	5.3	7.3
U.S. Service Schools	**0.9**	**1.0**	**1.2**	**1.3**

Note: Each year's data are for twelve months ending June 30.

Sources: 1 NCES, Digest of Education Statistics (Washington: GPO), 1983-84, tbl. 99;
1993, tbl. 236; 1996, tbl. 240.

2 _____, Earned Degrees Conferred, 1969-70, Summary Data (Washington: GPO, 1972), tbl. 3.

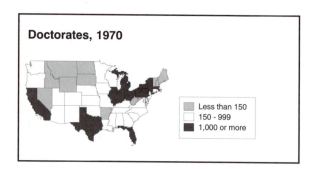

Doctorates, 1970

Less than 150
150 - 999
1,000 or more

Region and State	Doctoral Degrees			
	1969-70	1979-80	1989-90	1993-94
50 States & D.C.	**29,866**	**32,615**	**38,371**	**43,185**
New England	**2,480**	**2,652**	**3,060**	**3,380**
Connecticut	511	499	572	646
Maine	24	21	34	53
Massachusetts	1,676	1,839	2,122	2,228
New Hampshire	49	58	83	136
Rhode Island	187	203	190	255
Vermont	33	32	59	62
Mideast	**6,483**	**6,775**	**8,203**	**8,848**
Delaware	60	70	114	121
D.C.	498	487	540	489
Maryland	576	529	816	934
New Jersey	565	645	855	1,032
New York	3,292	3,375	3,842	4,025
Pennsylvania	1,492	1,669	2,036	2,247
Southeast	**3,707**	**5,441**	**6,354**	**7,531**
Alabama	221	249	354	476
Arkansas	124	110	135	146
Florida	668	1,536	1,251	1,644
Georgia	345	549	800	813
Kentucky	173	271	320	401
Louisiana	348	314	405	447
Mississippi	178	226	293	352
North Carolina	634	757	861	988
South Carolina	115	191	342	459
Tennessee	452	543	626	672
Virginia	306	550	839	1,006
West Virginia	143	145	128	127
Great Lakes	**6,970**	**6,490**	**7,333**	**8,261**
Illinois	1,884	1,872	2,409	2,592
Indiana	1,313	1,036	1,040	1,103
Michigan	1,577	1,334	1,313	1,483
Ohio	1,262	1,488	1,709	2,127
Wisconsin	934	760	862	956

Continued on next page.

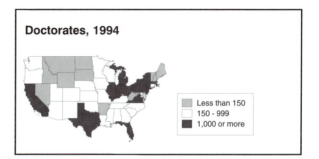

Doctorates, 1994

Less than 150
150 - 999
1,000 or more

Region and State	Doctoral Degrees			
	1969-70	1979-80	1989-90	1993-94
Plains	**2,547**	**2,401**	**2,664**	**3,177**
Iowa	620	532	604	689
Kansas	389	388	346	415
Minnesota	546	503	750	917
Missouri	630	637	619	778
Nebraska	213	221	230	244
North Dakota	86	83	71	74
South Dakota	63	37	44	60
Southwest	**2,290**	**2,620**	**3,444**	**4,116**
Arizona	383	417	545	754
New Mexico	182	166	223	243
Oklahoma	484	377	408	387
Texas	1,241	1,660	2,268	2,732
Rocky Mountains	**1,224**	**1,258**	**1,298**	**1,321**
Colorado	636	618	718	765
Idaho	45	55	90	88
Montana	63	56	71	57
Utah	413	453	361	338
Wyoming	67	76	58	73
Far West	**4,153**	**4,963**	**5,991**	**6,512**
Alaska	7	0	8	24
California	3,175	3,981	4,747	5,034
Hawaii	53	103	114	175
Nevada	11	21	38	52
Oregon	441	346	452	531
Washington	466	512	632	696
U.S. Service Schools	**12**	**15**	**24**	**39**

Note: Each year's data are for twelve months ending June 30. Degrees tabulated here include Ph.D.'s, Ed.D.'s, and their equivalents. Excluded are honorary doctorates and first-professional degrees such as M.D.'s, D.D.S.'s, etc.

Sources: 1 NCES, Digest of Education Statistics (Washington: GPO), 1983-84, tbl. 99; 1993, tbl. 236; 1996, tbl. 240.

2 _____, Earned Degrees Conferred, 1969-70, Summary Data (Washington: GPO, 1972), tbl. 3.

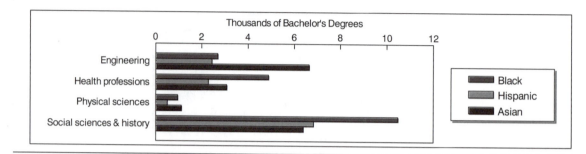

Thousands of Bachelor's Degrees

Academic Area	Black, non-His-panic	Ameri-can Indian	Asian	His-panic	Total Minor-ity	White, non-His-panic	Non-resident Alien	Total
					Number of Bachelor's Degrees			
All areas	83,576	6,189	55,660	50,241	195,666	936,227	34,080	1,165,973
Men	30,648	2,616	26,938	21,807	82,009	429,121	19,674	530,804
Women	52,928	3,573	28,722	28,434	113,657	507,106	14,406	635,169
Agriculture & natural resources	502	128	309	386	1,325	16,404	341	18,070
Architecture	348	36	717	479	1,580	6,961	434	8,975
Area and ethnic studies	636	53	479	484	1,652	3,737	184	5,573
Biological sciences	3,022	252	6,083	2,137	11,494	38,736	1,153	51,383
Business management	20,366	1,036	12,486	10,264	44,152	191,111	11,391	246,654
Communications & comm. tech.	4,210	225	1,312	1,952	7,699	42,988	1,140	51,827
Computer & info. sciences	2,455	79	2,301	899	5,734	16,191	2,275	24,200
Education	6,316	739	1,122	3,295	11,472	95,482	646	107,600
Engineering	2,712	223	6,652	2,452	12,039	45,639	4,542	62,220
Engineering technologies	1,190	98	726	651	2,665	12,682	476	15,823
English language & lit.	3,250	262	1,738	1,980	7,230	46,166	528	53,924
Foreign languages & lit.	510	55	588	1,798	2,951	10,963	464	14,378
Health professions	4,896	398	3,070	2,274	10,638	62,756	1,027	74,421
Home economics	959	87	476	394	1,916	13,369	237	15,522
Law and legal studies	208	14	87	121	430	1,735	6	2,171
Liberal arts, gen. studies	2,968	302	1,072	2,084	6,426	26,450	521	33,397
Library science	4	0	0	0	4	54	4	62
Mathematics	1,004	61	944	526	2,535	11,300	561	14,396
Multi/interdisciplinary studies	1,687	141	1,340	1,884	5,052	19,778	337	25,167
Parks, recreation, fitness	556	75	118	424	1,173	10,190	107	11,470
Philosophy and religion	319	35	336	305	995	6,416	135	7,546
Physical sciences	946	85	1,126	523	2,680	15,007	713	18,400
Protective services	3,482	160	403	1,412	5,457	17,393	159	23,009
Psychology	5,359	404	2,841	3,581	12,185	56,220	854	69,259
Public administration	2,717	188	396	1,067	4,368	13,253	194	17,815
Social sciences & history	10,460	783	6,408	6,851	24,502	105,776	3,402	133,680
Theological studies	188	20	159	121	488	4,770	176	5,434
Visual and performing arts	2,068	228	2,279	1,754	6,329	40,757	1,967	49,053
Other	238	22	92	143	495	3,943	106	4,544

Note: Data are for 50 states and D.C. Asian category includes Pacific Islanders. American Indian category includes Alaskan Natives.

Source: NCES, Digest of Education Statistics, 1996 (Washington: GPO, 1996), tbl. 260.

145 First-professional Degrees, by Race/Ethnicity and Academic Area, 1993–94

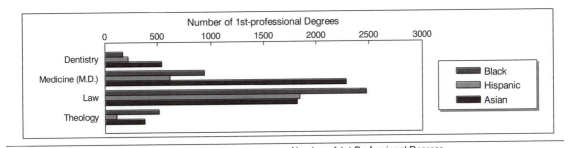

					Number of 1st Professional Degrees			
Profession	Black, non-His-panic	Ameri-can Indian	Asian	His-panic	Total Minor-ity	White, non-His-panic	Non-resident Alien	Total
All professions	4,444	371	5,892	3,134	13,841	60,140	1,437	75,418
Men	1,902	222	3,214	1,781	7,119	36,573	1,015	44,707
Women	2,542	149	2,678	1,353	6,722	23,567	422	30,711
Dentistry	171	17	538	218	944	2,559	284	3,787
Medicine (M.D.)	937	68	2,282	613	3,900	11,287	181	15,368
Optometry	36	3	153	38	230	818	55	1,103
Osteopathic medicine	48	8	182	70	308	1,478	12	1,798
Podiatry	32	2	43	41	118	339	8	465
Veterinary medicine	39	14	40	66	159	1,923	7	2,089
Chiropractic medicine	40	19	115	80	254	2,370	182	2,806
Pharmacy	155	1	347	54	557	1,297	82	1,936
Law	2,472	223	1,816	1,842	6,353	33,420	271	40,044
Theology	513	16	375	109	1,013	4,607	347	5,967
Other	1	0	1	3	5	42	8	55

Note: Data are for 50 states and D.C. Asian category includes Pacific Islanders. American Indian category includes Alaskan Natives.

Source: NCES, Digest of Education Statistics, 1996 (Washington: GPO, 1996), tbl. 269.

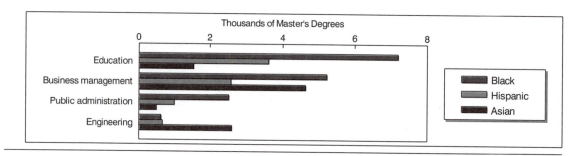

Academic Area	Black, non-His-panic	Ameri-can Indian	Asian	His-panic	Total Minor-ity	White, non-His-panic	Non-resident Alien	Total
All areas	21,937	1,697	15,267	11,913	50,814	288,288	46,317	385,419
Men	7,413	691	8,225	5,113	21,442	123,854	30,059	175,355
Women	14,524	1,006	7,042	6,800	29,372	164,434	16,258	210,064
Agriculture & natural resources	116	12	96	190	414	2,767	938	4,119
Architecture	144	12	221	135	512	2,676	755	3,943
Area and ethnic studies	113	17	103	96	329	1,129	175	1,633
Biological sciences	149	18	347	126	640	3,621	935	5,196
Business management	5,213	299	4,625	2,568	12,705	67,669	13,063	93,437
Communications & comm. tech.	364	23	149	117	653	3,872	894	5,419
Computer & info. sciences	391	19	1,317	176	1,903	4,605	3,908	10,416
Education	7,199	605	1,534	3,601	12,939	83,065	2,934	98,938
Engineering	623	64	2,586	670	3,943	15,327	9,351	28,621
Engineering technologies	59	1	37	30	127	820	186	1,133
English language & lit.	248	39	202	195	684	6,781	420	7,885
Foreign languages & lit.	49	9	137	307	502	2,158	628	3,288
Health professions	1,496	137	1,007	710	3,350	23,175	1,500	28,025
Home economics	139	7	70	56	272	1,928	221	2,421
Law and legal studies	47	7	61	76	191	1,218	1,023	2,432
Liberal arts, gen. studies	125	14	34	48	221	2,125	150	2,496
Library science	244	14	150	92	500	4,409	207	5,116
Mathematics	118	6	250	71	445	2,559	1,096	4,100
Multi/interdisciplinary studies	111	14	62	95	282	2,024	158	2,464
Parks, recreation, fitness	78	8	28	22	136	1,361	128	1,625
Philosophy and religion	38	3	38	53	132	1,102	116	1,350
Physical sciences	136	17	301	102	556	3,354	1,769	5,679
Protective services	220	7	23	48	298	1,092	47	1,437
Psychology	659	65	280	483	1,487	10,333	361	12,181
Public administration	2,506	143	495	990	4,134	16,891	808	21,833
Social sciences & history	737	71	481	459	1,748	10,247	2566	14,561
Theological studies	259	10	226	125	620	3,773	563	4,956
Visual and performing arts	327	51	388	253	1,019	7,496	1,410	9,925
Other	29	5	19	19	72	711	7	790

Note: Data are for 50 states and D.C. Asian category includes Pacific Islanders. American Indian category includes Alaskan Natives.

Source: NCES, Digest of Education Statistics, 1996 (Washington: GPO, 1996), tbl. 263.

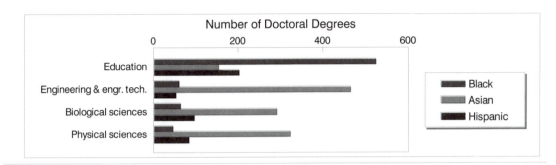

Number of Doctoral Degrees

Academic Area	Black, non-His-panic	Ameri-can Indian	Asian	His-panic	Total Minor-ity	White, non-His-panic	Non-resident Alien	Total
All areas	1,393	134	2,025	903	4,455	27,156	11,538	43,149
Men	631	66	1,373	465	2,535	15,126	8,870	26,531
Women	762	68	652	438	1,920	12,030	2,668	16,618
Agriculture & natural resources	16	2	34	18	70	596	612	1,278
Architecture	4	1	6	0	11	65	85	161
Area and ethnic studies	16	4	8	2	30	99	26	155
Biological sciences	64	9	291	96	460	2,828	1,246	4,534
Business management	38	7	66	13	124	847	393	1,364
Communications & comm. tech.	23	3	6	7	39	225	81	345
Computer & info. sciences	11	1	64	5	81	366	363	810
Education	523	42	152	201	918	5,393	597	6,908
Engineering & engr. tech.	60	5	464	52	581	2,210	3,188	5,979
English language & lit.	32	9	24	26	91	1,088	165	1,344
Foreign languages & lit.	8	0	24	73	105	514	267	886
Health professions	59	7	104	26	196	1,282	424	1,902
Home economics	10	1	9	5	25	279	61	365
Law and legal studies	1	0	3	7	11	16	52	79
Liberal arts, gen. studies	7	0	5	2	14	59	7	80
Library science	3	0	2	1	6	31	8	45
Mathematics	7	1	83	11	102	494	561	1,157
Multi/interdisciplinary studies	10	4	5	6	25	140	62	227
Parks, recreation, fitness	3	1	2	1	7	78	31	116
Philosophy and religion	22	0	16	5	43	417	68	528
Physical sciences	46	6	323	83	458	2,536	1,656	4,650
Protective services	2	0	0	1	3	19	3	25
Psychology	126	11	93	140	370	3,027	166	3,563
Public administration	44	4	14	14	76	356	87	519
Social sciences & history	123	12	130	73	338	2,318	971	3,627
Theological studies	113	2	66	17	198	1,058	192	1,448
Visual and performing arts	22	2	31	18	73	815	166	1,054

Note: Data are for 50 states and D.C. Asian category includes Pacific Islanders. American Indian category includes Alaskan Natives.

Source: NCES, Digest of Education Statistics, 1996 (Washington: GPO, 1996), tbl. 266.

Percentage Distribution of Bachelor's Degrees, by Academic Area and Race/Ethnicity, 1993–94

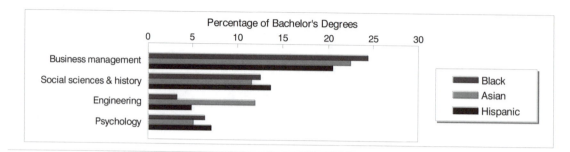

Academic Area	Black, non-His-panic	Ameri-can Indian	Asian	His-panic	Total Minor-ity	White, non-His-panic	Non-resident Alien	All Bachelor's Degrees
All areas	100.0	100.0	100.0	100.0	100.0	100.0	100.0	100.0
Men	36.7	42.3	48.4	43.4	41.9	45.8	57.7	45.5
Women	63.3	57.7	51.6	56.6	58.1	54.2	42.3	54.5
Agriculture & natural resources	0.6	2.1	0.6	0.8	0.7	1.8	1.0	1.5
Architecture	0.4	0.6	1.3	1.0	0.8	0.7	1.3	0.8
Area and ethnic studies	0.8	0.9	0.9	1.0	0.8	0.4	0.5	0.5
Biological sciences	3.6	4.1	10.9	4.3	5.9	4.1	3.4	4.4
Business management	24.4	16.7	22.4	20.4	22.6	20.4	33.4	21.2
Communications & comm. tech.	5.0	3.6	2.4	3.9	3.9	4.6	3.3	4.4
Computer & info. sciences	2.9	1.3	4.1	1.8	2.9	1.7	6.7	2.1
Education	7.6	11.9	2.0	6.6	5.9	10.2	1.9	9.2
Engineering	3.2	3.6	12.0	4.9	6.2	4.9	13.3	5.3
Engineering technologies	1.4	1.6	1.3	1.3	1.4	1.4	1.4	1.4
English language & lit.	3.9	4.2	3.1	3.9	3.7	4.9	1.5	4.6
Foreign languages & lit.	0.6	0.9	1.1	3.6	1.5	1.2	1.4	1.2
Health professions	5.9	6.4	5.5	4.5	5.4	6.7	3.0	6.4
Home economics	1.1	1.4	0.9	0.8	1.0	1.4	0.7	1.3
Law and legal studies	0.2	0.2	0.2	0.2	0.2	0.2	0.0	0.2
Liberal arts, gen. studies	3.6	4.9	1.9	4.1	3.3	2.8	1.5	2.9
Library science	0.0	0.0	0.0	0.0	0.0	0.0	0.0	0.0
Mathematics	1.2	1.0	1.7	1.0	1.3	1.2	1.6	1.2
Multi/interdisciplinary studies	2.0	2.3	2.4	3.7	2.6	2.1	1.0	2.2
Parks, recreation, fitness	0.7	1.2	0.2	0.8	0.6	1.1	0.3	1.0
Philosophy and religion	0.4	0.6	0.6	0.6	0.5	0.7	0.4	0.6
Physical sciences	1.1	1.4	2.0	1.0	1.4	1.6	2.1	1.6
Protective services	4.2	2.6	0.7	2.8	2.8	1.9	0.5	2.0
Psychology	6.4	6.5	5.1	7.1	6.2	6.0	2.5	5.9
Public administration	3.3	3.0	0.7	2.1	2.2	1.4	0.6	1.5
Social sciences & history	12.5	12.7	11.5	13.6	12.5	11.3	10.0	11.5
Theological studies	0.2	0.3	0.3	0.2	0.2	0.5	0.5	0.5
Visual and performing arts	2.5	3.7	4.1	3.5	3.2	4.4	5.8	4.2
Other	0.3	0.4	0.2	0.3	0.3	0.4	0.3	0.4

Note: Data are for 50 states and D.C. Asian category includes Pacific Islanders. American Indian category includes Alaskan Natives.

Source: Calculated from data in table 144.

Percentage Distribution of Bachelor's Degrees, by Race/Ethnicity and Academic Area, 1993–94

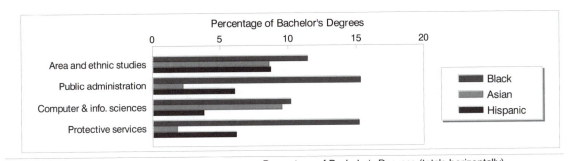

Percentage of Bachelor's Degrees

Academic Area	Black, non-His-panic	Ameri-can Indian	Asian	His-panic	Total Minor-ity	White, non-His-panic	Non-resident Alien	All Bachelor's Degrees
All areas	7.2	0.5	4.8	4.3	16.8	80.3	2.9	100.0
Men	5.8	0.5	5.1	4.1	15.4	80.8	3.7	100.0
Women	8.3	0.6	4.5	4.5	17.9	79.8	2.3	100.0
Agriculture & natural resources	2.8	0.7	1.7	2.1	7.3	90.8	1.9	100.0
Architecture	3.9	0.4	8.0	5.3	17.6	77.6	4.8	100.0
Area and ethnic studies	11.4	1.0	8.6	8.7	29.6	67.1	3.3	100.0
Biological sciences	5.9	0.5	11.8	4.2	22.4	75.4	2.2	100.0
Business management	8.3	0.4	5.1	4.2	17.9	77.5	4.6	100.0
Communications & comm. tech.	8.1	0.4	2.5	3.8	14.9	82.9	2.2	100.0
Computer & info. sciences	10.1	0.3	9.5	3.7	23.7	66.9	9.4	100.0
Education	5.9	0.7	1.0	3.1	10.7	88.7	0.6	100.0
Engineering	4.4	0.4	10.7	3.9	19.3	73.4	7.3	100.0
Engineering technologies	7.5	0.6	4.6	4.1	16.8	80.1	3.0	100.0
English language & lit.	6.0	0.5	3.2	3.7	13.4	85.6	1.0	100.0
Foreign languages & lit.	3.5	0.4	4.1	12.5	20.5	76.2	3.2	100.0
Health professions	6.6	0.5	4.1	3.1	14.3	84.3	1.4	100.0
Home economics	6.2	0.6	3.1	2.5	12.3	86.1	1.5	100.0
Law and legal studies	9.6	0.6	4.0	5.6	19.8	79.9	0.3	100.0
Liberal arts, gen. studies	8.9	0.9	3.2	6.2	19.2	79.2	1.6	100.0
Library science	6.5	0.0	0.0	0.0	6.5	87.1	6.5	100.0
Mathematics	7.0	0.4	6.6	3.7	17.6	78.5	3.9	100.0
Multi/interdisciplinary studies	6.7	0.6	5.3	7.5	20.1	78.6	1.3	100.0
Parks, recreation, fitness	4.8	0.7	1.0	3.7	10.2	88.8	0.9	100.0
Philosophy and religion	4.2	0.5	4.5	4.0	13.2	85.0	1.8	100.0
Physical sciences	5.1	0.5	6.1	2.8	14.6	81.6	3.9	100.0
Protective services	15.1	0.7	1.8	6.1	23.7	75.6	0.7	100.0
Psychology	7.7	0.6	4.1	5.2	17.6	81.2	1.2	100.0
Public administration	15.3	1.1	2.2	6.0	24.5	74.4	1.1	100.0
Social sciences & history	7.8	0.6	4.8	5.1	18.3	79.1	2.5	100.0
Theological studies	3.5	0.4	2.9	2.2	9.0	87.8	3.2	100.0
Visual and performing arts	4.2	0.5	4.6	3.6	12.9	83.1	4.0	100.0
Other	5.2	0.5	2.0	3.1	10.9	86.8	2.3	100.0

Note: Data are for 50 states and D.C. Asian category includes Pacific Islanders. American Indian category includes Alaskan Natives.

Source: Calculated from data in table 144.

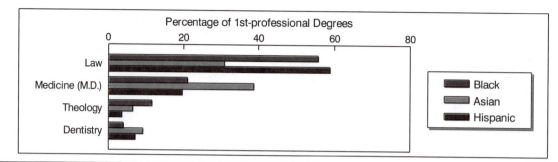

Academic Area	Black, non-His-panic	Ameri-can Indian	Asian	His-panic	Total Minor-ity	White, non-His-panic	Non-resident Alien	Total
All areas	100.0	100.0	100.0	100.0	100.0	100.0	100.0	100.0
Men	42.8	59.8	54.5	56.8	51.4	60.8	70.6	59.3
Women	57.2	40.2	45.5	43.2	48.6	39.2	29.4	40.7
Dentistry	3.8	4.6	9.1	7.0	6.8	4.3	19.8	5.0
Medicine (M.D.)	21.1	18.3	38.7	19.6	28.2	18.8	12.6	20.4
Optometry	0.8	0.8	2.6	1.2	1.7	1.4	3.8	1.5
Osteopathic medicine	1.1	2.2	3.1	2.2	2.2	2.5	0.8	2.4
Podiatry	0.7	0.5	0.7	1.3	0.9	0.6	0.6	0.6
Veterinary medicine	0.9	3.8	0.7	2.1	1.1	3.2	0.5	2.8
Chiropractic medicine	0.9	5.1	2.0	2.6	1.8	3.9	12.7	3.7
Pharmacy	3.5	0.3	5.9	1.7	4.0	2.2	5.7	2.6
Law	55.6	60.1	30.8	58.8	45.9	55.6	18.9	53.1
Theology	11.5	4.3	6.4	3.5	7.3	7.7	24.1	7.9
Other	<.1	0.0	<.1	0.1	<.1	0.1	0.6	0.1

Note: Data are for 50 states and D.C. Asian category includes Pacific Islanders. American Indian category includes Alaskan Natives.

Source: Calculated from data in table 145.

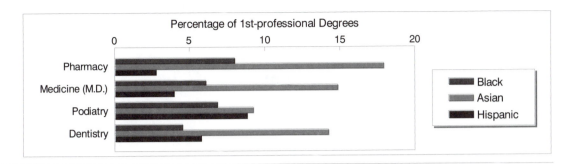

Academic Area	Black, non-His-panic	Ameri-can Indian	Asian	His-panic	Total Minor-ity	White, non-His-panic	Non-resident Alien	Total
All areas	5.9	0.5	7.8	4.2	18.4	79.7	1.9	100.0
Men	4.3	0.5	7.2	4.0	15.9	81.8	2.3	100.0
Women	8.3	0.5	8.7	4.4	21.9	76.7	1.4	100.0
Dentistry	4.5	0.4	14.2	5.8	24.9	67.6	7.5	100.0
Medicine (M.D.)	6.1	0.4	14.8	4.0	25.4	73.4	1.2	100.0
Optometry	3.3	0.3	13.9	3.4	20.9	74.2	5.0	100.0
Osteopathic medicine	2.7	0.4	10.1	3.9	17.1	82.2	0.7	100.0
Podiatry	6.9	0.4	9.2	8.8	25.4	72.9	1.7	100.0
Veterinary medicine	1.9	0.7	1.9	3.2	7.6	92.1	0.3	100.0
Chiropractic medicine	1.4	0.7	4.1	2.9	9.1	84.5	6.5	100.0
Pharmacy	8.0	0.1	17.9	2.8	28.8	67.0	4.2	100.0
Law	6.2	0.6	4.5	4.6	15.9	83.5	0.7	100.0
Theology	8.6	0.3	6.3	1.8	17.0	77.2	5.8	100.0
Other	1.8	0.0	1.8	5.5	9.1	76.4	14.5	100.0

Note: Data are for 50 states and D.C. Asian category includes Pacific Islanders. American Indian category includes Alaskan Natives.

Source: Calculated from data in table 145.

Percentage Distribution of Master's Degrees, by Academic Area and Race/Ethnicity, 1993–94

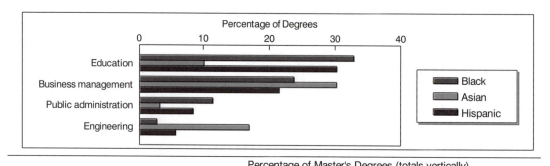

Percentage of Degrees

	Black, non-His-panic	Ameri-can Indian	Asian	His-panic	Total Minor-ity	White, non-His-panic	Non-resident Alien	All Master's Degrees
	Percentage of Master's Degrees (totals vertically)							
Academic Area								
All areas	100.0	100.0	100.0	100.0	100.0	100.0	100.0	100.0
Men	33.8	40.7	53.9	42.9	42.2	43.0	64.9	45.5
Women	66.2	59.3	46.1	57.1	57.8	57.0	35.1	54.5
Agriculture & natural resources	0.5	0.7	0.6	1.6	0.8	1.0	2.0	1.1
Architecture	0.7	0.7	1.4	1.1	1.0	0.9	1.6	1.0
Area and ethnic studies	0.5	1.0	0.7	0.8	0.6	0.4	0.4	0.4
Biological sciences	0.7	1.1	2.3	1.1	1.3	1.3	2.0	1.3
Business management	23.8	17.6	30.3	21.6	25.0	23.5	28.2	24.2
Communications & comm. tech.	1.7	1.4	1.0	1.0	1.3	1.3	1.9	1.4
Computer & info. sciences	1.8	1.1	8.6	1.5	3.7	1.6	8.4	2.7
Education	32.8	35.7	10.0	30.2	25.5	28.8	6.3	25.7
Engineering	2.8	3.8	16.9	5.6	7.8	5.3	20.2	7.4
Engineering technologies	0.3	0.1	0.2	0.3	0.2	0.3	0.4	0.3
English language & lit.	1.1	2.3	1.3	1.6	1.3	2.4	0.9	2.0
Foreign languages & lit.	0.2	0.5	0.9	2.6	1.0	0.7	1.4	0.9
Health professions	6.8	8.1	6.6	6.0	6.6	8.0	3.2	7.3
Home economics	0.6	0.4	0.5	0.5	0.5	0.7	0.5	0.6
Law and legal studies	0.2	0.4	0.4	0.6	0.4	0.4	2.2	0.6
Liberal arts, gen. studies	0.6	0.8	0.2	0.4	0.4	0.7	0.3	0.6
Library science	1.1	0.8	1.0	0.8	1.0	1.5	0.4	1.3
Mathematics	0.5	0.4	1.6	0.6	0.9	0.9	2.4	1.1
Multi/interdisciplinary studies	0.5	0.8	0.4	0.8	0.6	0.7	0.3	0.6
Parks, recreation, fitness	0.4	0.5	0.2	0.2	0.3	0.5	0.3	0.4
Philosophy and religion	0.2	0.2	0.2	0.4	0.3	0.4	0.3	0.4
Physical sciences	0.6	1.0	2.0	0.9	1.1	1.2	3.8	1.5
Protective services	1.0	0.4	0.2	0.4	0.6	0.4	0.1	0.4
Psychology	3.0	3.8	1.8	4.1	2.9	3.6	0.8	3.2
Public administration	11.4	8.4	3.2	8.3	8.1	5.9	1.7	5.7
Social sciences & history	3.4	4.2	3.2	3.9	3.4	3.6	5.5	3.8
Theological studies	1.2	0.6	1.5	1.0	1.2	1.3	1.2	1.3
Visual and performing arts	1.5	3.0	2.5	2.1	2.0	2.6	3.0	2.6
Other	0.1	0.3	0.1	0.2	0.1	0.2	0.0	0.2

Note: Data are for 50 states and D.C. Asian category includes Pacific Islanders. American Indian category includes Alaskan Natives.

Source: Calculated from data in table 146.

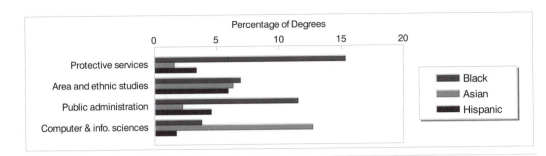

Academic Area	Black, non-His-panic	Ameri-can Indian	Asian	His-panic	Total Minor-ity	White, non-His-panic	Non-resident Alien	All Master's Degrees
					Percentage of Master's Degrees (totals horizontally)			
All areas	5.7	0.4	4.0	3.1	13.2	74.8	12.0	100.0
Men	4.2	0.4	4.7	2.9	12.2	70.6	17.1	100.0
Women	6.9	0.5	3.4	3.2	14.0	78.3	7.7	100.0
Agriculture & natural resources	2.8	0.3	2.3	4.6	10.1	67.2	22.8	100.0
Architecture	3.7	0.3	5.6	3.4	13.0	67.9	19.1	100.0
Area and ethnic studies	6.9	1.0	6.3	5.9	20.1	69.1	10.7	100.0
Biological sciences	2.9	0.3	6.7	2.4	12.3	69.7	18.0	100.0
Business management	5.6	0.3	4.9	2.7	13.6	72.4	14.0	100.0
Communications & comm. tech.	6.7	0.4	2.7	2.2	12.1	71.5	16.5	100.0
Computer & info. sciences	3.8	0.2	12.6	1.7	18.3	44.2	37.5	100.0
Education	7.3	0.6	1.6	3.6	13.1	84.0	3.0	100.0
Engineering	2.2	0.2	9.0	2.3	13.8	53.6	32.7	100.0
Engineering technologies	5.2	0.1	3.3	2.6	11.2	72.4	16.4	100.0
English language & lit.	3.1	0.5	2.6	2.5	8.7	86.0	5.3	100.0
Foreign languages & lit.	1.5	0.3	4.2	9.3	15.3	65.6	19.1	100.0
Health professions	5.3	0.5	3.6	2.5	12.0	82.7	5.4	100.0
Home economics	5.7	0.3	2.9	2.3	11.2	79.6	9.1	100.0
Law and legal studies	1.9	0.3	2.5	3.1	7.9	50.1	42.1	100.0
Liberal arts, gen. studies	5.0	0.6	1.4	1.9	8.9	85.1	6.0	100.0
Library science	4.8	0.3	2.9	1.8	9.8	86.2	4.0	100.0
Mathematics	2.9	0.1	6.1	1.7	10.9	62.4	26.7	100.0
Multi/interdisciplinary studies	4.5	0.6	2.5	3.9	11.4	82.1	6.4	100.0
Parks, recreation, fitness	4.8	0.5	1.7	1.4	8.4	83.8	7.9	100.0
Philosophy and religion	2.8	0.2	2.8	3.9	9.8	81.6	8.6	100.0
Physical sciences	2.4	0.3	5.3	1.8	9.8	59.1	31.1	100.0
Protective services	15.3	0.5	1.6	3.3	20.7	76.0	3.3	100.0
Psychology	5.4	0.5	2.3	4.0	12.2	84.8	3.0	100.0
Public administration	11.5	0.7	2.3	4.5	18.9	77.4	3.7	100.0
Social sciences & history	5.1	0.5	3.3	3.2	12.0	70.4	17.6	100.0
Theological studies	5.2	0.2	4.6	2.5	12.5	76.1	11.4	100.0
Visual and performing arts	3.3	0.5	3.9	2.5	10.3	75.5	14.2	100.0
Other	3.7	0.6	2.4	2.4	9.1	90.0	0.9	100.0

Note: Data are for 50 states and D.C. Asian category includes Pacific Islanders. American Indian category includes Alaskan Natives.

Source: Calculated from data in table 146.

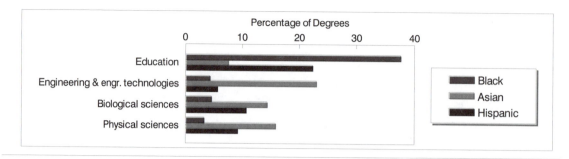

Academic Area	Black, non-His-panic	Ameri-can Indian	Asian	His-panic	Total Minor-ity	White, non-His-panic	Non-resident Alien	All Doctoral Degrees
						Percentage of Doctoral Degrees (totals vertically)		
All areas	100.0	100.0	100.0	100.0	100.0	100.0	100.0	100.0
Men	45.3	49.3	67.8	51.5	56.9	55.7	76.9	61.5
Women	54.7	50.7	32.2	48.5	43.1	44.3	23.1	38.5
Agriculture & natural resources	1.1	1.5	1.7	2.0	1.6	2.2	5.3	3.0
Architecture	0.3	0.7	0.3	0.0	0.2	0.2	0.7	0.4
Area and ethnic studies	1.1	3.0	0.4	0.2	0.7	0.4	0.2	0.4
Biological sciences	4.6	6.7	14.4	10.6	10.3	10.4	10.8	10.5
Business management	2.7	5.2	3.3	1.4	2.8	3.1	3.4	3.2
Communications & comm. tech.	1.7	2.2	0.3	0.8	0.9	0.8	0.7	0.8
Computer & info. sciences	0.8	0.7	3.2	0.6	1.8	1.3	3.1	1.9
Education	37.5	31.3	7.5	22.3	20.6	19.9	5.2	16.0
Engineering & engr. tech.	4.3	3.7	22.9	5.8	13.0	8.1	27.6	13.9
English language & lit.	2.3	6.7	1.2	2.9	2.0	4.0	1.4	3.1
Foreign languages & lit.	0.6	0.0	1.2	8.1	2.4	1.9	2.3	2.1
Health professions	4.2	5.2	5.1	2.9	4.4	4.7	3.7	4.4
Home economics	0.7	0.7	0.4	0.6	0.6	1.0	0.5	0.8
Law and legal studies	0.1	0.0	0.1	0.8	0.2	0.1	0.5	0.2
Liberal arts, gen. studies	0.5	0.0	0.2	0.2	0.3	0.2	0.1	0.2
Library science	0.2	0.0	0.1	0.1	0.1	0.1	0.1	0.1
Mathematics	0.5	0.7	4.1	1.2	2.3	1.8	4.9	2.7
Multi/interdisciplinary studies	0.7	3.0	0.2	0.7	0.6	0.5	0.5	0.5
Parks, recreation, fitness	0.2	0.7	0.1	0.1	0.2	0.3	0.3	0.3
Philosophy and religion	1.6	0.0	0.8	0.6	1.0	1.5	0.6	1.2
Physical sciences	3.3	4.5	16.0	9.2	10.3	9.3	14.4	10.8
Protective services	0.1	0.0	0.0	0.1	0.1	0.1	0.0	0.1
Psychology	9.0	8.2	4.6	15.5	8.3	11.1	1.4	8.3
Public administration	3.2	3.0	0.7	1.6	1.7	1.3	0.8	1.2
Social sciences & history	8.8	9.0	6.4	8.1	7.6	8.5	8.4	8.4
Theological studies	8.1	1.5	3.3	1.9	4.4	3.9	1.7	3.4
Visual and performing arts	1.6	1.5	1.5	2.0	1.6	3.0	1.4	2.4

Note: Data are for 50 states and D.C. Asian category includes Pacific Islanders. American Indian category includes Alaskan Natives.

Source: Calculated from data in table 147.

Percentage Distribution of Doctoral Degrees, by Race/Ethnicity and Academic Area, 1993–94

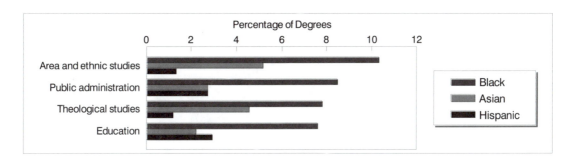

Academic Area	Black, non-His-panic	Ameri-can Indian	Asian	His-panic	Total Minor-ity	White, non-His-panic	Non-resident Alien	All Doctoral Degrees
All areas	3.2	0.3	4.7	2.1	10.3	62.9	26.7	100.0
Men	2.4	0.2	5.2	1.8	9.6	57.0	33.4	100.0
Women	4.6	0.4	3.9	2.6	11.6	72.4	16.1	100.0
Agriculture & natural resources	1.3	0.2	2.7	1.4	5.5	46.6	47.9	100.0
Architecture	2.5	0.6	3.7	0.0	6.8	40.4	52.8	100.0
Area and ethnic studies	10.3	2.6	5.2	1.3	19.4	63.9	16.8	100.0
Biological sciences	1.4	0.2	6.4	2.1	10.1	62.4	27.5	100.0
Business management	2.8	0.5	4.8	1.0	9.1	62.1	28.8	100.0
Communications & comm. tech.	6.7	0.9	1.7	2.0	11.3	65.2	23.5	100.0
Computer & info. sciences	1.4	0.1	7.9	0.6	10.0	45.2	44.8	100.0
Education	7.6	0.6	2.2	2.9	13.3	78.1	8.6	100.0
Engineering & engr. tech.	1.0	0.1	7.8	0.9	9.7	37.0	53.3	100.0
English language & lit.	2.4	0.7	1.8	1.9	6.8	81.0	12.3	100.0
Foreign languages & lit.	0.9	0.0	2.7	8.2	11.9	58.0	30.1	100.0
Health professions	3.1	0.4	5.5	1.4	10.3	67.4	22.3	100.0
Home economics	2.7	0.3	2.5	1.4	6.8	76.4	16.7	100.0
Law and legal studies	1.3	0.0	3.8	8.9	13.9	20.3	65.8	100.0
Liberal arts, gen. studies	8.8	0.0	6.3	2.5	17.5	73.8	8.8	100.0
Library science	6.7	0.0	4.4	2.2	13.3	68.9	17.8	100.0
Mathematics	0.6	0.1	7.2	1.0	8.8	42.7	48.5	100.0
Multi/interdisciplinary studies	4.4	1.8	2.2	2.6	11.0	61.7	27.3	100.0
Parks, recreation, fitness	2.6	0.9	1.7	0.9	6.0	67.2	26.7	100.0
Philosophy and religion	4.2	0.0	3.0	0.9	8.1	79.0	12.9	100.0
Physical sciences	1.0	0.1	6.9	1.8	9.8	54.5	35.6	100.0
Protective services	8.0	0.0	0.0	4.0	12.0	76.0	12.0	100.0
Psychology	3.5	0.3	2.6	3.9	10.4	85.0	4.7	100.0
Public administration	8.5	0.8	2.7	2.7	14.6	68.6	16.8	100.0
Social sciences & history	3.4	0.3	3.6	2.0	9.3	63.9	26.8	100.0
Theological studies	7.8	0.1	4.6	1.2	13.7	73.1	13.3	100.0
Visual and performing arts	2.1	0.2	2.9	1.7	6.9	77.3	15.7	100.0

Note: Data are for 50 states and D.C. Asian category includes Pacific Islanders. American Indian category includes Alaskan Natives.

Source: Calculated from data in table 147.

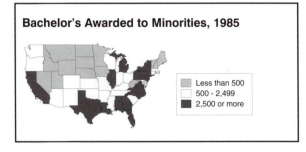

Bachelor's Awarded to Minorities, 1985

Less than 500
500 - 2,499
2,500 or more

Region and State	1984-85			1993-94		
	All Races	Total Minority	Black, non-Hispanic	All Races	Total Minority	Black, non-Hispanic
50 States & D.C.	**979,477**	**107,404**	**54,874**	**1,169,275**	**191,970**	**82,183**
New England	**77,018**	**4,140**	**1,758**	**83,818**	**8,210**	**2,511**
Connecticut	13,516	901	393	14,152	1,602	602
Maine	5,019	95	55	5,953	234	59
Massachusetts	40,458	2,414	938	42,351	5,122	1,474
New Hampshire	6,313	221	120	7,546	304	81
Rhode Island	7,636	412	207	9,145	752	241
Vermont	4,076	97	45	4,671	196	54
Mideast	**194,222**	**23,564**	**13,475**	**216,977**	**39,219**	**18,817**
Delaware	3,137	286	230	4,187	505	395
D.C.	7,093	2,143	1,656	7,184	2,683	2,078
Maryland	15,761	2,415	1,762	21,657	4,935	3,130
New Jersey	23,764	3,185	1,614	25,234	4,978	1,963
New York	87,596	12,270	6,090	94,389	20,396	8,434
Pennsylvania	56,871	3,265	2,123	64,326	5,722	2,817
Southeast	**195,777**	**28,660**	**22,753**	**251,308**	**46,871**	**34,557**
Alabama	16,334	2,719	2,507	21,150	3,869	3,494
Arkansas	7,153	829	680	8,549	1,027	854
Florida	31,289	5,002	2,241	44,075	10,171	4,253
Georgia	18,401	2,708	2,380	26,283	5,626	4,698
Kentucky	11,572	661	408	14,629	877	649
Louisiana	16,070	3,235	2,702	17,787	4,635	3,963
Mississippi	8,644	2,061	1,977	10,524	2,591	2,480
North Carolina	25,008	4,216	3,686	32,730	6,290	5,193
South Carolina	12,422	1,931	1,784	15,318	2,730	2,421
Tennessee	17,029	1,978	1,702	19,992	2,536	2,116
Virginia	23,958	3,006	2,457	31,226	6,104	4,203
West Virginia	7,897	314	229	9,045	415	233
Great Lakes	**178,057**	**12,218**	**7,599**	**206,490**	**21,779**	**11,457**
Illinois	46,304	4,805	2,829	52,330	8,848	4,049
Indiana	26,390	1,384	810	30,769	2,369	1,232
Michigan	38,132	2,820	1,962	44,925	4,727	2,801
Ohio	43,080	2,440	1,649	50,982	4,245	2,814
Wisconsin	24,151	769	349	27,484	1,590	561

Continued on next page.

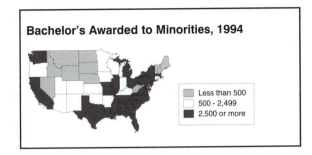

Bachelor's Awarded to Minorities, 1994

Less than 500
500 - 2,499
2,500 or more

Region and State	1984-85			1993-94		
	All Races	Total Minority	Black, non-Hispanic	All Races	Total Minority	Black, non-Hispanic
Plains	**87,964**	**3,793**	**1,834**	**103,494**	**6,636**	**2,882**
Iowa	15,268	426	193	17,846	837	346
Kansas	12,179	651	311	14,599	1,062	414
Minnesota	20,673	468	148	24,746	1,230	346
Missouri	23,200	1,658	1,014	27,494	2,730	1,518
Nebraska	8,330	392	131	10,087	457	217
North Dakota	4,189	104	15	4,558	166	27
South Dakota	4,125	94	22	4,164	154	14
Southwest	**86,631**	**12,772**	**3,970**	**107,243**	**23,331**	**6,046**
Arizona	12,236	1,229	216	16,093	2,432	385
New Mexico	4,603	1,164	65	6,118	1,996	133
Oklahoma	13,287	1,187	557	15,734	2,380	943
Texas	56,505	9,192	3,132	69,298	16,523	4,585
Rocky Mountains	**34,176**	**1,602**	**237**	**44,518**	**3,467**	**607**
Colorado	14,921	991	176	19,973	2,415	476
Idaho	2,986	137	13	4,203	216	30
Montana	4,324	127	12	4,357	175	17
Utah	10,337	307	31	14,191	575	70
Wyoming	1,608	40	5	1,794	86	14
Far West	**121,839**	**20,378**	**3,140**	**155,427**	**42,457**	**5,306**
Alaska	820	78	20	1,396	174	31
California	87,397	16,179	2,694	111,848	35,369	4,563
Hawaii	3,269	1,840	29	4,314	2,560	52
Nevada	1,962	154	39	3,276	360	108
Oregon	10,842	741	93	13,272	1,178	154
Washington	17,549	1,386	265	21,321	2,816	398
U.S. Service Schools	**3,793**	**277**	**108**	**nr**	**nr**	**nr**

nr: Not reported; data for U.S. Service Schools are included in state data.

Note: "All Races" column includes data for degree recipients who are minorities; "white, non-Hispanic"; "nonresident alien"; or for whom race/ethnicity was unknown.

Sources: 1 U.S. Department of Education, Office for Civil Rights (OCR), unpublished data.

2 NCES, E.D. Tabs, Degrees and Other Awards Conferred by Institutions of Higher Education, 1993-94, NCES 96-015 (Washington: GPO, 1996), tbl. 7b.

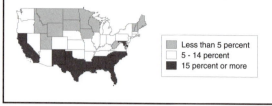

Percentage of Minority Bachelor's Degrees, 1985

Less than 5 percent
5 - 14 percent
15 percent or more

Region and State	Percentage of All Bachelor's Degrees						
	1984-85		1993-94				
	Total Minority	Black, non-Hispanic	Total Minority	Black, non-Hispanic	Hispanic	Asian or Pac. Isldr.	American Indian
50 States & D.C.	11	6	16	7	4	5	1
New England	5	2	10	3	2	4	< 1
Connecticut	7	3	11	4	3	4	< 1
Maine	2	1	4	1	1	1	1
Massachusetts	6	2	12	3	3	6	< 1
New Hampshire	4	2	4	1	1	2	< 1
Rhode Island	5	3	8	3	2	3	< 1
Vermont	2	1	4	1	1	1	< 1
Mideast	12	7	18	9	4	5	< 1
Delaware	9	7	12	9	1	1	< 1
D.C.	30	23	37	29	4	5	< 1
Maryland	15	11	23	14	2	6	< 1
New Jersey	13	7	20	8	6	6	< 1
New York	14	7	22	9	6	6	< 1
Pennsylvania	6	4	9	4	1	3	< 1
Southeast	15	12	19	14	3	2	< 1
Alabama	17	15	18	17	1	1	< 1
Arkansas	12	10	12	10	1	1	< 1
Florida	16	7	23	10	10	3	< 1
Georgia	15	13	21	18	1	2	< 1
Kentucky	6	4	6	4	0	1	< 1
Louisiana	20	17	26	22	2	2	< 1
Mississippi	24	23	25	24	0	1	< 1
North Carolina	17	15	19	16	1	2	1
South Carolina	16	14	18	16	1	1	< 1
Tennessee	12	10	13	11	1	1	< 1
Virginia	13	10	20	13	2	4	< 1
West Virginia	4	3	5	3	1	1	< 1
Great Lakes	7	4	11	6	2	3	< 1
Illinois	10	6	17	8	4	5	< 1
Indiana	5	3	8	4	2	2	< 1
Michigan	7	5	11	6	1	2	< 1
Ohio	6	4	8	6	1	2	< 1
Wisconsin	3	1	6	2	1	2	1

Continued on next page.

Percentage of Minority Bachelor's Degrees, 1994

Less than 5 percent
5 - 14 percent
15 percent or more

Region and State	Percentage of All Bachelor's Degrees						
	1984-85		1993-94				
	Total Minority	Black, non-Hispanic	Total Minority	Black, non-Hispanic	Hispanic	Asian or Pac. Isldr.	American Indian
Plains	4	2	6	3	1	2	1
Iowa	3	1	5	2	1	1	< 1
Kansas	5	3	7	3	2	2	1
Minnesota	2	1	5	1	1	2	1
Missouri	7	4	10	6	2	2	< 1
Nebraska	5	2	5	2	1	1	< 1
North Dakota	2	0	4	1	1	1	2
South Dakota	2	1	4	0	0	1	2
Southwest	15	5	22	6	11	3	1
Arizona	10	2	15	2	8	3	1
New Mexico	25	1	33	2	26	2	3
Oklahoma	9	4	15	6	1	2	6
Texas	16	6	24	7	13	4	< 1
Rocky Mountains	5	1	8	1	4	2	1
Colorado	7	1	12	2	6	3	1
Idaho	5	0	5	1	2	2	1
Montana	3	0	4	0	1	1	2
Utah	3	0	4	0	2	1	1
Wyoming	2	0	5	1	3	0	1
Far West	17	3	27	3	8	15	1
Alaska	10	2	12	2	2	1	7
California	19	3	32	4	11	16	1
Hawaii	56	1	59	1	1	57	< 1
Nevada	8	2	11	3	4	4	1
Oregon	7	1	9	1	2	5	1
Washington	8	2	13	2	2	8	1
U.S. Service Schools	7	3	nr	nr	nr	nr	nr

nr: Not reported; data for U.S. Service Schools are included in state data.

Sources: 1 U.S. Department of Education, Office for Civil Rights (OCR), unpublished data.
   2 NCES, E.D. Tabs, Degrees and Other Awards Conferred by Institutions of Higher Education, 1993-94, NCES 96-015 (Washington: GPO, 1996), tbl. 7b.

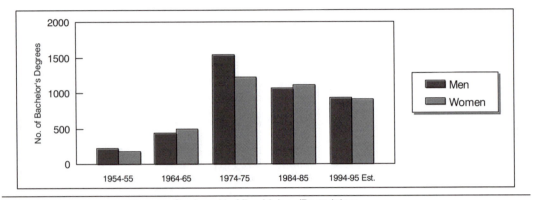

	Degrees Conferred in Microbiology/Bacteriology				
	Bachelor's				
Year	Total	Men	Women	Master's	Doctor's
1947-48	624	227	397	174	65
1949-50	870	563	307	327	74
1954-55	414	233	181	233	131
1959-60	533	245	288	248	141
1964-65	938	441	497	341	225
1969-70	1,411	741	670	469	359
1974-75	2,767	1,538	1,229	554	345
1979-80	2,631	1,281	1,350	596	376
1981-82	2,377	1,131	1,246	470	350
1983-84	2,329	1,072	1,257	447	360
1984-85	2,180	1,070	1,110	413	302
1985-86	2,217	1,084	1,133	353	336
1987-88	2,014	922	1,092	357	386
1989-90	1,814	834	980	366	409
1990-91	1,757	799	958	324	419
1991-92	1,722	842	880	336	454
1992-93	1,769	872	897	328	520
1993-94	1,841	916	925	332	478
Estimates					
1994-95	1,851	938	913	325	499
1995-96	1,880	977	903	325	522

Note: Data prior to 1979-80 are for aggregate U.S. For later years, data are for 50 states and D.C. Figures
through 1964-65 generally exclude those master's degrees that are considered first-professional degrees,
such as master's of social work, etc. Data for later years include all master's degrees.
Data for 1994-95 and later are Fact Book estimates based on data for the previous 4 years.

Sources: See Guide to Sources.

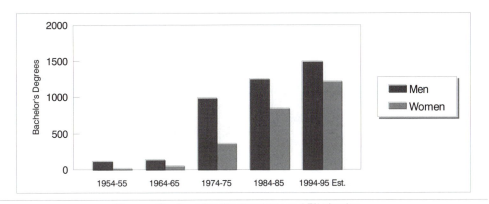

Degrees Conferred in Biochemistry and Biophysics

Year	Bachelor's			Master's	Doctor's
	Total	Men	Women		
1947-48	270	226	44	131	65
1949-50	175	160	15	144	116
1954-55	144	124	20	142	147
1959-60	108	84	24	143	165
1964-65	200	143	57	236	290
1969-70	455	332	123	240	449
1974-75	1,355	996	359	270	437
1979-80	1,686	1,090	596	268	475
1981-82	1,865	1,197	668	273	462
1983-84	2,052	1,209	843	254	490
1984-85	2,111	1,261	850	257	464
1985-86	2,109	1,242	867	279	468
1987-88	2,060	1,144	916	248	533
1989-90	2,030	1,128	902	290	588
1990-91	2,094	1,177	917	254	650
1991-92	2,148	1,204	944	239	620
1992-93	2,327	1,370	957	207	692
1993-94	2,570	1,420	1,150	276	659
Estimates					
1994-95	2,731	1,505	1,225	277	680
1995-96	2,923	1,602	1,320	287	689

Note: Data prior to 1979-80 are for aggregate U.S. For later years, data are for 50 states and D.C. Figures through 1964-65 generally exclude thoise master's degrees that are considered first-professional degrees, such as master of social work, etc. Data for later years include all master's degrees. Figures for 1994-95 and later are Fact Book estimates based on data for the previous 4 years. later are Fact Book estimates based on data for the previous 4 years.

Sources: See Guide to Sources.

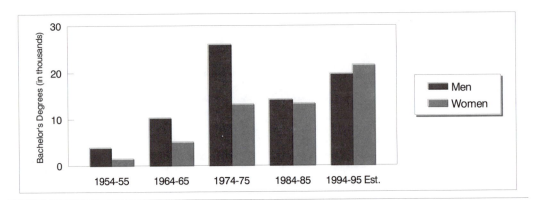

	Degrees Conferred in Biology				
	Bachelor's				
Year	Total	Men	Women	Master's	Doctor's
1947-48	6,739	4,294	2,445	246	65
1949-50	10,428	8,121	2,307	549	81
1954-55	5,493	3,946	1,547	446	150
1959-60	8,426	5,730	2,696	630	159
1964-65	15,577	10,316	5,261	1,340	219
1969-70	24,684	17,037	7,647	2,632	588
1974-75	39,289	26,050	13,239	3,210	769
1979-80	33,880	19,388	14,492	2,982	1,218
1981-82	31,836	17,337	14,499	2,904	1,308
1983-84	27,379	14,408	12,971	2,313	617
1984-85	27,593	14,205	13,388	2,130	658
1985-86	27,618	14,135	13,483	1,131	574
1987-88	26,838	13,187	13,651	1,981	576
1989-90	27,213	13,138	14,075	1,998	551
1990-91	29,285	14,085	15,200	1,956	632
1991-92	31,909	15,109	16,800	1,995	657
1992-93	34,932	16,500	18,432	2,000	671
1993-94	38,103	18,252	19,851	2,178	665
	Estimates				
1994-95	41,451	19,817	21,634	2,227	698
1995-96	45,216	21,584	23,631	2,302	716

Note: Data prior to 1979-80 are for aggregate U.S. For later years, data are for 50 states and D.C. Figures through 1964-65 generally exclude those master's degrees that are considered first-professional degrees, such as master of social work, etc. Data for later years include all master's degrees. Beginning in 1983-84, figures show only "general biology." Data for 1994-95 and later are Fact Book estimates based on data for the previous 4 years.

Sources: See Guide to Sources.

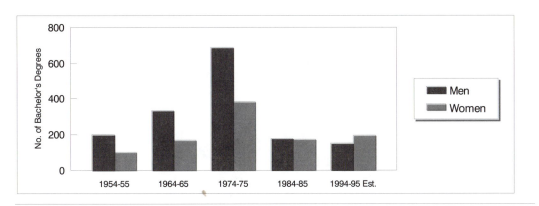

Degrees Conferred in Botany					
	Bachelor's				
Year	Total	Men	Women	Master's	Doctor's
1947-48	353	179	174	169	73
1949-50	494	385	109	299	126
1954-55	302	199	103	173	151
1959-60	385	289	96	248	208
1964-65	503	335	168	433	304
1969-70	597	413	184	528	368
1974-75	1,075	689	386	428	289
1979-80	820	410	410	489	274
1981-82	718	366	352	400	303
1983-84	454	223	231	370	257
1984-85	348	176	172	304	271
1985-86	302	155	147	306	270
1987-88	242	125	117	324	284
1989-90	206	101	105	253	288
1990-91	175	99	76	236	267
1991-92	222	93	129	220	293
1992-93	263	135	128	224	223
1993-94	303	138	165	220	264
Estimates					
1994-95	346	152	194	213	262
1995-96	421	171	250	207	264

Note: Data prior to 1979-80 are for aggregate U.S. For later years, data are for 50 states and D.C.
Figures through 1964-65 generally exclude those master's degrees that are considered first-professional degrees such as master of social work, etc. Data for later years include all master's degrees.
Data for 1994-95 and later are Fact Book estimates based on data for the previous 4 years.

Sources: See Guide to Sources.

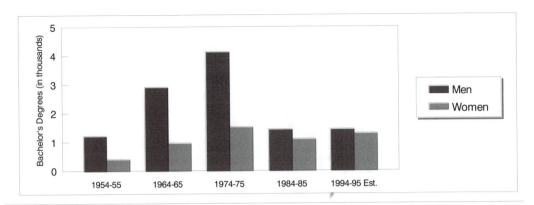

Degrees Conferred in Zoology					
	Bachelor's				
Year	Total	Men	Women	Master's	Doctor's
1947-48	2,306	1,499	807	358	83
1949-50	3,289	2,727	562	551	125
1954-55	1,648	1,218	430	264	196
1959-60	2,250	1,685	565	364	185
1964-65	3,880	2,912	968	575	239
1969-70	5,584	4,412	1,172	730	412
1974-75	5,686	4,150	1,536	608	284
1979-80	3,653	2,350	1,303	431	245
1981-82	3,089	1,802	1,287	413	223
1983-84	2,616	1,483	1,133	347	188
1984-85	2,544	1,438	1,106	329	175
1985-86	2,395	1,330	1,065	289	201
1987-88	2,095	1,095	1,000	224	190
1989-90	2,016	1,004	1,012	226	166
1990-91	2,217	1,124	1,093	211	164
1991-92	2,350	1,183	1,167	214	161
1992-93	2,552	1,268	1,284	208	134
1993-94	2,592	1,354	1,238	278	156
Estimates					
1994-95	2,763	1,460	1,304	296	155
1995-96	2,922	1,558	1,364	324	154

Note: Data prior to 1979-80 are for aggregate U.S. For later years, data are for 50 states and D.C.
Figures through 1964-65 generally exclude those master's degrees that are considered first-professional degrees such as social work, etc. Data for later years include all master's degrees.
Data for 1994-95 and later are Fact Book estimates based on data for the previous 4 years.

Sources: See Guide to Sources.

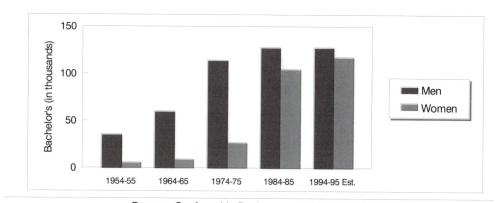

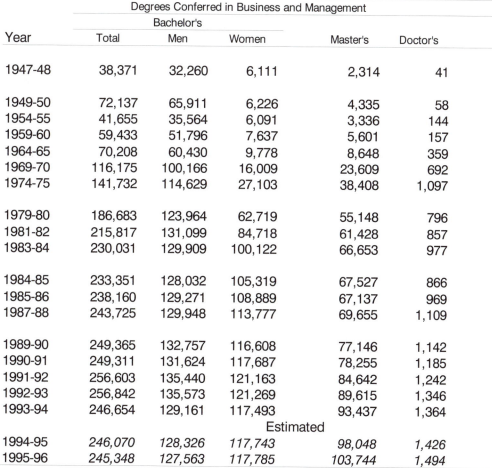

	Degrees Conferred in Business and Management				
	Bachelor's				
Year	Total	Men	Women	Master's	Doctor's
1947-48	38,371	32,260	6,111	2,314	41
1949-50	72,137	65,911	6,226	4,335	58
1954-55	41,655	35,564	6,091	3,336	144
1959-60	59,433	51,796	7,637	5,601	157
1964-65	70,208	60,430	9,778	8,648	359
1969-70	116,175	100,166	16,009	23,609	692
1974-75	141,732	114,629	27,103	38,408	1,097
1979-80	186,683	123,964	62,719	55,148	796
1981-82	215,817	131,099	84,718	61,428	857
1983-84	230,031	129,909	100,122	66,653	977
1984-85	233,351	128,032	105,319	67,527	866
1985-86	238,160	129,271	108,889	67,137	969
1987-88	243,725	129,948	113,777	69,655	1,109
1989-90	249,365	132,757	116,608	77,146	1,142
1990-91	249,311	131,624	117,687	78,255	1,185
1991-92	256,603	135,440	121,163	84,642	1,242
1992-93	256,842	135,573	121,269	89,615	1,346
1993-94	246,654	129,161	117,493	93,437	1,364
		Estimated			
1994-95	246,070	128,326	117,743	98,048	1,426
1995-96	245,348	127,563	117,785	103,744	1,494

Note: Data prior to 1979-80 are for aggregate U.S. For later years, data are for 50 states and D.C. Figures through 1964-65 generally exclude those master's degrees that are considered first-professional degrees such as master of library science and social work. Data for later years include all master's degrees. Over the years, various subfields have been listed separately in NCES reports. The most recent listing includes: "business management and administrative services" and "marketing operations and distribution." Figures for 1994-95 and later are Fact Book estimates based on data for the four previous years.
Sources: See Guide to Sources.

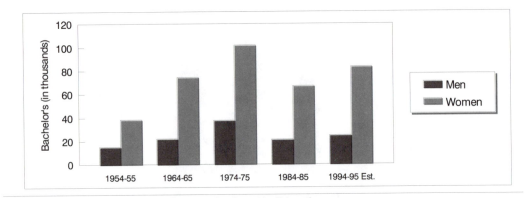

Degrees Conferred in Education

Year	Bachelor's			Master's	Doctor's
	Total	Men	Women		
1947-48	36,385	12,971	23,414	13,098	521
1949-50	61,725	31,490	30,235	20,069	953
1954-55	53,254	14,871	38,383	27,620	1,470
1959-60	71,820	19,920	51,900	30,424	1,474
1964-65	96,387	21,743	74,644	39,296	2,372
1969-70	133,258	32,403	100,855	71,803	5,224
1974-75	139,716	37,615	102,101	111,574	6,714
1979-80	118,102	30,896	87,206	103,453	7,940
1981-82	101,063	24,385	76,678	93,104	7,676
1983-84	92,382	22,215	70,167	77,187	7,473
1984-85	88,161	21,264	66,897	76,137	7,151
1985-86	87,221	20,986	66,235	76,353	7,110
1987-88	91,287	21,028	70,259	77,867	6,553
1989-90	105,267	23,020	82,247	86,399	6,991
1990-91	110,807	23,417	87,390	87,343	6,187
1991-92	108,006	22,686	85,320	92,668	6,864
1992-93	107,781	23,233	84,548	96,028	7,030
1993-94	107,600	24,450	83,150	98,938	6,908
Estimates					
1994-95	108,258	24,832	83,426	102,363	6,910
1995-96	107,678	25,210	82,467	106,512	7,112

Note: Data prior to 1979-80 are for aggregate U.S. For later years, data are for 50 states and D.C. Figures through 1964-65 generally exclude those master's degrees that are considered first-professional degrees, such as master of social work, etc. Data for later years include all master's degrees. Between 1959-60 and 1979-80, data for certain specialized teaching fields were excluded from the figures shown in this table. Data for 1979-80 and subsequent years, all education degrees as reported by NCES, including those specialized teaching fields, are shown in this table.

Sources: See Guide to Sources.

Degrees Conferred in Engineering: Chemical Engineering,
Selected Years, 1950–1996

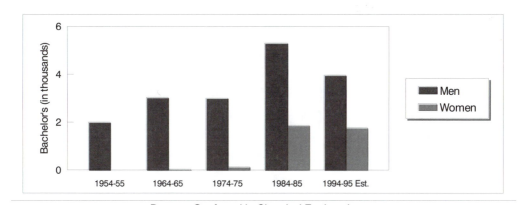

Degrees Conferred in Chemical Engineering					
	Bachelor's				
Year	Total	Men	Women	Master's	Doctor's
1949-50	4,529	4,509	20	712	178
1954-55	2,027	2,014	13	470	139
1959-60	2,966	2,935	31	617	170
1964-65	3,076	3,050	26	806	364
1969-70	3,720	3,663	57	1,045	438
1974-75	3,142	3,001	141	990	346
1979-80	6,320	5,113	1,207	1,270	284
1981-82	6,740	5,273	1,467	1,285	311
1983-84	7,475	5,604	1,871	1,514	330
1984-85	7,146	5,289	1,857	1,277	418
1985-86	5,877	4,425	1,452	1,361	446
1987-88	3,917	2,864	1,053	1,088	579
1989-90	3,430	2,398	1,032	1,035	562
1990-91	3,444	2,338	1,106	903	611
1991-92	3,754	2,576	1,178	956	590
1992-93	4,459	2,995	1,464	990	595
1993-94	5,163	3,588	1,575	1,032	604
Estimates					
1994-95	5,735	3,980	1,754	1,034	616
1995-96	6,522	4,549	1,973	1,070	617

Note: Data prior to 1979-80 are for aggregate U.S. For later years, data are for 50 states and D.C. Figures through 1964-65 generally exclude those master's degrees that are considered first-professional degrees such as master of library science and social work. Data for later years include all master's degrees. Bachelor degree figures include degrees from four- and five-year programs. Estimates are based on average percentage changes in the last four years.

Sources: See Guide to Sources.

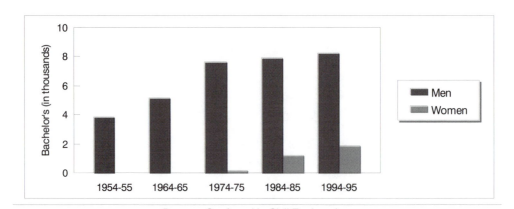

	Degrees Conferred in Civil Engineering				
	Bachelor's				
Year	Total	Men	Women	Master's	Doctor's
1949-50	7,772	7,761	11	729	32
1954-55	3,868	3,860	8	693	29
1959-60	5,287	5,272	15	1,024	73
1964-65	5,200	5,187	13	1,686	252
1969-70	6,524	6,477	47	2,242	411
1974-75	7,790	7,640	150	2,771	356
1979-80	10,326	9,349	977	2,683	270
1981-82	10,524	9,333	1,191	2,995	329
1983-84	9,693	8,390	1,303	3,146	369
1984-85	9,162	7,931	1,231	3,172	377
1985-86	8,679	7,538	1,141	2,926	395
1987-88	7,488	6,429	1,059	2,836	481
1989-90	7,252	6,134	1,118	2,812	516
1990-91	7,314	6,193	1,121	2,927	536
1991-92	8,034	6,712	1,322	3,113	540
1992-93	8,868	7,291	1,577	3,610	577
1993-94	9,479	7776	1703	3873	651
Estimates					
1994-95	10,151	8,255	1,897	4,199	691
1995-96	11,035	8,870	2,165	4,598	736

Note: Data prior to 1979-80 are for aggregate U.S. For later years, data are for 50 states and D.C. Figures through 1964-65 generally exclude those master's degrees that are considered first-professional degrees such as master of library science and social work. Data for later years include all master's degrees. Bachelor degree figures include degrees from four- and five-year programs. Estimates are based on average percentage changes in the last four years.

Sources: See Guide to Sources.

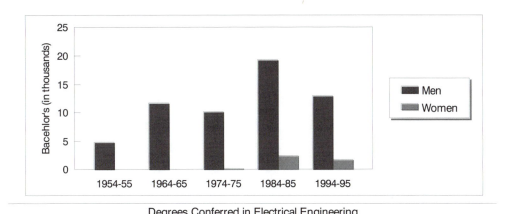

Degrees Conferred in Electrical Engineering					
	Bachelor's				
Year	Total	Men	Women	Master's	Doctor's
1949-50	13,270	13,258	12	1,168	85
1954-55	4,860	4,847	13	1,074	141
1959-60	10,631	10,599	32	1,993	203
1964-65	11,730	11,694	36	3,505	511
1969-70	12,288	12,220	68	4,138	882
1974-75	10,246	10,116	130	3,471	701
1979-80	13,821	12,923	898	3,836	525
1981-82	16,455	15,046	1,409	4,462	526
1983-84	19,943	17,919	2,024	5,078	585
1984-85	21,691	19,275	2,416	5,153	660
1985-86	23,742	20,906	2,836	5,534	722
1987-88	23,597	20,425	3,172	6,688	860
1989-90	20,711	18,138	2,573	7,225	1,162
1990-91	19,320	16,848	2,472	7,095	1,220
1991-92	17,958	15,811	2,147	7,360	1,282
1992-93	17,281	15,314	1,967	7,870	1,413
1993-94	15,823	13,892	1,931	7,791	1,470
Estimates					
1994-95	14,799	13,000	1,799	7,944	1,559
1995-96	13,850	12,187	1,664	8,175	1,658

Note: Data prior to 1979-80 are for aggregate U.S. For later years, data are for 50 states and D.C. Figures through 1964-65 generally exclude those master's degrees that are considered first-professional degrees such as master of library science and social work. Data for later years include all master's degrees. Bachelor degree figures include degrees from four- and five-year programs. Estimates are based on average percentage changes. Includes electrical, electronic, and communications engineering.

Sources: See Guide to Sources.

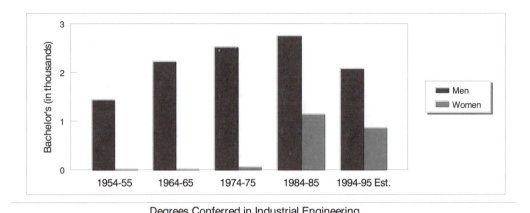

	Degrees Conferred in Industrial Engineering				
	Bachelor's				
Year	Total	Men	Women	Master's	Doctor's
1949-50	3,369	3,364	5	258	3
1954-55	1,448	1,444	4	373	9
1959-60	2,242	2,232	10	468	13
1964-65	2,236	2,230	6	1,013	61
1969-70	3,199	3,178	21	1,763	126
1974-75	2,583	2,524	59	1,687	119
1979-80	3,175	2,636	539	1,313	116
1981-82	3,992	3,049	943	1,656	116
1983-84	3,937	2,883	1,054	1,557	119
1984-85	3,914	2,766	1,148	1,462	139
1985-86	4,163	2,903	1,260	1,653	130
1987-88	4,082	2,886	1,196	1,815	162
1989-90	3,915	2,760	1,155	1,841	194
1990-91	3,736	2,686	1,050	2,029	217
1991-92	3,679	2,623	1,056	2,012	220
1992-93	3,300	2,354	946	2,058	267
1993-94	3,122	2207	915	2098	253
Estimates					
1994-95	2,952	2,088	864	2,169	272
1995-96	2,786	1,962	824	2,206	288

Note: Data prior to 1979-80 are for aggregate U.S. For later years, data are for 50 states and D.C. Figures through 1964-65 generally exclude those master's degrees that are considered first-professional degree such as master of library science and social work. Data for later years include all master's degrees. Bachelor degree figures include degrees from four- and five-year programs. Estimates are based on average percentage changes.

Sources: See Guide to Sources.

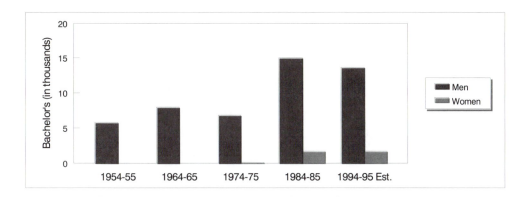

Degrees Conferred in Mechanical Engineering

Year	Bachelor's Total	Bachelor's Men	Bachelor's Women	Master's	Doctor's
1949-50	14,332	14,312	20	835	48
1954-55	5,876	5,867	9	759	79
1959-60	9,597	9,577	20	1,179	107
1964-65	8,035	8,019	16	2,036	265
1969-70	9,310	9,271	39	2,298	435
1974-75	6,949	6,867	82	1,860	340
1979-80	11,808	10,927	881	2,060	281
1981-82	13,922	12,702	1,220	2,399	333
1983-84	16,629	14,868	1,761	2,794	319
1984-85	16,794	15,045	1,749	3,053	409
1985-86	16,194	14,525	1,669	3,075	426
1987-88	14,900	13,182	1,718	3,329	596
1989-90	14,336	12,646	1,690	3,424	742
1990-91	13,977	12,423	1,554	3,516	757
1991-92	17,067	15,545	1,522	3,653	851
1992-93	14,464	12,863	1,601	3,982	871
1993-94	15,030	13,327	1,703	4,099	887
Estimates					
1994-95	15,360	13,651	1,709	4,289	928
1995-96	15,877	14,126	1,751	4,508	978

Note: Data prior to 1979-80 are for aggregate U.S. For later years, data are for 50 states and D.C. Figures through 1964-65 generally exclude those master's degrees that are considered first-professional degrees such as master of social work. Data for later years include all master's degrees. Bachelor degree figures include degrees from four-and five-year programs. Estimates are based on average percentage changes.

Source: See "Guide to Sources."

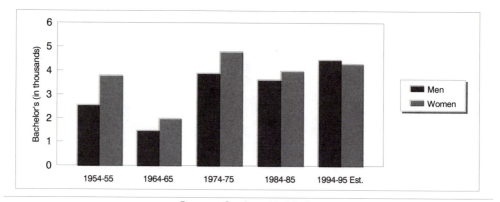

	Degrees Conferred in Music				
	Bachelor's				
Year	Total	Men	Women	Master's	Doctor's
1947-48	5,284	1,766	3,518	1,043	27
1949-50	7,934	4,069	3,865	1,489	34
1954-55	6,339	2,553	3,786	1,677	68
1959-60	2,988	1,254	1,734	1,171	119
1964-65	3,469	1,475	1,994	1,463	141
1969-70	5,433	2,424	3,009	2,130	278
1974-75	8,675	3,879	4,796	3,104	403
1979-80	8,920	4,139	4,781	3,417	402
1980-81	8,657	4,103	4,554	3,332	381
1982-83	7,910	3,701	4,209	3,551	421
1984-85	7,613	3,612	4,001	3,533	432
1985-86	7,175	3,387	3,788	3,453	476
1987-88	6,708	3,263	3,445	3,183	502
1989-90	6,879	3,411	3,468	3,260	574
1990-91	6,989	3,355	3,634	3,267	567
1991-92	7,724	3,805	3,919	3,458	623
1992-93	7,853	3,962	3,891	3,488	609
1993-94	8,268	4,151	4,117	3,619	708
		Estimated			
1994-95	8,754	4,460	4,295	3,745	764
1995-96	9,132	4,702	4,429	3,847	820

Note: Data prior to 1979-80 are for aggregate U.S. For later years, data are for 50 states and D.C. Figures through 1964-65 generally exclude those master's degrees that are considered first-professional degrees such as master of library science. Data for later years include all master's degrees. Prior to 1959-60, data include music education degrees; from 1959-60, music education degrees are excluded from these data. Figures for 1994-95 and later are Fact Book estimates based on percentage changes in the previous 3 years.

Sources: See Guide to Sources.

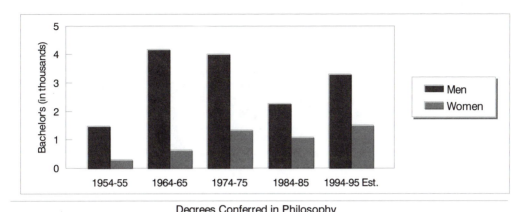

Degrees Conferred in Philosophy					
	Bachelor's				
Year	Total	Men	Women	Master's	Doctor's
1947-48	1,726	1,397	329	241	37
1949-50	2,835	2,449	386	277	83
1954-55	1,774	1,473	301	231	84
1959-60	3,466	3,052	414	383	137
1964-65	4,810	4,175	635	581	144
1969-70	5,717	4,631	1,086	729	359
1974-75	5,348	4,003	1,345	699	375
1979-80	3,695	2,647	1,048	509	246
1981-82	3,391	2,408	983	445	247
1983-84	3,300	2,305	995	477	219
1984-85	3,354	2,269	1,085	431	234
1985-86	3,265	2,193	1,072	437	242
1987-88	3,565	2,411	1,154	465	222
1989-90	4,287	2,926	1,361	550	248
1990-91	4,588	3,074	1,514	539	281
1991-92	4,846	3,293	1,553	555	282
1992-93	4,842	3,310	1,532	707	266
1993-94	4,691	3,218	1,473	727	301
Estimated					
1994-95	4,803	3,298	1,505	784	317
1995-96	4,861	3,358	1,503	864	327

Note: Data prior to 1979-80 are for aggregate U.S. For later years, data are for 50 states and D.C. Figures through 1964-65 generally exclude those master's degrees that are considered first-professional degrees, such as master of social work, etc. Data for later years include all master's degrees. Figures for 1994-95 and later are Fact Book estimates based on data for the previous four years.

Sources: See Guide to Sources.

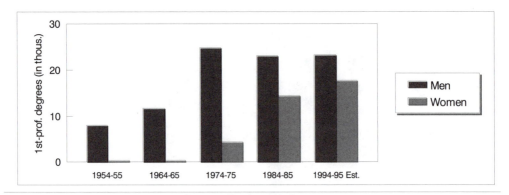

Degrees Conferred in Law

Year	First-professional			Master's	Doctor's
	Total	Men	Women		
1947-48	10,990	10,570	420	394	247
1949-50	14,312	13,891	421	531	27
1954-55	8,226	7,937	289	373	22
1959-60	9,314	9,073	241	520	24
1964-65	12,000	11,596	404	672	29
1969-70	14,916	14,115	801	884	35
1974-75	29,296	24,881	4,415	1,245	21
1979-80	35,647	24,893	10,754	1,817	40
1981-82	35,991	23,965	12,026	1,893	22
1983-84	37,012	23,382	13,630	1,802	121
1984-85	37,491	23,070	14,421	1,796	105
1985-86	35,844	21,874	13,970	1,922	54
1987-88	35,397	21,067	14,330	1,878	89
1989-90	36,485	21,079	15,406	1,888	111
1990-91	37,945	21,643	16,302	1,050	86
1991-92	38,848	22,260	16,588	2,369	68
1992-93	40,302	23,182	17,120	2,172	86
1993-94	40,044	22,826	17,218	2,335	43
Estimated					
1994-95	40,997	23,290	17,707	2,804	36
1995-96	41,803	23,726	18,077	3,820	30

Note: Data prior to 1969-70 are for aggregate U.S. For later years, data are for 50 states and D.C. First-professional data prior to 1969-70 are not entirely comparable with subsequent figures inasmuch as they include some bachelor's degrees. Data for 1969-70 and later include only first-professional degrees, such as LL.B. & J.D. Figures for 1994-95 and later are Fact Book estimates based on data for the previous four years.

Sources: See Guide to Sources.

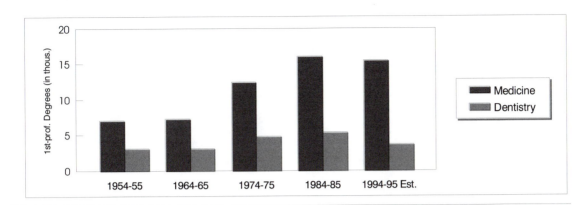

Year	Medicine (M.D. only)			Dentistry (D.D.S. or D.M.D only)		
	Total	Men	Women	Total	Men	Women
1949-50	5,612	5,028	584	2,579	2,561	18
1954-55	7,056	6,718	338	3,099	3,071	28
1959-60	7,032	6,645	387	3,247	3,221	26
1964-65	7,347	6,869	478	3,135	3,112	23
1969-70	8,314	7,615	699	3,718	3,684	34
1974-75	12,447	10,818	1,629	4,773	4,627	146
1979-80	14,902	11,416	3,486	5,258	4,558	700
1981-82	15,814	11,867	3,947	5,282	4,467	815
1983-84	15,813	11,359	4,454	5,353	4,302	1,051
1984-85	16,041	11,167	4,874	5,339	4,233	1,106
1985-86	15,938	11,022	4,916	5,046	3,907	1,139
1987-88	15,358	10,278	5,080	4,477	3,300	1,177
1989-90	15,075	9,923	5,152	4,100	2,834	1,266
1990-91	15,043	9,629	5,414	3,699	2,510	1,189
1991-92	15,243	9,796	5,447	3,593	2,431	1,162
1992-93	15,531	9,679	5,852	3,605	2,383	1,222
1993-94	15,368	9,544	5,824	3,787	2,330	1,457
Estimated						
1994-95	15,461	9,453	6,008	3,736	2,221	1,515
1995-96	15,580	9,410	6,169	3,768	2,154	1,614

Note: Data are for 50 states and D.C. Figures for 1994-95 and later are based on data for the previous four years.

Sources: See Guide to Sources.

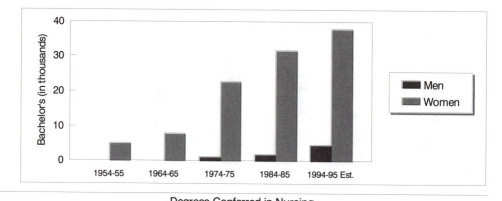

	Degrees Conferred in Nursing				
	Bachelor's				
Year	Total	Men	Women	Master's	Doctor's
1947-48	3,351	27	3,324	200	0
1949-50	3,292	23	3,269	368	2
1954-55	5,240	61	5,179	550	3
1959-60	6,661	81	6,580	599	0
1964-65	7,908	77	7,831	809	8
1969-70	11,280	160	11,120	1,549	11
1974-75	23,813	1,104	22,709	2,220	16
1979-80	32,441	1,785	30,656	4,616	118
1981-82	33,177	1,695	31,482	5,312	134
1983-84	33,092	1,829	31,263	5,744	220
1984-85	33,654	1,937	31,717	5,761	273
1985-86	34,097	1,958	32,139	6,050	277
1987-88	31,793	1,640	30,153	6,500	283
1989-90	28,681	1,695	26,986	6,731	319
1990-91	29,361	1,911	27,450	7,129	408
1991-92	31,029	2,381	28,648	7,512	408
1992-93	34,792	2,934	31,858	8,151	396
1993-94	39,076	3,735	35,341	8,991	382
			Estimated		
1994-95	42,390	4,555	37,834	9,668	402
1995-96	46,670	5,661	41,009	10,434	401

Note: Data prior to 1979-80 are for aggregate U.S. For later years, data are for 50 states and D.C. Figures for 1994-95 and later are Fact Book estimates based on data for the previous four years.

Sources: See Guide to Sources.

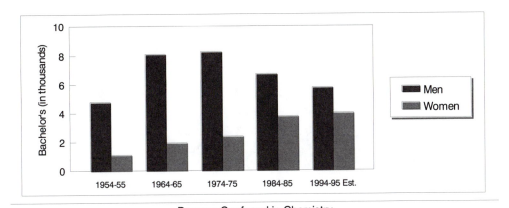

Degrees Conferred in Chemistry

Year	Bachelor's Total	Men	Women	Master's	Doctor's
1947-48	7,429	5,361	2,068	1,360	569
1949-50	10,619	9,134	1,485	1,576	953
1954-55	5,920	4,781	1,139	1,173	1,005
1959-60	7,603	6,005	1,598	1,228	1,048
1964-65	10,047	8,111	1,936	1,715	1,414
1969-70	11,221	9,105	2,116	2,146	2,208
1974-75	10,649	8,264	2,385	2,066	1,824
1979-80	11,232	8,050	3,182	1,723	1,545
1981-82	11,055	7,566	3,489	1,683	1,682
1983-84	10,704	6,973	3,731	1,667	1,744
1984-85	10,482	6,691	3,791	1,719	1,789
1985-86	10,116	6,483	3,633	1,754	1,908
1987-88	9,052	5,452	3,600	1,708	1,995
1989-90	8,132	4,893	3,239	1,682	2,183
1990-91	8,321	4,983	3,338	1,665	2,238
1991-92	8,641	5,155	3,486	1,780	2,280
1992-93	8,914	5,288	3,626	1,842	2,261
1993-94	9,425	5,591	3,834	1,999	2,353
Estimated					
1994-95	9,780	5,781	3,999	2,088	2,398
1995-96	10,184	6,000	4,184	2,211	2,440

Note: Data prior to 1979-80 are for aggregate U.S. For later years, data are for 50 states and D.C. Figures through 1964-65 generally exclude those master's degrees that are considered first-professional degrees such as master of library science and social work. Data for later years include all master's degrees. Over the years, various subfields of chemistry have been listed in NCES reprints in addition to "Chemistry, general." Data for the subfields have been included in these data. Figures for 1994-95 and later are Fact Book estimates based on data for the previous four years.

Sources: See Guide to Sources.

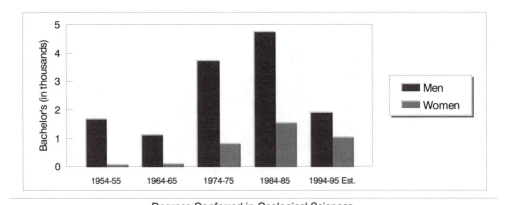

Degrees Conferred in Geological Sciences					
	Bachelor's				
Year	Total	Men	Women	Master's	Doctor's
1947-48	1,172	1,037	135	318	57
1949-50	3,043	2,934	109	493	113
1954-55	1,795	1,703	92	507	154
1959-60	2,564	2,485	79	620	214
1964-65	1,258	1,127	131	618	291
1969-70	3,002	2,668	334	847	355
1974-75	4,559	3,738	821	1,314	387
1979-80	5,924	4,476	1,448	1,556	352
1981-82	6,425	4,728	1,697	1,682	346
1983-84	6,549	4,934	1,615	1,514	315
1984-85	6,308	4,750	1,558	1,692	289
1985-86	4,974	3,871	1,103	1,767	271
1987-88	2,551	1,930	621	1,523	350
1989-90	1,767	1,252	515	1,200	414
1990-91	1,784	1,233	551	1,089	446
1991-92	2,078	1,382	696	735	314
1992-93	2,299	1,554	745	925	406
1993-94	2,677	1766	911	937	422
Estimated					
1994-95	2,981	1,928	1,054	903	434
1995-96	3,397	2,156	1,241	882	441

Note: Data prior to 1979-80 are for aggregate U.S. For later years, data are for 50 states and D.C. Figures through 1964-65 generally exclude those master's degrees that are considered first-professional degrees such as master of library science and social work. Data for later years include all master's degrees. Over the years, various subfields of geological sciences have been listed separately in NCES reports in addition to "Geology." The most recent listing includes: geology, geochemistry, geophysics and seismology, and "other geological sciences."
Figures for 1994-95 and later are Fact Book estimates based on data for the previous four years.

Sources: See Guide to Sources.

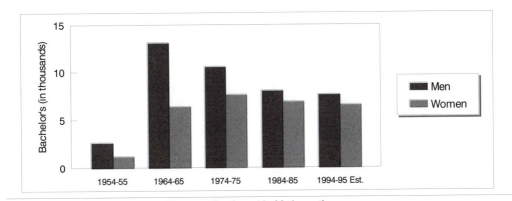

Degrees Conferred in Mathematics

Year	Bachelor's			Master's	Doctor's
	Total	Men	Women		
1947-48	4,266	2,619	1,647	711	128
1949-50	6,392	4,946	1,446	974	160
1954-55	4,034	2,724	1,310	761	250
1959-60	11,437	8,312	3,125	1,765	303
1964-65	19,581	13,132	6,449	4,148	682
1969-70	27,565	17,248	10,317	5,648	1,236
1974-75	18,346	10,646	7,700	4,338	975
1979-80	11,378	6,562	4,816	2,860	724
1981-82	11,599	6,593	5,006	2,727	681
1983-84	13,211	7,366	5,845	2,741	695
1984-85	15,146	8,164	6,982	2,882	699
1985-86	16,306	8,725	7,581	3,159	742
1987-88	15,904	8,523	7,381	3,442	750
1989-90	14,509	7,808	6,701	3,676	917
1990-91	15,310	8,178	7,132	4,041	1,036
1991-92	14,783	7,888	6,895	4,011	1,082
1992-93	14,812	7,827	6,985	4,067	1,189
1993-94	14,396	7,735	6,661	4,100	1,157
Estimated					
1994-95	14,378	7,720	6,657	4,217	1,228
1995-96	14,156	7,611	6,546	4,262	1,283

Note: Data prior to 1979-80 are for aggregate U.S. For later years, data are for 50 states and D.C. Figures through 1964-65 generally exclude those master's degrees that are considered first-professional degrees, such as master of social work, etc. Data for later years include all master's degrees.

Figures for data for 1994-95 and later are Fact Book estimates based on data for the previous four years.

Sources: See Guide to Sources.

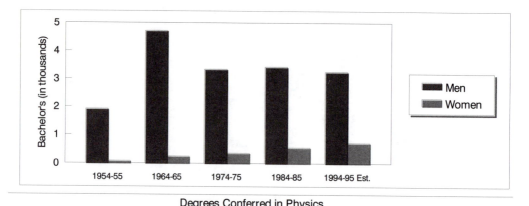

	Degrees Conferred in Physics				
	Bachelor's				
Year	Total	Men	Women	Master's	Doctor's
1947-48	2,126	1,962	164	706	198
1949-50	3,414	3,287	127	922	358
1954-55	1,996	1,920	76	729	511
1959-60	4,338	4,166	172	1,073	487
1964-65	4,954	4,708	246	1,906	942
1969-70	5,333	5,004	329	2,205	1,439
1974-75	3,716	3,354	362	1,577	1,080
1979-80	3,396	2,962	434	1,192	830
1981-82	3,472	3,012	460	1,282	863
1983-84	3,731	3,198	533	1,440	863
1984-85	3,988	3,443	545	1,445	874
1985-86	4,056	3,467	589	1,422	947
1987-88	4,100	3,488	612	1,675	1,093
1989-90	4,155	3,479	676	1,831	1,192
1990-91	4,236	3,572	664	1,725	1,209
1991-92	4,098	3,427	671	1,834	1,337
1992-93	4,063	3,390	673	1,777	1,277
1993-94	4,001	3,292	709	1,945	1,465
Estimated					
1994-95	3,966	3,248	718	1,978	1,546
1995-96	3,904	3,172	732	2,050	1,648

Note: Data prior to 1979-80 are for aggregate U.S. For later years, data are for 50 states and D.C. Figures through 1964-65 generally exclude those master's degrees that are considered first-professional degrees such as master of library science and social work. Data for later years include all master's degrees.

Sources: See Guide to Sources.

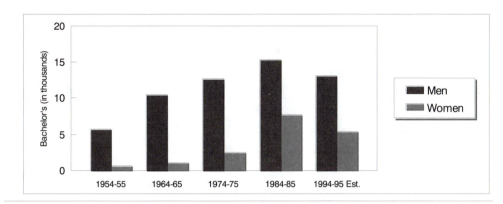

	Degrees Conferred in Economics				
	Bachelor's				
Year	Total	Men	Women	Master's	Doctor's
1947-48	9,002	7,684	1,318	922	116
1949-50	14,573	13,471	1,102	921	200
1954-55	6,364	5,678	686	617	241
1959-60	8,101	7,422	679	995	313
1964-65	11,538	10,496	1,042	1,597	538
1969-70	18,325	16,436	1,889	2,396	975
1974-75	15,160	12,677	2,483	2,522	974
1979-80	19,643	13,956	5,687	2,382	841
1981-82	21,785	14,975	6,810	2,499	837
1983-84	22,813	15,312	7,501	2,477	890
1984-85	23,015	15,356	7,659	2,514	905
1985-86	23,746	15,811	7,935	2,488	953
1987-88	22,911	15,412	7,499	1,847	770
1989-90	23,923	16,467	7,456	1,950	806
1990-91	23,488	16,374	7,114	1,951	802
1991-92	23,423	16,416	7,007	2,106	866
1992-93	21,321	14,965	6,356	2,292	879
1993-94	19,496	13,747	5,749	2,521	869
			Estimated		
1994-95	18,544	13,153	5,391	2,690	886
1995-96	17,493	12,461	5,032	2,915	909

Note: Data prior to 1979-80 are for aggregate U.S. For later years, data are for 50 states and D.C. Figures through 1964-65 generally exclude those master's degrees that are considered first-professional degrees such as master of library science and social work. Data for later years include all master's degrees. Figures for 1994-95 and later are Fact Book estimates based on data for the previous four years.

Sources: See Guide to Sources.

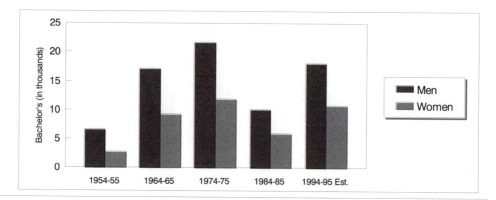

Degrees Conferred in History					
	Bachelor's				
Year	Total	Men	Women	Master's	Doctor's
1947-48	9,245	5,669	3,576	1,566	162
1949-50	13,567	10,242	3,325	1,801	275
1954-55	9,540	6,707	2,833	1,199	310
1959-60	15,227	10,294	4,933	1,861	366
1964-65	26,421	17,128	9,293	3,234	600
1969-70	44,784	29,019	15,765	5,287	1,087
1974-75	33,524	21,653	11,871	4,552	1,192
1979-80	20,589	12,540	8,049	2,566	790
1981-82	18,397	11,133	7,264	2,418	692
1983-84	16,642	10,363	6,279	1,937	561
1984-85	16,048	10,075	5,973	1,921	468
1985-86	16,413	10,409	6,004	1,959	497
1987-88	18,207	11,388	6,819	2,090	517
1989-90	22,476	14,053	8,423	2,365	570
1990-91	24,541	15,133	9,408	2,591	606
1991-92	26,966	16,434	10,532	2,754	644
1992-93	27,774	17,212	10,562	2,952	690
1993-94	27,503	17,260	10,243	3,009	752
			Estimated		
1994-95	28,957	18,179	10,778	3,197	806
1995-96	30,207	19,039	11,167	3,370	866

Note: Data prior to 1979-80 are for aggregate U.S. For later years, data are for 50 states and D.C. Figures through 1964-65 generally exclude those master's degrees that are considered first-professional degrees such as master of library science and social work. Data for later years include all master's degrees. From 1955-56 thru 1982-83, data include "American studies." Beginning 1983-84, figures show only "history." Figures for 1994-95 and later are Fact Book estimates based on data for the previous four years.

Sources: See Guide to Sources.

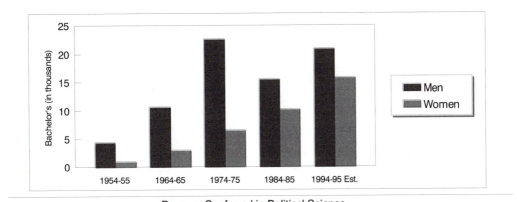

Degrees Conferred in Political Science					
	Bachelor's				
Year	Total	Men	Women	Master's	Doctor's
1947-48	4,874	3,727	1,147	806	99
1949-50	6,346	5,366	980	710	127
1954-55	5,500	4,415	1,085	498	181
1959-60	6,657	5,401	1,256	722	201
1964-65	13,693	10,655	3,038	1,210	304
1969-70	25,856	20,698	5,158	2,105	525
1974-75	29,314	22,704	6,610	2,333	680
1979-80	25,457	16,315	9,142	1,938	535
1981-82	25,658	15,883	9,775	1,954	513
1983-84	25,719	15,655	10,064	1,769	457
1984-85	25,834	15,640	10,194	1,500	441
1985-86	26,439	15,959	10,480	1,704	439
1987-88	27,207	16,297	10,910	1,579	391
1989-90	33,560	19,885	13,675	1,580	480
1990-91	35,737	20,806	14,931	1,772	468
1991-92	37,805	22,044	15,761	1,908	535
1992-93	37,931	22,052	15,879	1,943	529
1993-94	36,097	20,741	15,356	2,147	616
Estimated					
1994-95	36,808	20,983	15,824	2,320	658
1995-96	37,111	21,047	16,064	2,482	718

Note: Data prior to 1979-80 are for aggregate U.S. For later years, data are for 50 states and D.C. Figures through 1964-65 generally exclude those master's degrees that are considered first-professional degrees, such as master of social work, etc. Data for later years include all master's degrees. Figures for 1994-95 and later are Fact Book estimates based on data for the previous four years.

Sources: See Guide to Sources.

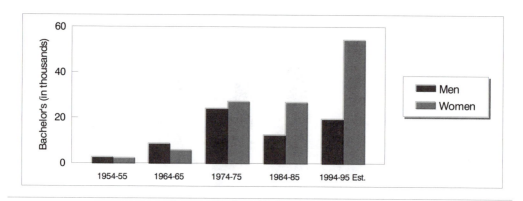

| | Degrees Conferred in Psychology | | | | |
| Year | Bachelor's | | | Master's | Doctor's |
	Total	Men	Women		
1947-48	6,402	2,808	3,594	1,200	154
1949-50	9,582	6,058	3,524	1,316	283
1954-55	5,532	3,009	2,523	1,293	688
1959-60	8,111	4,785	3,326	1,406	641
1964-65	14,771	8,729	6,042	2,708	1,004
1969-70	33,927	19,148	14,779	5,167	1,962
1974-75	51,693	24,427	27,266	9,432	2,913
1979-80	42,093	15,440	26,653	9,938	3,395
1981-82	41,031	13,623	27,408	7,791	2,780
1983-84	39,872	12,792	27,080	8,002	2,973
1984-85	39,811	12,694	27,117	8,408	2,908
1985-86	40,521	12,578	27,943	8,293	3,088
1987-88	45,003	13,497	31,506	7,872	2,987
1989-90	53,794	15,322	38,472	9,192	3,322
1990-91	58,655	16,067	42,588	11,349	3,932
1991-92	63,513	17,031	46,482	10,215	3,373
1992-93	66,728	17,908	48,820	10,957	3,651
1993-94	69,259	18642	50617	12181	3563
Estimated					
1994-95	73,809	19,579	54,230	13,153	3,652
1995-96	78,190	20,572	57,619	13,693	3,598

Note: Data prior to 1979-80 are for aggregate U.S. For later years, data are for 50 states and D.C. Figures through 1964-65 generally exclude those master's degrees that are considered first-professional degrees such as master of library science and social work. Data for later years include all master's degrees. From 1964-65 thru 1980-81, figures include degrees in educational psychology that were reported in 2 major categories--education and psychology. Beginning with 1981-82, data show only degrees reported in "psychology." Figures for 1994-95 and later are Fact Book estimates based on data for the previous four years.

Sources: See Guide to Sources.

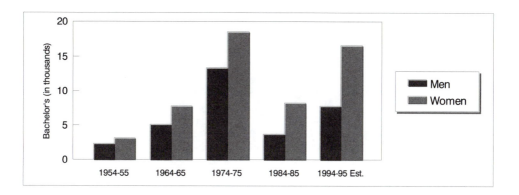

Degrees Conferred in Sociology				
	Bachelor's			
Year	Total	Men	Women	Master's	Doctor's
1947-48	6,271	1,787	4,484	430	66
1949-50	7,887	3,848	4,039	552	98
1954-55	5,533	2,333	3,200	474	167
1959-60	7,182	3,171	4,011	440	161
1964-65	12,896	5,123	7,773	789	230
1969-70	30,848	12,445	18,403	1,716	534
1974-75	31,817	13,330	18,487	2,112	693
1979-80	18,881	6,270	12,611	1,341	583
1981-82	16,042	4,771	11,271	1,145	558
1983-84	13,145	4,218	8,927	1,008	520
1984-85	11,968	3,701	8,267	1,022	480
1985-86	12,271	3,811	8,460	965	504
1987-88	13,024	4,065	8,959	984	452
1989-90	16,035	5,083	10,952	1,198	432
1990-91	17,550	5,398	12,152	1,260	465
1991-92	19,568	6,096	13,472	1,347	501
1992-93	20,896	6,605	14,291	1,521	536
1993-94	22,368	7,114	15,254	1,639	530
Estimated					
1994-95	24,315	7,740	16,575	1,773	558
1995-96	26,386	8,471	17,915	1,932	585

Note: Data prior to 1979-80 are for aggregate U.S. For later years, data are for 50 states and D.C. Figures through 1964-65 generally exclude those master's degrees that are considered first-professional degrees such as master of library science and social work. Data for later years include all master's degrees. Figures for 1994-95 and later are Fact Book estimates based on data for the previous four years.

Sources: See Guide to Sources.

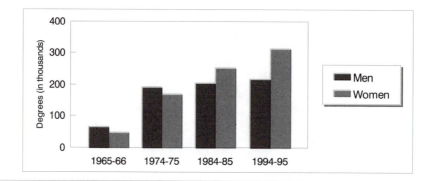

Year	Number of Associate Degrees (in thousands)				
	Total	Men	Women	Public	Independent
1965-66	111.7	63.8	47.9	82.4	29.3
1969-70	206.0	117.4	88.6	171.0	35.1
1974-75	360.2	191.0	169.2	318.5	41.7
1979-80	400.9	183.7	217.2	344.5	56.4
1981-82	434.5	196.9	237.6	366.7	67.8
1983-84	452.2	202.7	249.5	379.2	73.0
1984-85	454.7	202.9	251.8	377.6	77.1
1985-86	446.0	196.2	249.9	369.1	77.0
1987-88	435.1	190.0	245.0	354.2	80.9
1989-90	455.1	191.2	263.9	375.6	79.5
1990-91	481.7	198.6	283.1	398.1	83.7
1991-92	504.2	207.5	296.8	420.3	84.0
1992-93	514.8	212.0	302.8	430.3	84.4
1993-94	542.4	221.0	321.5	456.2	86.3
Projected					
1994-95	530.0	216.0	314.0	442.0	88.0
1995-96	534.0	212.0	323.0	445.0	89.0

Note: Public/independent projections are based on the average percentage distribution of the 1991-1994 period.

Source: NCES, Digest of Education Statistics, 1996 (Washington: GPO, 1996), tbls. 239, 249.

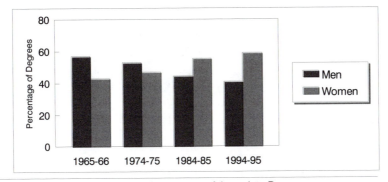

| Year | Percentage of Associate Degrees | | | |
	Men	Women	Public	Independent
1965-66	57.1	42.9	73.8	26.2
1969-70	57.0	43.0	83.0	17.0
1974-75	53.0	47.0	88.4	11.6
1979-80	45.8	54.2	85.9	14.1
1981-82	45.3	54.7	84.4	15.6
1983-84	44.8	55.2	83.9	16.1
1984-85	44.6	55.4	83.0	17.0
1985-86	44.0	56.0	82.8	17.3
1987-88	43.7	56.3	81.4	18.6
1989-90	42.0	58.0	82.5	17.5
1990-91	41.2	58.8	82.6	17.4
1991-92	41.2	58.9	83.4	16.7
1992-93	41.2	58.8	83.6	16.4
1993-94	40.7	59.3	84.1	15.9
Projected				
1994-95	41.0	59.0	83.0	17.0
1995-96	40.0	60.0	83.0	17.0

Note: Public/independent projections are based on the average percentage
distribution of the 1991-1994 period.

Source: Calculated from data on the preceding table.

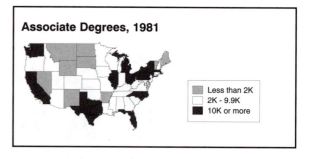

Associate Degrees, 1981

Region and State	Number of Associate Degrees (in thousands)				Percent Change
	1969-70	1980-81	1989-90	1993-94	1989-90 to 1993-94
50 States & D.C.	**206.0**	**416.4**	**455.1**	**542.4**	**19**
New England	**14.4**	**28.2**	**27.3**	**29.3**	**7**
Connecticut	2.7	5.4	4.7	5.1	9
Maine	0.3	1.7	1.9	2.5	32
Massachusetts	9.1	14.6	13.4	13.1	-2
New Hampshire	0.5	2.0	2.5	3.4	36
Rhode Island	1.0	3.2	3.5	3.9	11
Vermont	0.8	1.3	1.3	1.3	0
Mideast	**42.6**	**83.4**	**85.8**	**97.4**	**14**
Delaware	1.0	1.2	1.3	1.2	-8
D.C.	0.7	0.6	0.4	0.3	-25
Maryland	2.5	6.8	7.4	8.3	12
New Jersey	3.5	9.8	9.9	12.6	27
New York	27.2	48.7	49.0	53.8	10
Pennsylvania	7.8	16.3	17.8	21.2	19
Southeast	**35.4**	**86.1**	**95.7**	**116.8**	**22**
Alabama	1.8	4.8	6.3	7.8	24
Arkansas	0.4	1.8	2.6	2.8	8
Florida	17.1	31.5	33.8	40.6	20
Georgia	3.1	6.0	7.4	9.4	27
Kentucky	1.4	4.8	5.4	6.4	19
Louisiana	0.3	2.1	2.6	3.3	27
Mississippi	3.3	4.2	5.0	5.5	10
North Carolina	3.2	10.6	10.6	13.6	28
South Carolina	1.1	5.5	5.2	6.2	19
Tennessee	1.0	5.7	5.6	6.9	23
Virginia	1.9	6.8	8.4	11.3	35
West Virginia	0.8	2.4	2.8	3.0	7
Great Lakes	**25.2**	**69.7**	**79.5**	**102.1**	**28**
Illinois	8.4	21.2	23.3	27.0	16
Indiana	1.9	6.9	8.9	9.6	8
Michigan	8.1	18.9	21.2	36.0	70
Ohio	4.6	15.5	17.6	20.1	14
Wisconsin	2.3	7.2	8.5	9.4	11

Continued on next page.

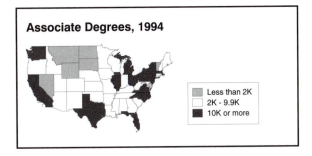

Associate Degrees, 1994

Less than 2K
2K - 9.9K
10K or more

Region and State	Number of Associate Degrees (in thousands)				Percent Change 1989-90 to 1993-94
	1969-70	1980-81	1989-90	1993-94	
Plains	**14.3**	**28.4**	**33.4**	**38.9**	**16**
Iowa	2.8	5.6	7.9	8.3	5
Kansas	2.4	4.6	5.5	6.7	22
Minnesota	4.0	6.6	7.7	9.7	26
Missouri	3.2	6.4	6.9	8.4	22
Nebraska	0.6	2.3	2.7	3.2	19
North Dakota	0.9	1.7	1.9	1.7	-11
South Dakota	0.3	1.3	0.8	0.9	13
Southwest	**10.7**	**28.1**	**37.9**	**42.4**	**12**
Arizona	2.3	5.2	6.4	6.8	6
New Mexico	0.4	1.3	2.5	3.1	24
Oklahoma	1.9	3.9	6.2	6.7	8
Texas	6.2	17.6	22.8	25.8	13
Rocky Mountains	**5.2**	**10.3**	**15.3**	**19.0**	**24**
Colorado	1.9	4.5	6.1	6.7	10
Idaho	1.2	2.0	3.0	4.1	37
Montana	0.1	0.5	0.8	1.0	25
Utah	1.3	2.4	3.8	5.3	39
Wyoming	0.6	0.8	1.6	1.9	19
Far West	**58.2**	**78.2**	**71.2**	**85.5**	**20**
Alaska	0.1	0.5	0.6	1.0	67
California	51.3	59.5	48.4	56.4	17
Hawaii	0.7	2.1	2.2	2.4	9
Nevada	0.2	0.6	0.9	1.3	44
Oregon	1.8	4.3	4.8	6.0	25
Washington	4.1	11.1	14.3	18.4	29
U.S. Service Schools	**-**	**4.0**	**9.1**	**11.0**	**21**

Note: Each year's data are for twelve months ending June 30. Detail may not sum to totals because of rounding.

Sources: 1 NCES, "Associate Degrees and Other Formal Awards below the Baccalaureate" and "Degrees and Other Formal Awards Conferred" surveys.

2 _____, Digest of Education Statistics (Washington: GPO), 1993, tbl. 236; 1996, tbl. 240.

Guide to Sources

The information presented in *Fact Book* was obtained from many sources, including federal and state agencies, private research organizations, and professional associations. The data collected by these agencies were gathered by using many research methods, including surveys of a "universe" (such as all colleges) or of a "sample" (such as households), and statistical projections. *Fact Book* users should use caution when comparing data from different sources. Differences in procedures, timing, phrasing of questions, interviewer training, and so forth mean that the results from the different sources are not always strictly comparable. Following the brief note on data accuracy below, there are descriptions of the major information sources used in this edition of *Fact Book*.

ACCURACY OF DATA

The accuracy of any statistic is determined by the joint effects of sampling and nonsampling errors. Estimates based on a sample will differ somewhat from the figures that would have been obtained if a complete census had been taken using the same survey instruments, instructions, and procedures. In addition to such sampling errors, all surveys, both universe and sample, are subject to design, reporting, and processing errors, and errors due to nonresponse. To the greatest extent possible, these nonsampling errors are kept to a minimum by methods built into the survey procedures. In general, however, the effects of nonsampling errors are more difficult to determine than those produced by sampling variability.

DEMOGRAPHIC AND ECONOMIC DATA SOURCES

Current Population Survey (CPS)

Current population estimates of school enrollment as well as social and economic characteristics of the nation's population are presented in the Demographic and Economic Data section of *Fact Book*. They are based on data collected in the Census Bureau's monthly household survey of about 60,000 households. The sample is periodically updated to reflect data from decennial censuses.

The monthly CPS deals primarily with labor force data for the civilian noninstitutional population (excluding military personnel and their families living on-post, and inmates of institutions). In addition, supplemental questions are asked about the education of all eligible members of the household; information on enrollment status by grade is gathered each October.

The estimation procedure employed for the monthly CPS data involves inflating weighted sample results to independent estimates of characteristics of the civilian noninstitutional population in the United States by age, sex, and race. These independent estimates are based on statistics from decennial censuses; statistics on birth, deaths, immigration, and emigration; and statistics on the population in the armed forces. Generalized standard error tables are provided in the Current Population Reports. The data are subject to both nonsampling and sampling errors.

School Enrollment. Each October, the Current Population Survey includes questions on the enrollment status of the population 3 years old and over. The main sources of nonsampling variability in the responses to these questions are those inherent in the survey instrument. The question concerning educational attainment may be sensitive for some respondents, who may not want to acknowledge the lack of a high school diploma. The question of current enrollment may not be answered accurately for various reasons. Some respondents may not know current grade information for every student in the household, a problem especially prevalent for households with members in college or in nursery school. Confusion over college credits or hours taken by a student may make it difficult to determine the year in which the student is enrolled.

Educational Attainment. Data on years of school completed are derived from two questions on the CPS instrument. In addition to the general constraints of the CPS, some data indicate that the respondents have a tendency to overestimate the educational level of members of their household. Some inaccuracy may be due to the respondent's lack of knowledge of the exact educational attainment of each household member and the hesitancy to acknowledge anything less than a high school education.

Questions concerning "educational attainment" or "school enrollment" based on the CPS may be directed to:

Education and Social Stratification Branch
Bureau of the Census
U.S. Department of Commerce
Washington, DC 20212

Bureau of Labor Statistics
U.S. Department of Labor
Washington, DC 20212

National Center for Education Statistics
U.S. Department of Education
555 New Jersey Avenue
Washington, DC 20208

GED Testing Service
American Council on Education
One Dupont Circle
Washington, DC 20036

Center for Higher Education
College of Education
Illinois State University
Normal, IL 61761

National Association of State Universities and Land-grant Colleges
One Dupont Circle
Washington, DC 20036

National Center for Health Statistics
3700 East-West Highway
Hyattsville, MD 20782

Western Interstate Commission on Higher Education
P.O. Drawer P
Boulder, CO 80301-9752

Most of the sources published by various government agencies are available from:

Superintendent of Documents
U.S. Government Printing Office
Washington, DC 20402.

SURVEYS OF THE NATIONAL CENTER FOR EDUCATION STATISTICS (NCES) OF THE U.S. DEPARTMENT OF EDUCATION

Higher Education General Information Survey (HEGIS)

HEGIS was a coordinated data collection effort of NCES designed to acquire and maintain statistical data on the characteristics and operation of institutions of higher education. Prior to HEGIS's beginning in 1966, the U.S. Office of Education (USOE, the precedent agency of today's U.S. Department of Education) gathered much of the same types of data through a variety of separate surveys. The HEGIS concept was to pull the various surveys together into a more coordinated system of surveys. HEGIS was an annual universe survey of institutions listed in the NCES's latest *Education Directory, Colleges and Universities.*

The information presented in *Fact Book* draws on HEGIS surveys that gathered information concerning institutional characteristics, finance, enrollment, and degrees. Because the surveys covered all institutions in the universe, the data were not subject to sampling error. They were, however, subject to nonsampling error, the sources of which vary with the survey instrument. Information concerning the nonsampling error of the enrollment and earned degree surveys is described in the *HEGIS Post-Survey Validation Study* conducted in 1979.

Integrated Postsecondary Education Data System (IPEDS)

Beginning with surveys for the 1986–87 academic year, NCES expanded its collection of postsecondary data. The Integrated Postsecondary Education Data System (IPEDS) includes all institutions of higher education —universities and colleges accredited at the college level by an agency recognized by the Secretary, U.S. Department of Education—plus other postsecondary institutions: those offering technical and vocational education beyond high school but whose instruction is not usually creditable to college degrees. IPEDS makes possible comprehensive coverage of education data for all education beyond high school. The higher education portion of IPEDS is a census of all education institutions similar to those included in HEGIS. The tabulations on institutional characteristics from IPEDS surveys shown in this edition of *Fact Book* are based on data from HEGIS-type institutions and in nearly every case are not subject to sampling errors. IPEDS data for the non-higher education portion of postsecondary education are collected through sample surveys and would be subject to both sampling and nonsampling errors.

Enrollment Data Sources

The Fall Enrollment survey has been part of the HEGIS/IPEDS series since its development. Prior to 1965, the U.S. Office of Education had conducted an annual Opening Fall Enrollment survey for over fifteen years and also conducted a comprehensive enrollment survey that provided data for its biennial reports on education. The enrollment survey does not appear to suffer significantly from problems associated with nonresponse, according to NCES. The 1995 survey response rate was 97 percent. Nonsampling errors may appear because of institutions' difficulty in classifying students by

attendance status (full-time, part-time), race, and first-time status. Problems of comparability may arise as a result of the change from HEGIS to IPEDS inasmuch as the "universe" of the latter was expanded somewhat. Comparability is also limited because institutions may change their classification from two-year to four-year institution categories as their missions and academic programs change.

Data on Institutions

The IPEDS and the earlier HEGIS surveys provide the basis for the universe of institutions presented in the *Directory of Postsecondary Institutions*. This is the directory on which the Department of Education surveys are based and is comprised of institutions that are accredited at the college level by an agency recognized by the Secretary of Education. Further data concerning the institutional surveys may be obtained from the NCES address.

The Carnegie Foundation for the Advancement of Teaching publishes *A Classification of Institutions of Higher Education*, most recently in 1994. This classification groups colleges and universities on the basis of their missions and educational functions. Copies of the publication may be obtained from:

California/Princeton Fulfillment Services
1445 Lower Ferry Road
Ewing, NJ 08618

Financial Data

NCES's financial surveys have been conducted by the HEGIS and IPEDS. Changes were made in the survey instruments in fiscal years (FY) 1976, 1982, and 1987. The FY 1976 survey form contained numerous revisions to earlier survey forms and made direct comparisons of line items difficult. The introduction of IPEDS in FY 1987 included several changes to the survey instrument and data processing procedures. The financial tables from which the data shown in *Fact Book* have been drawn underwent significant adjustments to present reasonably comparable data over time. Response rates for this survey range from 85 percent to 90 percent for most years reported. In most cases IPEDS estimates for nonreporting institutions were made by using data from peer institutions selected for location, control, level, and enrollment size.

To reduce reporting error, NCES uses rational standards for reporting finance statistics. These standards are contained in *College and University Business Administration: Administrative Services* (1974 edition) and *Financial Accounting and Reporting Manual for Higher Education* (1990 edition), published by the National Association of College and University Business Officers; *Audits of Colleges and Universities* (as amended August 1974), by the American Institute of Certified Public Accountants; and *HEGIS Financial Reporting Guide* (1980), by NCES.

Faculty and Staff Data Sources

The NCES survey of salaries and tenure status of full-time faculty was conducted intermittently from 1966 to 1987, and annually since 1989. The survey form changed a number of times during those years. However, the data sources from which figures shown in *Fact Book* were taken were adjusted to provide comparability. Data for the NCES surveys come from administrative offices of the institutions. They may not always agree with data published by the AAUP (see below), whose chapters, in many cases, are the sources of the data that the organization publishes.

NCES's Fall Staff survey is one of the components of its IPEDS. Between 1987 and 1991 the staff data were collected in cooperation with the U.S. Equal Employment Opportunity Commission (EEOC). In 1993, schools formerly surveyed by EEOC were surveyed by NCES, which will continue the survey through IPEDS.

NCES also sponsors the *National Survey of Postsecondary Faculty* which was conducted in 1988 and 1993. It is a representative sample survey that provides information on postsecondary faculty and departments.

The American Association of University Professors (AAUP) has been collecting and re-

porting faculty salary data for decades. Annual reports concerning salary and compensation are published regularly—usually in a spring issue—in the organization's publication, *Academe*. Further information may be obtained from:

American Association of University Professors
1012 16th Street, N.W.
Washington, DC 20005

Student Data Sources

The annual survey of first-time freshmen conducted by the Higher Education Research Institute at the University of California, Los Angeles (UCLA), is the nation's largest continuing empirical study of higher education. The survey covers an array of demographic, experiential, and attitudinal issues. The 1996 survey was based on questionnaires completed by a sample of freshmen entering two- and four-year institutions. The data collected are statistically adjusted to represent the nation's total population of an estimated 1.5 million first-time, full-time entering freshmen.

For additional information about the survey, contact:

The American Freshman Program
Higher Education Research Institute
UCLA Graduate School of Education and
Information Studies
3005 Moore Hall/Mail Box 951521
Los Angeles, CA 90095-1521

NCES conducts the *National Postsecondary Student Aid Study* (NPSAS). The survey is designed to learn how students and their families pay for postsecondary education. Its higher education component involves a national representative sample of students attending two-year and four-year colleges and universities, and is conducted every three years. The first survey was conducted in the 1986–87 academic year.

NCES also conducts longitudinal studies of high school and junior high school students to learn about their educational experiences from high school through postsecondary eduction to the workplace. Several studies are underway—*Beginning Postsecondary Student Longitudinal Study, High School and Beyond*, and a *National Longitudinal Study*. Further information concerning both the financial aid study and the longitudinal studies may be obtained from:

> Data Development and Longitudinal
>   Studies Group
> National Center for Education Statistics
> U.S. Department of Education
> 555 New Jersey Avenue
> Washington, DC 20208

The College Entrance Examination Board (CEEB), through its Washington office, publishes *Trends in Student Aid*, an annual monograph concerning student financial aid programs. Concentrating primarily on federal programs that provide grants, loans, and work-study funds, the report also shows average cost data for college attendance. For further information, contact:

> The Washington Office of the College
>   Board
> 1717 Massachusetts Avenue, N.W.
> Washington, DC 20036

Earned Degree Data Sources

Earned degree data have been collected annually by the Department of Education and its precedent agencies since the 1940s. Until the mid-1980s, reports were published annually showing the number of degrees awarded by level and field of study. Since the cessation of those annual publications, the data have been published annually in the *Digest of Education Statistics*. More detailed data by institution have been available in electronic form. Comparability of the data over the years is limited by changes in the field of study taxonomy, which has become increasingly more detailed. Furthermore, differences in institutions' departmental organization and degree-granting traditions tend to reduce comparability.

Prior to 1960–61, data for bachelor's and first-professional degrees were combined and reported as a single figure. Beginning in 1960–61, the degrees were reported separately, and this differentiation is reflected in *Fact Book*.

The comparability of master's, bachelor's, and first-professional degrees for years prior to 1965–66 is limited due to the fact that master's degrees that were considered to be first-professional degrees—for example, those in library science and social work administration—were included with the bachelor's or first-professional degree count, not with master's degrees. Beginning in 1965–66, institutions were instructed to count all master's degrees as master's degrees, even if they were generally considered to be first-professional degrees. For a more complete discussion of this change, see Paul L. Mason and Mabel Rice, *Earned Degrees Conferred*, Washington, DC, National Center for Education Statistics, 1965, p. 1.

NCES's current taxonomy includes the over 400 specific fields of study identified in its most recent *Classification of Instructional Programs*. These fields have been grouped by NCES into the 28 major academic areas that are shown in several of the *Fact Book* summary tables. Other *Fact Book* tables show more traditional fields of study, such as philosophy or chemistry. In preparing these tables, care has been taken to include recently specified subfields in order to provide a reasonable degree of comparability over time.

Earned degree data from other sources such as the National Science Foundation and the National Research Council may not agree with NCES figures. This is due to differences in survey methodology, disciplinary definitions, and data sources.

Projections of Education Statistics

Since 1964, NCES has published its annual *Projections of Education Statistics*, which shows projections of key statistics for all levels of education (elementary, secondary, and higher education). These data include enrollment, instructional staff, graduates, degrees, and expenditures. The projections include several alternative series;

however, the data in this edition of *Fact Book* show only the middle/intermediate series. Projections of enrollment and earned degrees are for only the higher education portion of the postsecondary education enterprise.

Because projections of time-series data are subject to errors both by the nature of statistics and the properties of projection methodologies, *Fact Book* users are cautioned not to overemphasize the numerical values of the projections. Important but unforeseeable economic and social changes may lead to differences, particularly at the higher education level. Projections should be considered as indicators of broad trends, not precise predictions. Each edition of *Projections* has a section explaining the methodology used and tables showing some of the basic demographic and financial data used in developing the projections.

Further information may be obtained from:

Data Development and Longitudinal
    Studies
National Center for Education Statistics
555 New Jersey Avenue
Washington, DC 20208

Index

Note: Figures refer to TABLE NUMBERS, not page numbers.

A

Administrative personnel, 118–121
Age
    of labor force, 29
    of population, 3, 4, 5, 9, 13, 15
    of students, 21
Appropriations (state) for higher education, 24
Associate degrees, 186–188
    by control of institution, 186, 187
    by region and state, 188
    by sex of recipient, 186, 187

B

Bachelor's degrees, 131, 133, 137, 138, 140, 158–185
    See also Earned Degrees
    by control of institution, 133, 138
    by field of study, 144, 158–185
    by race/ethnicity, 144, 148, 149, 156, 157
    by region and state, 140, 156, 157
    by sex of recipient, 133, 137
Birth rate, 8
Births, number of, 8

C

Carnegie classification of institutions, 92, 93
Characteristics of faculty, 113
Characteristics of freshmen, 126–129
Charges to undergrad. students, 122
College participation rates, 13, 141
College work-study financial assistance, 123, 124
Colleges and univs., number of, 86–93
    by control of institution, 86
    by highest level of offering, 89, 90
    by region and state, 91
    by size, 88
    by type, 87
Compensation of faculty, 116
Consumer price index (CPI), 27
Cost of attendance, 122
Current-fund expenditures, 101–107
Current-fund revenues, 94–100

D

Death rate, 8
Deaths, number of, 8
Degree attainment, 126
Degrees awarded. *See* Earned Degrees and type of
    degree (bachelor's, master's, etc.).
Disability status of students, 129

Doctoral degrees, 131, 136–139, 147, 158–185
    awarded to women, 139
    by control of institution, 136, 138
    by field of study, 139, 158–185
    by race/ethnicity, 147, 154, 155
    by region and state, 143
    by sex of recipient, 136, 137
    held by faculty, 113
    held by population, 15, 16

E

Earned degrees, 131–188
    associate degrees, 186–188
    bachelor's, 133, 137, 138, 140, 158–185
    by level, 131
    by race/ethnicity, 144–157
    by region and state, 140–143
    by sex of recipient, 132–137, 158–185
    bachelor's and higher in
        bacteriology, 158
        biochemistry, 159
        biological sciences, 158–162
        biology, 160
        biophysics, 158
        botany, 161
        business and management, 163
        chemical engineering, 165
        chemistry, 177
        civil engineering, 166
        dentistry, 175
        economics, 181
        education, 164
        electrical engineering, 167
        engineering, 165–169
        English, 170
        foreign languages, 171
        geology and earth sciences, 178
        history, 182
        humanities, 170–173
        industrial engineering, 168
        law, 174
        mathematics, 179
        mechanical engineering, 169
        medicine, 175
        microbiology, 158
        music, 172
        nursing, 176
        philosophy, 173
        physical sciences, 177–180
        physics, 180
        political science, 183
        psychology, 184

Earned degrees (*continued*)
 social sciences, 181–185
 sociology, 185
 zoology, 162
 doctoral degrees, 136–139, 143
 first-professional degrees, 134, 137, 138, 141
 master's degrees, 135, 137, 138, 142, 158–185
Educational attainment, 9, 15, 16, 37, 38
 and income, 16
 region and state, 9
Elementary school enrollment, 39, 40
Employees in higher education, 118–121
Employment, 28, 30–32
Endowment income, 94–100
Enrollment in higher education, 39, 41–86
 all students at all institutions, 42
  by attendance status, 44
  by control of institution, 45, 48, 50
  by level, 42
  by race/ethnicity, 52–55
  by region and state, 46–55
  by sex of student, 43
  by type of institution, 45
 first-time students, 41, 68–71, 74–76
  by control of institution, 69–71
  by region and state, 72–76
  by sex of student, 68
 four-year institutions, 42, 56, 58, 60, 70, 78
  all students, 56, 58, 60, 70
  by attendance status, 60
  by control of institution, 58
  by sex of student, 56, 62, 63
  first-time students, 70
 full-time students, 44, 66, 67, 83
 full-time equivalents (FTE), 77–80
  by control of institution, 79, 80
  by type of institution, 78
 graduate students,
  all, 81
  by attendance status, 83
  by control of institution, 82
  by field of study, 84
  by region and state, 85
  by sex of student, 81
 in independent institutions, 45, 50, 51
 in-state students, 74
 out-of-state students, 75, 76
 part-time students, 44
 as a percentage of high school graduates, 41
 in public institutions, 45, 48, 49, 64, 65
 race/ethnicity, 52–55
 secondary school, 39, 40
 two-year institutions, 42, 57, 59, 61, 71, 78
  all students, 42, 57, 59, 61
  by attendance status, 61
  by control of institution, 59
  first-time students, 71
  by sex of student, 57, 62, 63

Expenditures
 for education as a percentage of GDP, 26
 by institutions of higher education, 101–107
Expenses for undergraduates, 122

F

Faculty
 by control of institution, 118–121
 compensation, 116
 and enrollment, 110
 characteristics, 113
 full- and/or part-time, 108–113, 118
 by highest degrees, 113
 by minority status, 111, 119, 120, 121
 by rank, 109, 111, 112, 117
 by region and state, 112
 salaries, 115, 116
 sex, 109, 111
 with tenure, 117
 work time distribution, 114
Families, 7
Family income, 17, 18, 19, 21, 22
Federal support for education, 123–125, 130
Finances of higher education, 94–107, 130
Financial aid, 123–125
First-professional degrees, 131, 134, 137, 138, 141
 by control of institution, 134, 138
 by field of study, 145, 174, 175
 by race/ethnicity, 145, 150, 151
 by region and state, 141
 by sex of recipient, 134, 137
First-time enrollment. *See* Enrollment, first-time
  students.
Four-year institutions
 enrollment. *See* Enrollment, four-year institutions.
 number of, 87
Freshman characteristics, 127, 128
Fringe benefits for faculty, 116
Full-time enrollment, 44, 60, 61, 66, 67, 83
Full-time equivalent (FTE) enrollment, 77–80
Full-time faculty, 108–119

G

GED tests, 14
Graduate enrollment, 42, 81–85
Grants (student aid), 123, 124
Gross domestic product (GDP), 25
 educational expenditures as a percent of, 26
Guaranteed student loans, 123, 124

H

High school graduates
 and college enrollment, 11, 13, 41
 by control of institution, 10
 as a percentage of the population, 9
 by race/ethnicity, 11–13, 15
 by sex of graduate, 11
Higher Education Price Index (HEPI), 27

Highest degrees earned,
    by faculty, 113
    by population, 9, 15
Households, 6, 7
    income, 20

I

Income,
    families of first-time students, 22
    family, 17–19, 21, 22
    household, 20
    individual, 16
    personal, per capita,
        by region and state, 23
Independent institutions,
    degrees conferred, 132–136, 138, 186, 187
    enrollment, 45, 50, 51
        first-time students, 69, 70, 71
        full-time equivalent (FTE) enrollment, 80
        graduate, 82
        sex of student, 64, 65
    expenditures, 106, 107
    number of, 86, 88
    revenue, 99, 100
In-state student enrollment, 74
Institutions,
    by Carnegie classification, 92, 93
    by control, 86
    by highest level of degree, 89, 90
    by region and state, 91
    by size of enrollment, 88
    by type, 87

J

Job growth, 29–32

L

Labor force, 28, 29
    by age, 29
    employment status, 28
    by occupational group, 30–34
    by race/ethnicity, 29, 33
    by sex, 29, 33
Loans for higher education, 123, 124

M

Master's degrees, 131, 132, 135, 137, 138, 142, 146,
    152, 153, 158–185
    See also Earned degrees, bachelor's and higher.
    by control of institution, 135, 138
    by field of study, 146, 158–185
    held by population, 15, 16
    by race/ethnicity, 146, 152, 153
    by region and state, 142
    by sex of recipient, 135, 137
    held by faculty, 113
Men
    earned degrees, 132–137, 144–155, 158–187
    enrolled in higher education,

        all institutions, 43, 62
        by attendance status, 66
        by control of institution, 45, 64
        first-time students, 68
        four-year institutions, 62
        graduate study, 81
        two-year institutions, 62
    faculty, 109, 111, 115, 117
    income, 16
    labor force participation, 29
Migration of students between states, 75
Minorities
    educational attainment, 15
    earned degrees, 144–157
    employees in higher ed., 119, 120, 121
    employment, 29, 33
    enrollment, 52–55
    faculty, 119, 120
    high school graduates, 11–13
    income, 16–19, 21
    labor force, 29
    occupations, 33
    population, 1, 3, 4, 13
    unemployment, 36, 38

O

Occupations, number of individuals in, 30–34
    participation by minorities & women, 33
    projections for job growth, 30–34
Out-of-state first-time students, 76

P

Part-time enrollment, 44, 60, 61, 66, 67, 83
Part-time faculty, 108, 110, 113
Pell Grants, 123
Perkins Loans, 123
Population
    age groups, 1, 3–5, 13
    educational attainment, 9
    families, 7
    households, 7
        by region and state, 6
    labor force, 28–34
    race/ethnicity, 1, 3, 4
    region and state, 2, 5, 8, 9
    sex, 1, 3, 4
Price indexes, 27
Private institutions. *See* independent institutions.
Public institutions
    degrees conferred, 132–136, 138, 186, 187
    enrollment, 45, 48, 49, 58, 59
        first-time students, 69–71
        full-time-equivalent (FTE), 79
        graduate, 82
        by sex of student, 64, 65
    expenditures, 104, 105
    number of, 86, 88
    revenue, 97, 98

R

Race/Ethnicity. *See* Minorities.
Residence and migration of undergraduates, 74–76
Revenue, current-fund, 94–100

S

Salaries, faculty, 115, 116
Secondary school enrollment, 39, 40
Staff in higher ed. 118–121
States
    appropriations for higher education, 24
    earned degrees, 140–143
    educational attainment, 9
    enrollment, 46–55, 72–76
    faculty, 112
    households, 7
    income, family and per capita, 20, 23
    institutions, 91
    population, 2, 5
Student aid, 123–125
Student characteristics, 127–129
Student charges, 122

T

Tenure, 117
Tuition and fees, 122

Two-year institutions
    enrollment. See Enrollment, two-year institutions.
    number of, 87

U

Undergraduates, 42
Unemployment rates, 28, 35, 36
    and educational attainment, 37, 38

W

Women
    doctorate recipients, 139
    earned degrees, 132–137, 144–155, 158–187
    enrolled in higher education
        all institutions, 43, 63
        by attendance status, 67
        by control of institution, 45, 65
        first-time, 68
        four-year institutions, 63
        graduate, 81
        two-year institutions, 63
    faculty, 109, 111, 115, 117
    income, 16
    labor force, 29
    occupations, 33
    unemployment rate, 25
Work time of faculty, 114